THE POLITICAL WRITINGS
OF THOMAS JEFFERSON

D1562453

The American Heritage Series
OSKAR PIEST, FOUNDER

THE POLITICAL WRITINGS OF THOMAS JEFFERSON

Representative Selections

Edited, with an introduction, by
EDWARD DUMBAULD

• •

The American Heritage Series
published by

THE BOBBS-MERRILL COMPANY, INC.
INDIANAPOLIS • NEW YORK

Thomas Jefferson: 1743-1826

COPYRIGHT ©, 1955

THE LIBERAL ARTS PRESS, INC.

A Division of

THE BOBBS-MERRILL COMPANY, INC.

Printed in the United States of America

Library of Congress Catalog Card Number: 55-2881

ISBN 0-672-60012-9 (pbk)

ISBN 0-672-50966-0

Tenth Printing

CONTENTS

THOMAS JEFFERSON'S WRITINGS

CHAPTER ONE
FUNDAMENTALS OF RIGHTFUL GOVERNMENT

CHAPTER TWO
THE BLESSINGS OF A FREE GOVERNMENT

CHAPTER THREE

GOVERNMENT FOUNDED ON THE WILL OF THE PEOPLE

CHAPTER FOUR

THE VALUE OF CONSTITUTIONS

CHAPTER FIVE

THE TRUE PRINCIPLES OF THE UNITED STATES CONSTITUTION

CHAPTER SIX

THE GREAT FAMILY OF MANKIND

INTRODUCTION

I. JEFFERSON'S POLITICAL SIGNIFICANCE

An intelligent understanding of American traditions and institutions is more important today in the light of world events than ever before. Indispensable in that connection is a thorough knowledge of Thomas Jefferson's political philosophy and his impact upon American life during its formative years. If there is any unique or distinctively significant contribution which America has made or can make to modern civilization, it is Jeffersonian democracy. Jefferson gave to America what America is giving to the world. His achievements as a foremost figure in the nation's public life and as spokesman of "the American mind" [1] overshadow his accomplishments in other fields. Yet little of all that has been written about the varied aspects of his many-sided genius has concerned itself specifically with Jefferson's political principles. Hitherto no convenient volume has brought together the strands of his thought on this vital topic.

The central feature of Jefferson's political creed was his concern for human freedom. He constantly proclaimed "the happy truth that man is capable of self-government." A succinct summary of his beliefs was embodied in his statement: "I have sworn on the altar of God eternal hostility to every form of tyranny over the mind of man." [2]

He epitomized the true significance of his life when he chose to be remembered on his tombstone as "Author of the Declaration of American Independence, of the Statute of Virginia for religious freedom, and Father of the University of Virginia." [3] It was

[1] To Henry Lee, May 8, 1825. Paul L. Ford, ed., *The Works of Thomas Jefferson* (New York, 1904), XII, 409.

[2] To François de Marbois, June 14, 1817, Andrew A. Lipscomb and A. Ellery Bergh, eds., *The Writings of Thomas Jefferson* (Washington, 1903), XV, 130; to Benjamin Rush, September 3, 1800, *Works*, IX, 148.

[3] *Works*, XII, 483.

characteristic of his thinking that he enumerated as most important among the events of his career not his incumbency of high
offices of state where he wielded power over his fellow men, but
his contributions to the cause of liberty. He believed that mankind should be free; that human conduct should be guided and
governed by reason, not by arbitrary authority or tyrannical
mandates of rulers; and that the purpose of government was to
protect the safety and happiness of the people by guaranteeing
their God-given natural rights. To be subject to a government
of unlimited powers he regarded as the greatest of political evils.[4]
Throughout his life he remained true to this political faith
which had animated the American Revolution and which received
its noblest formulation at his hands in the Declaration of Independence. That document gave to the world not only a deathless
presentation of Jefferson's own political opinions but a true
"expression of the American mind."

The tradition of freedom to which it gave voice has never
lost its vitality. It is an imperishable feature of America's national
heritage. That this is so is largely due to Jefferson. It was not
inevitable that upon liberation from English domination America
should become a self-governing republic. There might have been
established one or more new monarchies. Nor did the achievement
of federal union and the avoidance of schism among the States
necessarily mean that the national government would be a democratic polity. The fact that a single government (whether federal
or consolidated) is established within a particular area instead
of a multitude of separate sovereignties does not inevitably neces-
sitate that the political structure so erected will be based on the
consent of the governed. Self-government is not guaranteed by
having a single government within a country, as many nations
in modern Europe to their sorrow can testify. The United States
might have had an autocratic or tyrannical national government,
as other peoples have been obliged to endure, if it had not been

[4] Edward Dumbauld, *The Declaration of Independence and What It
Means Today* (Norman, 1950), p. 48; to Gilbert Merritt, July 10, 1821.
W. C. Ford, ed., *Thomas Jefferson's Correspondence Printed from the Orig-
inals in the Collections of William K. Bixby* (New York, 1916), p. 261.

for Jefferson's influence on American life. Thanks to his tenure of public office, citizens of the United States could declare, "We are all federalists, we are all republicans," and could adopt as their slogan "federal union and republican government." [5] So, too, in the struggle of competing ideologies today for control of the modern world, it is certain that if American policies, based on the tradition of Jefferson, prevail, whatever regime for the government of international affairs is established will recognize the right of mankind to be free.

World government must be self-government if the insistent voice of Jefferson and America is heeded. And that voice can never be silenced, for it proclaims the indubitable aspirations of human nature itself. In honor of the fiftieth anniversary of the Declaration of Independence, its author sent forth from his Virginia mountainside these ringing final words: "May it be to the world what I believe it will be (to some parts sooner, to others later, but finally to all), the signal . . . to assume the blessings and security of self-government. . . . All eyes are opened, or opening, to the rights of man. The general spread of the light of science has already laid open to every view the palpable truth that the mass of mankind has not been born with saddles on their backs, nor a favored few booted and spurred, ready to ride them legitimately, by the grace of God. These are grounds of hope for others. For ourselves, let the annual return of this day forever refresh our recollections of these rights, and an undiminished devotion to them." [6]

II. JEFFERSON'S LIFE

Born on April 13, 1743, at Shadwell, in what is now Albemarle County, Virginia, Jefferson was "a typical American of his region and generation. . . . Living among planters and frontiersmen who knew and controlled their own lives with an easy mastery,

[5] *Works*, I, 182; Dumbauld, *The Declaration of Independence and What It Means Today*, p. 28.
[6] To Roger C. Weightman, June 24, 1826. *Works*, XII, 477 (Cf. p. 9.).

he believed in the capacity of the free people of the whole country to see their own interests and pursue them as his own neighbors about him did." [1] From March 25, 1760, to April 25, 1762, he was enrolled in William and Mary College. At the conclusion of his formal schooling he continued to live in the brilliant colonial capital of Williamsburg for the next nineteen years, as a law student and lawmaker. His preceptor in the legal profession was the learned and distinguished George Wythe. Jefferson was admitted to the bar in 1767 and practiced his profession until the courts were closed at the outbreak of the American Revolution. In 1769 he was elected for his first term as a legislator. He continued to serve in the Virginia House of Burgesses until that body ceased to function in 1775. Prevented by illness from participating in the first Virginia Convention in 1774, he forwarded for perusal by its members his *Summary View of the Rights of British America*, which impressed contemporary statesmen so strongly that it was published in Williamsburg as a pamphlet.

Jefferson attended the second Virginia Convention at Richmond in 1775. He was chosen as a delegate of the Old Dominion to the second Continental Congress in Philadelphia, where he took his seat on June 21, 1775. The young Virginian had previously visited the Quaker metropolis in 1766 in order to be inoculated for smallpox by the celebrated Doctor Shippen. In 1776 Jefferson won lasting renown as author of the Declaration of Independence. In the fall of that year he left Congress and returned to Virginia, where he entered the House of Delegates.

He had hoped to be recalled to take part in framing the first Constitution of Virginia. "Should our Convention propose to establish now a form of government, perhaps it might be agreeable to recall for a short time their delegates. It is a work of the most interesting nature and such as every individual would wish to have his voice in. In truth it is the whole object of the present controversy; for, should a bad government be instituted for us in future, it had been as well to have accepted at first the bad

[1] Woodrow Wilson, "The Spirit of Jefferson," *Princeton Alumni Weekly*, VI (1906), 551f.

one offered to us from beyond the water without the risk and expense of contest." [2] From Philadelphia he did forward a draft for a proposed constitution. Of this the preamble was accepted and prefixed to the declaration of rights and frame of government which were chiefly the work of George Mason.[3] Jefferson believed that the instrument so adopted was not really a "constitution," because it had been enacted by the ordinary legislature instead of by a constitutional convention. Only an assembly upon which the people had specially conferred "a power superior to that of the ordinary legislature" could create a basic or fundamental law binding upon all branches of the government and unalterable by them.[4] Anything less than this would not be a constitution.[5]

In the Virginia Assembly Jefferson pursued his memorable program of legislative reform, seeking to bring the law of that Commonwealth into conformity with republican principles and to eliminate those features which were the vestiges of English monarchical institutions. Jefferson was convinced that "our whole code must be reviewed, adapted to our republican form of government, and, now that we had no negatives of councils, governors and kings to restrain us from doing right, that it should be corrected, in all its parts, with a single eye to reason and the good of those for whose government it was framed." [6]

The *Report of the Committee of Revisors,* printed in 1784, containing 126 bills, was largely the product of Jefferson's industry. From time to time, through Madison's efforts, some of these

[2] To Thomas Nelson, May 16, 1776. Julian P. Boyd, ed., *The Papers of Thomas Jefferson* (Princeton, 1950), I, 292.

[3] *Ibid.,* I, 329–386.

[4] *Ibid.,* VI, 295ff. Jefferson appended to his *Notes on Virginia* a proposed constitution of Virginia which he prepared in 1783 when there was talk of holding a convention. See also *ibid.,* VII, 293; and *Notes on Virginia,* Query XIII, *Works,* IV, 17ff.

[5] The British Constitution, which can be changed by any act passed by Parliament, Jefferson regarded as "no constitution at all." To A. Coray, October 31, 1823, *Writings,* XV, 488. Similarly, if the French king had power to "model the constitution at will," it meant "that his government is a pure despotism." To James Madison, July 31, 1788, *Writings,* VII, 96.

[6] Paul L. Ford, ed., *Autobiography of Thomas Jefferson* (New York, 1914), pp. 66f.

bills became law, especially the world-famous Act of Religious Freedom, passed in 1786. Two important measures enacted during Jefferson's service in the House of Delegates were the laws for abolition of primogeniture and entail. These statutes promoted equal distribution of property, instead of permitting the whole estate of a landholder to pass intact to his eldest son, and so on for generation after generation. These reforms, along with freedom of religion and diffusion of knowledge, he considered as forming a system by which every fiber would be eradicated of ancient or future aristocracy "and a foundation laid for a government truly republican." [7]

Not until late in Jefferson's life did he see his proposal for general education put into force. "A system of general instruction, which shall reach every description of our citizens, from the richest to the poorest, as it was the earliest, so will it be the latest of all the public concerns in which I shall permit myself to take an interest." [8] Convinced that "no nation is permitted to live in ignorance with impunity," [9] he vigorously proclaimed that: "If a nation expects to be ignorant and free, . . . it expects what never was and never will be." [10] From Europe he exhorted his law teacher, George Wythe: "Preach, my dear Sir, a crusade against ignorance; establish and improve the law for educating the common people."[11] To George Washington he wrote: "It is an axiom in my mind that our liberty can never be safe but in the hands of the people themselves, and that, too, of the people with a certain degree of instruction. This it is the business of the state to effect, and on a general plan." [12] Of the University of

[7] *Ibid.*, p. 77.

[8] To Joseph C. Cabell, January 14, 1818. In Roy J. Honeywell, *The Educational Work of Thomas Jefferson* (New York, 1931), p. 247.

[9] Minutes of Board of Visitors of University of Virginia, November 29, 1821. *Writings*, XIX, 408.

[10] To Charles Yancey, January 6, 1816. *Works*, XI, 497.

[11] To George Wythe, August 13, 1786. *Works*, V, 154. Cf. p. 65.

[12] To George Washington, January 4, 1786. *Writings*, XIX, 24. See also to Edward Carrington, January 16, 1787, *Works*, V, 252ff; and to William C. Jarvis, September 28, 1820, *Works*, XII, 163. Cf. to John Norvell, June 11, 1807. *Works*, X, 417f.

Virginia, established as the fruition of his lifelong efforts, he said: "This institution will be based on the illimitable freedom of the human mind. For here we are not afraid to follow truth wherever it may lead, nor to tolerate any error so long as reason is left free to combat it." [13]

On June 1, 1779, Jefferson was chosen as the second republican Governor of Virginia (succeeding Patrick Henry in that office) and retired from the House of Delegates. He served two one-year terms as chief executive, after which he held no public office until after his wife's death in 1782. He then accepted an appointment as envoy to the peace conference ending the Revolutionary War. But when news came that negotiations were already so far advanced that his attendance would not be required, he returned to his home. Shortly afterward, he was re-elected to Congress. He took his seat in that body on November 4, 1783, at Princeton, New Jersey. On May 7, 1784, he was chosen by Congress as a plenipotentiary, in conjunction with John Adams and Benjamin Franklin, to negotiate treaties of commerce with European nations. On July 5, 1784, he sailed for Europe, landing at Cowes on July 25, 1784. The following year Jefferson succeeded Franklin as minister to the French court. He remained abroad until 1789.[14] On October 8, 1789, he "left Havre at half before one o'clock in the morning" and, after a delay at Cowes awaiting favorable winds, he sailed on the *Clermont* for Norfolk on October 23, 1789, arriving exactly a month later.

Jefferson had expected, after settling some personal affairs in America, to return to Paris; but found that President George Washington wished him to serve as first Secretary of State under the new Constitution. He resigned that office effective December 31, 1793, but returned to Philadelphia in 1797 as Vice-President. On March 4, 1801, he was sworn in as third President of the

[13] To William Roscoe, December 27, 1820. *Writings*, XV, 303.
[14] For an account of Jefferson's interesting experiences in Europe, though in large part unrelated to his political or diplomatic activities, see Edward Dumbauld, *Thomas Jefferson: American Tourist* (Norman, Okla., 1946), pp. 60–153.

United States. He served two terms, leaving the rustic capital of Washington on March 11, 1809, after the inauguration of his successor, James Madison. Thereafter he lived in retirement in Virginia, holding no public trust except as Rector of the University of Virginia, to the establishment of which Jefferson devoted his later years. During this period he was fond of saying that politics was a subject "which . . . I . . . leave to the generation which it concerns. They are to feel the good and evil of measures, and therefore have the right to direct them." [15] Nevertheless, it was heartening to the aged statesman to learn that his tenets of republicanism were not being abandoned. "It is a comfort to me when I find the sound principles of the Revolution cherished and avowed by the rising generation." [16]

Jefferson died on July 4, 1826, as did John Adams. The passing of these two venerable patriarchs on the date marking a half century since the fruition of their labors for independence seemed to awaken throughout the land a deeper sense of national destiny. It was as if that solemn moment marked the end of childhood and the beginning of maturity for the rising young republic.[17]

III. JEFFERSON AND POLITICAL PARTIES

Though Jefferson repeatedly expressed his distaste for public life [1] and political partisanship,[2] the fact remains that it was as

[15] To J. A. Bingham, July 2, 1822. Massachusetts Historical Society, Jefferson Papers. Cf. to James Monroe, January 28, 1809. *Works*, XI, 96.

[16] To Leonard M. Parker, July 24, 1821. Massachusetts Historical Society, Jefferson Papers. Cf. to John Holmes, April 22, 1820. *Works*, XII, 159.

[17] Lyman H. Butterfield, "The Jubilee of Independence," *Virginia Magazine of History and Biography*, LXI (April, 1953), 119.

[1] "I have no ambition to govern men. It is a painful and thankless office." To John Adams, Monticello, December 28, 1796. *Works*, VIII, 261. See also to Destutt de Tracy, Monticello, January 26, 1811. *Works*, XI, 186. For Jefferson's comments on the torments of public life, see Edward Dumbauld, *Thomas Jefferson: American Tourist*, pp. 21, 23f.

[2] To Francis Hopkinson, Paris, March 13, 1789. *Works*, V, 456.

a party leader that he displayed his most distinctive talents. His influence was greatest, not as an orator, but as an organizer.[3]

Jefferson early became prominent as a political leader. Before independence, the chief political division in most of the Colonies was between the frontiersmen and the wealthy tidewater families who held offices of profit and power under the British colonial government or were engaged as merchants in trade with England. Jefferson allied himself with Patrick Henry as a champion of the backwoodsmen, who defended their settlements against the attacks of Indians but were denied an equal representation in the government.[4] Their struggle for self-government and the right to manage their own affairs led gradually to the movement for independence from Great Britain.[5] In this struggle, as is well known, Jefferson played a prominent part. He was active in the work of the Continental Congress, where he supported the measures of John and Samuel Adams of Massachusetts. When at length the views of these advocates of complete separation from England prevailed, Jefferson as author of the Declaration of Independence became the spokesman of American sentiments to the world.

In the period between the end of the Revolution and the adoption of the Constitution framed in 1787, the same political divisions continued. Jefferson remained sympathetic to the interests of the Western pioneers. Navigation of the Mississippi was one of the important issues to this group, who feared that it

[3] Charles F. Adams, ed., *Works of John Adams* (Boston, 1850–1854), II, 511, 514.

[4] In his *Notes on Virginia* Jefferson demonstrated statistically that "nineteen thousand men, living below the falls of the rivers . . . in one part of the country, give law to upwards of thirty thousand living in another, and appoint all their chief officers executive and judiciary. From the difference of their situation and circumstances, their interests will often be very different." *Works*, IV, 18f. Likewise Quaker merchants in Philadelphia controlled Pennsylvania and refused to provide funds for defense of the Western frontiers. In Massachusetts it happened that the city of Boston was the center of agitation for popular rights. Jefferson in Congress supported the measures of John and Sam Adams.

[5] See Edward Dumbauld, *The Declaration of Independence and What It Means Today*, p. 16.

might be sacrificed for the sake of promoting the navigation and commerce of Eastern states. Jefferson's appointment to the diplomatic mission negotiating treaties of commerce with European nations gave reassurance that no treaty provisions detrimental to the agricultural states would be adopted.[6]

The next great party struggle in America took place while Jefferson was in Europe. This was the battle over adoption of the Constitution drawn up at Philadelphia in 1787. It was with respect to the partisan divisions on this question that Jefferson made the statement to Francis Hopkinson that he belonged to neither faction, and that "if I could not go to heaven but with a party, I would not go there at all." [7] Concerning the Constitution, Jefferson's position was ambivalent. As a "Continentalist" and especially in the light of his experience in Europe, he had long recognized the need of an effective federal government, particularly in the field of foreign affairs. On the other hand, he saw possibilities of danger in the polity formulated by the Philadelphia Convention. There was no Bill of Rights to protect the citizens against abuse of power by the government; and the possibility of perpetual re-election of the president might result

[6] Anthony M. Lewis, "Jefferson and Virginia's Pioneers, 1774–1781," *Mississippi Valley Historical Review*, XXXIV (1948), 551; Charles Warren, "The Mississippi River and the Treaty Clause of the Constitution," *George Washington Law Review*, II (1934), 271; Dumas Malone, *Jefferson, The Virginian* (Boston, 1948), p. 419. Speaking of the period after independence, Charles Warren fixes July 4, 1778, as the date "that there arose the first division of Americans into political parties" (p. 273). On that day George Rogers Clark captured Kaskaskia, commencing the conquest of the western territory, access to which depended upon control of the Mississippi; and preparations were afoot in Philadelphia to welcome the French minister, Gérard. That diplomat sought to discourage American expansion westward. His intrigues led to formation of a "Gallican" party among representatives of eastern States. New England, in order to obtain support for its fisheries, which France also opposed, at first voted with the Southern "anti-Gallican" party; but after the interests of that region in the fisheries had been definitely secured by the terms of the peace treaty with Great Britain, New England's commercial interests aligned it with the eastern commercial States who thought the Mississippi comparatively unimportant (pp. 278, 282f).

[7] See note 2 *supra*.

in monarchy. Generally speaking, Jefferson favored the adoption of the Constitution and the simultaneous addition thereto of a Bill of Rights.[8] Through his influence on James Madison, the latter offered in Congress proposals which resulted in the adoption of the Bill of Rights contained in the first ten amendments to the Constitution.

Though Jefferson was thus more of a "federalist" than an "anti-federalist" during the controversies over the Constitution, the situation was different in the next partisan struggle which arose. Here the name "Federalist" continued to be employed to designate one of the contending parties. The leader of this group was Alexander Hamilton, Secretary of the Treasury in the administration of President George Washington. The leader of the other contending party was Jefferson himself. As Secretary of State in Washington's official family, the Virginian found that he and Hamilton "were daily pitted in the cabinet like two cocks." [9]

Hamilton's party was pro-British in its sympathies. It found its chief strength among merchants and financial speculators, whose support for the new government it sought to assure by policies which would afford them pecuniary advantage. It endeavored to increase the powers of the federal government at the expense of the States, and of the executive branch at the expense of the legislative. Distrusting and fearing the people as "a great beast," it looked for the coming of a "crisis" when, through military dictatorship, popular licentiousness might be curbed and the "frail and worthless fabric" of the Constitution might be replaced by a more "energetic" government after the pattern of the English monarchy.[10]

Jefferson's party (which came to be known as "Republican" or "Democratic"), on the other hand, favored popular government. Protection for the rights of individuals against arbitrary action

[8] Edward Dumbauld, "Thomas Jefferson and American Constitutional Law," Emory University *Journal of Public Law,* II (1953), 370, 378ff.

[9] To Walter Jones, Monticello, March 5, 1810. *Works,* XI, 138.

[10] John Sharp Williams, *Thomas Jefferson: His Permanent Influence on American Institutions* (New York, 1913), pp. 152ff.

by officials was regarded as more important than "energy" and authority in the government. Predominance was given to civil over military power. Agricultural rather than mercantile interests were encouraged and, until the vexatious bungling of the French envoy, Edmond Charles Genêt, caused embarrassment to the Jeffersonians, they were sympathetic toward the French Revolution, seeing in it a kindred movement to the American Revolution, and believing that the success of the former would be of help in guaranteeing the permanence of the fruits of the latter.[11]

The triumph of Jefferson at the polls in 1800 marked the death knell of the Federalist party. It never revived from the shock of this defeat, and never regained popular favor. The democratic character of the American polity was assured. The Jeffersonian party continued in power for decades. Apart from a brief interlude caused by the election of the individualistic John Quincy Adams by the House of Representatives in 1825, the democratizing tendency continued with increasing intensity under Andrew Jackson and his successor, Martin Van Buren. But the election of 1840 brought into the presidency General William Henry Harrison, as representative of the "Whig" party which had been formed in 1834 out of a motley aggregation of groups antagonistic to Jackson.[12] Harrison died shortly thereafter, and John Tyler succeeded to the office of Chief Executive. He soon lost the support of the Whigs. In 1844 the Whig candidate, Henry Clay, was defeated by the Democrat, James K. Polk. A Whig president, Zachary Taylor, was elected in 1848. But in 1852 the election of Franklin K. Pierce gave a death blow to the

[11] To Edward Rutledge, Philadelphia, August 29, 1791. *Works,* VI, 309. See also note 2 *supra* and Jefferson's First Inaugural Address.

[12] Edward Stanwood, *A History of the Presidency from 1788 to 1897* (New York, 1898), pp. 179f. Use of the term "Whig" to describe this nineteenth-century party of opposition to the Democrats should be distinguished from its use to describe the Patriots during the Revolutionary period. In that earlier era opponents of the "Loyalists" or "Tories" were often known as "Whigs." This usage survived from the English practice, according to which the "court" and "country" parties were called Tories and Whigs, respectively.

Whig party. The Whigs could not face squarely the burning issue of slavery.

In 1856 there appeared on the national scene a new party (the present Republican Party) whose candidate, John C. Frémont, lost to the Democrat, James Buchanan. But four years later Abraham Lincoln carried the Republican banner to victory.

As a result of the war of 1861–65, the Republican Party remained in power for many years. The first Democrat to hold office thereafter was Grover Cleveland, elected in 1884 and 1892. Woodrow Wilson, chosen in 1912 and 1916, was the second. The third was Franklin D. Roosevelt, who began in 1932 a twenty-year period of Democratic success. In 1952 a Republican, Dwight D. Eisenhower, became president.

The present Democratic Party, it will be noted, claims ancestry extending back to the Republican-Democratic party founded by Jefferson.[13] But it must be observed that when that party, in the post-Jackson period, had come to be dominated by slave-owning sections of the country, it was the principles of Jefferson that inspired the founders of the Republican Party. Its early activities were animated by a zealous determination to revitalize Jefferson's "self-evident truths" regarding human freedom and equality. Abraham Lincoln declared repeatedly that his own opinions were based upon the teachings of Jefferson. "The principles of Jefferson are the definitions and axioms of free society," Lincoln affirmed. Speaking at Independence Hall in Philadelphia on February 22, 1861, he avowed that "all the political sentiments I entertain have been drawn . . . from the sentiments which originated and were given to the world from this hall. I have never had a feeling politically that did not spring from the sentiments embodied in the Declaration of Independence."[14]

The enduring influence of Jefferson on American political parties is thus manifest. Equally plain is his own skill as a

[13] Frank R. Kent, *The Democratic Party: A History* (New York, 1928), p. 14.
[14] Edward Dumbauld, *The Declaration of Independence and What It Means Today*, p. 58.

politician in his own time. Besides liberating his country from
foreign rule, he was successful in holding, among other important
positions of public trust, the highest office in the gift of his state
and of his nation. His policies molded the measures of his successors. This was the effect of gifted political leadership.

The continuance of Jefferson's influence over succeeding generations is doubtless due to the inherent value and validity of his
political philosophy rather than to his skill in the management
of men. Later thinkers revere him because his teachings have
won their own assent rather than because they are dominated
by his political contrivances. But his record in public life is evidence of his superlative skill as a practitioner of the political art.

Jefferson believed that, at any time and place where men are
free to think and to speak, differences of opinion will lead to
formation of political parties.[15] He believed also that there was
a natural division into two parties, one of which fears and dis-
trusts the people, the other of which has faith in the people and
seeks to protect them from abuse and misgovernment on the part
of their rulers.[16]

IV. JEFFERSON'S POLITICAL WRITINGS

Though prominent in political life and as advocate of democratic theories of government, Jefferson produced no systematic
treatise containing a statement of his political principles.[1] These
must be studied in his state papers[2] and in his voluminous correspondence,[3] which often contains luminous and stirring discussion of political topics.

[15] To John Adams, Monticello, June 27, 1813. *Writings*, XIII, 279.
[16] See p. 195, note 8.
[1] Cf. Charles E. Merriam, *A History of American Political Theories*
(New York, 1903), p. 145.
[2] Jefferson advised a publisher proposing to reprint his writings that
"these . . . would no more find readers now, than the journals and statute
books in which they are deposited." To John W. Campbell, September 3,
1809. *Works*, XI, 115ff.
[3] "The letters of a person, especially of one whose business has been

The published books of which Jefferson was author were all, in whole or part, political and legal. These are listed in the bibliography appended to this volume. The only additional items which could have been added to this list would have been contemporary printings of laws, presidential messages, his report on decimal currency, and similar documents.[4] Perhaps the utilitarian compilation, *The Limits and Bounds of Louisiana,*[5] should have been excluded on similar grounds, and the posthumously published *Reports of Cases,* which entitle Jefferson to be numbered among the Virginia law reporters. The *Report of the Committee of Revisors* was prepared with the collaboration of George Wythe, and perhaps also of Edmund Pendleton, though Jefferson apparently performed the major part of the work.[6]

Of the books published during his lifetime and entirely of Jefferson's authorship, the *Summary View,* printed at Williamsburg by Clementina Rind in 1774, is of the greatest significance among his political writings. It was a prelude to the Declaration of Independence and was undoubtedly drawn upon by Jefferson when writing the more famous document of 1776.

The well-known *Notes on Virginia* contains portions which are of great importance from the political standpoint. Jefferson referred to it as "giving a general view of my principles of government." This work, "one which bibliographers love," was written by him in response to inquiries regarding the State propounded by François Marbois, secretary to the French minister in Philadelphia.[7] Later Jefferson printed an edition of 200 copies in Paris

---

chiefly transacted by letters, form the only full and true journal of his life." To Robert Walsh, April 5, 1823. Quoted in Malone, *Jefferson, the Virginian* (Boston, 1948), p. 127.

[4] Mention should perhaps be made of his printed memoir on whale oil, submitted to the French government. To Jay, Paris, November 19, 1788. *Writings,* VII, 192.

[5] Regarding this work, see to P. S. Duponceau, December 30, 1817. *Ibid.,* XV, 159f.

[6] Regarding the revisal of the laws, see Boyd, *Papers of Thomas Jefferson,* II, 305–664.

[7] To Jeremiah Moor, August 14, 1800. *Works,* IX, 142. See also Randolph G. Adams, "Thomas Jefferson, Librarian," in *Three Americanists*

in 1785. A French translation appeared there in 1786, and in 1787 an authorized trade edition in English was issued by Stockdale in London. Numerous other editions have since been published.

Jefferson's *Manual*, published in 1801, he characterized as "a mere compilation, into which nothing entered of my own but the arrangement, and a few observations necessary to explain that and some of the cases."[8] Later editions appeared during the author's lifetime in 1812, 1813, and 1822. The work is still reissued from time to time and regarded as authoritative by the United States Senate.

The *Proceedings of the Government of the United States* was a collection of legal authorities originally gathered by Jefferson for use of his counsel in a lawsuit[9] brought by Edward Livingston against Jefferson seeking damages of $100,000 on account of the latter's official action, while President, in using force to eject Livingston from the *batture* or beach at New Orleans, of which the federal government claimed ownership. The case was decided on a question of jurisdiction, the court holding that an action of that sort could be brought only in a court where the land was situated, and not in Virginia, the residence of the defendant. After the case was thus disposed of, Jefferson published the volume in order to present to the public his justification of his conduct on the merits. The book is an erudite discussion of questions arising under French and Roman law, and a detailed treatment of the facts and documents in the case. "It is merely a law argument, and a very dry one."[10]

The foregoing description of Jefferson's work as an author

(Philadelphia, 1939), p. 78; and Alice H. Lerch, "Who Was the Printer of Jefferson's *Notes?*" in Deoch Fulton, ed., *Bookmen's Holiday* (1943), pp. 44–56. The list of 22 queries is printed in *Papers of Thomas Jefferson*, IV, 166.

[8] To John W. Campbell, September 3, 1809, cited in note 2 *supra*.

[9] *Livingston v. Jefferson*, 1 Brockenbrough 203 (1811), Fed. Cas. No. 8,411.

[10] To Ezra Sargent, February 3, 1812. *Writings*, XIII, 132.

indicates that these books are largely legalistic. Even the *Summary View* is a treatment of the constitutional rights of British America. It is obvious that the unforgettable statements of political theory which have made Jefferson the outstanding exponent of democracy and the American philosophy of government must chiefly be gleaned from his state papers and correspondence.

V. JEFFERSON'S POLITICAL THEORY

1. THE PURPOSE OF GOVERNMENT

Jefferson, as we have seen, proposed to reform the law of Virginia "with a single eye to reason, and the good of those for whose government it was framed." Late in life he wrote: "The equal rights of man and the happiness of every individual are now acknowledged to be the only legitimate objects of government. Modern times have the signal advantage, too, of having discovered the only device by which these rights can be secured, to wit: government by the people, acting not in person, but by representatives chosen by themselves." [1] While President of the United States he declared that "the will of the people . . . is the only legitimate foundation of any government, and to protect its free expression should be our first object." [2] In counseling students what books from his library they should read, Jefferson said: "I endeavor to keep their attention fixed on the main objects of all science, the freedom and happiness of man. So that, coming to bear a share in the councils and government of their country, they will keep ever in view the sole objects of all legitimate government." [3]

The classical Jeffersonian expression of the purpose of government is of course contained in the Declaration of Independence: that all men are created equal, endowed with certain natural rights; and "that to secure these rights, governments are instituted

[1] To A. Coray, October 31, 1823. *Writings*, XV, 482 (Cf. p. 60).
[2] To Benjamin Waring, March 23, 1801. *Ibid.*, X, 236.
[3] To Thaddeus Kosciusko, February 26, 1810. *Ibid.*, XII, 369f.

among men, deriving their just powers from the consent of the governed." [4]

The object of government is, therefore, the protection of pre-existing, God-given rights, which all men enjoy under the law of nature. The mode by which just government is created is consent.

The resemblances are obvious between Jefferson's theory and Locke's state of nature, governed by the law of nature, namely, reason, which state is superseded by civil society through the social compact. [5]

It follows from this conception of the nature of government and the method of establishing it that not all of the rights enjoyed by citizens under the "state of nature" before entering into the social compact were surrendered to the government when that compact was formed. Accordingly Jefferson lays great stress on constitutional limitations. The powers of government are not unlimited. [6] They extend only so far as provided by the constitution or basic fundamental law establishing the scope of governmental powers. An area of reserved natural rights remains after the government is created. Hence a bill of rights, specifying the boundaries of the area which the government may not invade, is an important feature of every constitution.

"There are rights which it is useless to surrender to the government, and which governments have yet always been found to invade. These are the rights of thinking, and publishing our thoughts by speaking or writing; the right of free commerce; the right of personal freedom. There are instruments for administering the government, [such as trial by jury], so peculiarly trustworthy that we should never leave the legislature at liberty to change them. . . . There are instruments [such as a standing army] so dangerous to the rights of the nation, and which place

[4] On another occasion Jefferson said that "it is to secure our just rights that we resort to government at all." To d'Ivernois, February 6, 1795. *Works*, VIII, 165.

[5] See Edward Dumbauld, *The Declaration of Independence and What It Means Today*, pp. 54–74; and Locke, *The Second Treatise of Government*, ed. by T. P. Peardon, "The Library of Liberal Arts," No. 31 (New York: The Liberal Arts Press), pp. 5, 54ff.

[6] *Works*, VIII, 471 (Jefferson's draft of Kentucky Resolutions).

them so totally at the mercy of their governors, that those governors, whether legislative or executive, should be restrained from keeping such instruments on foot, but in well defined cases." [7] These matters should be dealt with in a bill of rights.

Since "the purposes of society do not require a surrender of all our rights to our ordinary governors," [8] Jefferson concluded that "a bill of rights is what the people are entitled to against every government on earth, general or particular, and what no just government should refuse, or rest on inferences." [9] Even though "written constitutions may be violated in moments of passion or delusion, yet they furnish a text to which those who are watchful may again rally and recall the people; they fix too for the people the principles of their political creed." [10] Another important function of a bill of rights is "the legal check which it puts into the hands of the judiciary." [11]

A system of internal checks and balances which shall restrain the government from invading the sphere reserved by the bill of rights becomes an important feature of a well organized government. In view of the disproportionate strength of the government in comparison with the individual citizen, it is imperative that the structure of the government be such as to bring one

[7] To David Humphreys, March 18, 1789. *Works,* V, 470. Cf. to Francis W. Gilmer, June 7, 1816. *Works,* XI, 533f.

[8] To Noah Webster, December 4, 1790. *Works,* VI, 159. Natural rights may be taken away by express compact. To Horatio Gates, Paris, December 13, 1784, *Papers of Thomas Jefferson,* VII, 571; *Works,* VI, 571 (Opinion on residence bill).

[9] To James Madison, December 20, 1787. *Works,* V, 371f.

[10] To Joseph Priestley, June 19, 1802. *Works,* IX, 381f.

[11] To James Madison, March 15, 1789. *Works,* V, 461. Jefferson recognized the value of judicial enforcement of constitutional limitations upon the legislative power. To de Meusnier, January 24, 1786, *Works,* V, 15; to James Madison, June 20, 1787, *ibid.,* V, 284f; to A. H. Rowan, September 26, 1798, *ibid.,* VIII, 448. But he believed that each branch of the government must pass on questions of constitutionality, and that this function was not vested exclusively in the judiciary. To Abigail Adams, September 11, 1804, *ibid.,* X, 89; to W. H. Torrance, June 11, 1815, *ibid.,* XI, 471ff; to Spencer Roane, September 8, 1819, *ibid.,* XII, 136; to W. C. Jarvis, September 8, 1820, *ibid.,* XII, 162f.

organ of government into operation automatically as a counter-vailing force whenever another organ threatens to exceed its rightful powers. Therefore, according to Jefferson: "The first principle of a good government is certainly a distribution of its powers into executive, judiciary, and legislative, and a subdivision of the latter into two or three branches." Hence "the English constitution, acknowledged to be better than all which have preceded it, is only better in proportion as it has approached nearer to this distribution of powers." It is then easy to show "by a comparison of our constitutions with that of England, how much more perfect they are." Jefferson lamented that Americans "do not sufficiently know the value of their constitutions and how much happier they are rendered by them than any other people on earth by the governments under which they live." [12]

Freedom of religion, freedom of the press, trial by jury, habeas corpus, and a representative legislature were enumerated by Jefferson when specifying what he considered as "the essentials constituting free government." [13]

Included by Jefferson among natural rights were the following: life, liberty, and pursuit of happiness; [14] expatriation; [15] self-government; [16] freedom of religion; [17] freedom from retroactive legislation; [18] freedom from imprisonment for debt; [19] freedom from perpetual obligation; [20] freedom of communication between

[12] To John Adams, September 28, 1787. *Works*, V, 349f.

[13] To Dupont de Nemours, February 28, 1815. *Writings*, XIV, 255. Jefferson went on to say "that the organization of the Executive is interesting, as it may ensure wisdom and integrity in the first place, but next as it may favor or endanger the preservation of these fundamentals."

[14] *Works*, I, 35 (Declaration of Independence).

[15] To John Manners, June 12, 1817. *Works*, XII, 66. See also *ibid.*, II, 64 (*Summary View*).

[16] To John H. Pleasants, April 19, 1824. *Works*, XII, 353. See also *ibid.*, VI, 98.

[17] *Works*, II, 441 (Statute of Virginia for Religious Freedom).

[18] To Isaac McPherson, August 13, 1813. *Writings*, XIII, 326f.

[19] To George Hammond, May 29, 1792. *Works*, VII, 53.

[20] To Albert Gallatin, November 26, 1805. *Works*, X, 185.

constituents and representatives;[21] commerce with neighboring nations;[22] innocent navigation;[23] the right to labor for a livelihood;[24] self-defense against wrongdoers[25] and aggressors;[26] coercion against the delinquent party to a compact;[27] and the right to an impartial judge.[28]

2. THE FORM OF GOVERNMENT

What has been said demonstrates also Jefferson's belief that the best form of government is that in which popular participation is assured. For not only is protection of the rights of the people the only legitimate object of government, but the best form of government is that which most effectively affords such protection. Only a republican form of government, where the people themselves participate in political processes, meets this test. Jefferson was convinced that the people themselves were the only safe guardians of their own interests. Especially after his observations in Europe he was certain that kings and hereditary rulers brought nothing but unhappiness to the people upon whom they were saddled. He believed "that government to be the strongest of which every man feels himself a part." Hence he regarded the American republic as "the strongest government on earth" where every man at the call of the law would "meet invasions of public order as his own personal concern."[29]

[21] To James Monroe, September 7, 1797. *Works*, VIII, 339f. See also *ibid.*, 327.

[22] To George Washington, December 4, 1788. *Works*, V, 438.

[23] To Albert Gallatin, July 4, 1807. *Writings*, XI, 257. See also *Works*, VI, 425 (Report on negotiations with Spain, March 18, 1792).

[24] To James Madison, October 28, 1785. *Works*, VIII, 196. See also *ibid.*, XII, 436, 442 (Thoughts on lotteries).

[25] To W. C. Claiborne, May 3, 1810. *Writings*, XII, 383.

[26] To George Rogers Clark, January 29, 1780. *Papers of Thomas Jefferson*, III, 276.

[27] To Edward Carrington, August 4, 1787. *Works*, V, 319.

[28] To Francis W. Gilmer, June 7, 1816. *Works*, XI, 534.

[29] To Edward Tiffin, February 2, 1807, *Writings*, XI, 147; First Inaugural, *Works*, IX, 196 (Cf. p. 43.).

The people should share not only in the enactment of the laws, but also in their enforcement. This could be accomplished through the jury system, in combination with popular election of the legislative assembly and of the executive magistrate.[30] Jefferson regarded a government as republican only to the degree that "every member composing it has his equal voice in the direction of its concerns."[31] He declared also that "the republican is the only form of government which is not eternally at open or secret war with the rights of mankind."[32]

With regard to the machinery of government, Jefferson also favored the principle that all questions should be decided by those whom they concern. This meant the application of a system of federalism or "governmental gradation."[33] Local concerns would be dealt with at the local level. Jefferson favored the division of counties into "wards," for the administration of affairs affecting only groups of that size. County, state, national, and international concerns would be handled by progressively wider units in the political hierarchy.[34] "The natural right of self-government"[35] could thus be made applicable all the way from the individual citizen managing his own affairs to a democratic international organization embodying the modern notion of "world government," a notion implicit in Jefferson's own principle of "gradation" and not unfamiliar to Jeffersonian political thinkers, such as Richard Price and Joel Barlow. "Every man, and every

[30] To the Abbé Arnoux, July 19, 1789. *Works*, V, 483. Trial by jury Jefferson considered "as the only anchor yet imagined by man, by which a government can be held to the principles of its constitution." To Thomas Paine, July 11, 1789. *Writings*, VII, 408.

[31] To Samuel Kercheval, July 12, 1816. *Writings*, XII, 4; to P. S. Dupont de Nemours, April 24, 1816, *ibid.*, XI, 520, 523; to John Taylor, May 28, 1816, *ibid.*, XI, 529, 532.

[32] To William Hunter, March 11, 1790. *Writings*, VI, 34.

[33] Charles E. Merriam, *A History of American Political Theories*, p. 160.

[34] To Joseph C. Cabell, February 2, 1816, *Writings*, XIV, 421f; *Works*, I, 122f. (Autobiography); to Samuel Kercheval, July 12, 1816, *ibid.*, XII, 9; to John Adams, October 28, 1813, *ibid.*, XI, 347.

[35] To John Pleasants, April 19, 1824. *Works*, XII, 353.

body of men on earth, possesses the right of self-government. They receive it with their being from the hand of nature." [36]

The value of governmental institutions, in Jefferson's view, was measured by their effectiveness as a means of expressing the popular will. As Secretary of State, he instructed the ·American minister to France that: "It accords with our principles to acknowledge any government to be rightful which is formed by the will of the nation substantially declared." [37]

"The right of nations to self-government being my polar star," [38] Jefferson declared that "I do not indeed wish to see any nation have a form of government forced on them; but if it is to be done, I should rejoice at its being a freer one." [39] He criticized the French for "endeavoring to force liberty on their neighbors in their own form." [40] To Lafayette, writing of the Spanish American insurgents, he said: "No one, I hope, can doubt my wish to see them and all mankind exercising self-government and capable of exercising it. But the question is not what we wish, but what is practicable." [41] In his opinion, "the excellence of every government is its adaptation to the state of those who are governed by it." [42]

[36] *Works*, VI, 98. In his *Summary View* Jefferson wrote: "The God who gave us life gave us liberty at the same time; the hand of force may destroy, but cannot disjoin them." *Works*, II, 89. This sentiment is voiced in the Latin motto: *Ab eo libertas a quo spiritus.*

[37] To Gouverneur Morris, November 7, 1792. *Works*, VII, 175. See also *ibid.*, 198, 284f.

[38] To J. Correa, June 28, 1815. *Writings*, XIV, 330.

[39] To Peregrine Fitzhugh, February 23, 1798. *Works*, VIII, 378. See also to Albert Gallatin, June 16, 1817; to John Adams, May 17, 1818; to James Monroe, December 1, 1822. *Works*, XII, 71, 96, 273f.

[40] To Thomas M. Randolph, June 24, 1793. *Works*, VII, 410.

[41] To Lafayette, May 14, 1817. *Works*, XII, 63. Jefferson recognized that "the qualifications for self-government are not innate. They are the result of habit and long training." To Edward Everett, March 27, 1824. *Writings*, XVII, 22. See also to Joseph Priestley, Washington, November 29, 1802. *Works*, IX, 404.

[42] To P. S. Dupont de Nemours, April 24, 1816. *Works*, XI, 519. Not all peoples are ripe for liberty, rooted in reason, or for independence. To Lafayette, February 14, 1815, *ibid.*, p. 455; to Lafayette, November 30,

Likewise political institutions must keep pace with the progress of events and develop as science and enlightenment advance.[43] The earth belongs to the living and not to the dead. "Nothing then is unchangeable but the inherent and unalienable rights of man."[44]

3. The Spirit of Government

Jefferson recognized the distinction between the structure of government and the spirit with which it is administered.[45] He acknowledged that in Revolutionary Virginia "the spirit of our people . . . would oblige even a despot to govern us republicanly."[46]

His experience in Europe confirmed Jefferson's conviction that American conditions were far preferable to those in other countries and should be preserved from contamination by foreign influence and example. In Europe he observed "governments of force" that were governments "of wolves over sheep." The com-

1813, *ibid.*, 357; to Lafayette, May 14, 1817, *ibid.*, XII, 63f; to John Adams, May 17, 1818, *ibid.*, XII, 95f; to Dewitt Clinton, December 2, 1803, *ibid.*, X, 55; to Samuel Brown, July 14, 1813, *Writings*, XIII, 311.

[43] To Samuel Kercheval, July 12, 1816, *Works*, XII, 11f; to Robert Garnett, February 14, 1824, *ibid.*, 342. The same optimistic desire for progress and reform which colored Jefferson's views on the immutability of constitutions and his Revisal of Virginia legislation extended to international law. "Why should not this Law of Nations go on improving?" he inquired of a European diplomat with whom he was negotiating a treaty. To de Thulemeier, Passy, November 10, 1784. *Papers of Thomas Jefferson*, VII, 491. Jefferson sought "while we are reforming the principles to reform also the language of treaties . . . by simplifying their style and structure." *Ibid.*, VII, 463, 466, 476f.

[44] To John Cartwright, June 5, 1824. *Writings*, XVI, 48.

[45] To P. S. Dupont de Nemours, April 24, 1816. *Ibid.*, XI, 519, 522. Dupont loved the people as children, Jefferson as adults capable of managing their own affairs.

[46] It was his wish "to secure self-government by the republicanism of our constitution, as well as by the spirit of our people." To Samuel Kercheval, July 12, 1816. *Ibid.*, XII, 6, 10.

parison of American political institutions with those of Europe was "like a comparison of heaven and hell. England, like the earth, may be allowed to take the intermediate station." To George Washington he wrote: "I was much an enemy to monarchies before I came to Europe. I am ten thousand times more so, since I have seen what they are." Describing the policy he pursued as president, he said: "Having seen the people of other nations bowed down to the earth under the prodigalities of their rulers, I have cherished their opposites, peace, economy, and riddance of public debt, believing that these were the highroad to public as well as to private prosperity and happiness." [47]

Jefferson regarded "republicanism and Americanism" [48] as synonymous sentiments. The American system was a civilization based upon peace and productivity. Of the European countries he said: "They are nations of eternal war. All their energies are expended in the destruction of the labor, property, and lives of their people. On our part, never had a people so favorable a chance of trying the opposite system, of peace and fraternity with mankind, and the direction of all our means and faculties to the purposes of improvement instead of destruction." [49] Jefferson never forgot that: "The care of human life and happiness, and not their destruction, is the first and only legitimate object of good government." [50]

The triumph of Jefferson's party in the election of 1800 meant

[47] Edward Dumbauld, *Thomas Jefferson: American Tourist,* pp. 211ff.
[48] To Joshua Dodge, August 3, 1823. *Writings,* XVIII, 322.
[49] To James Monroe, June 11, 1823. *Works,* XII, 292. See also to James Madison, March 23, 1815, *Works,* XI, 464, 466; and to George Logan, March 21, 1801, *ibid.,* IX, 220. Though Jefferson believed that "our form of government is odious" to autocrats "as a standing contrast between republican and despotic rule," he did not fear attacks from European governments because: "They have too many jealousies of one another to engage in distant wars for a matter of opinion only." To Thomas Leiper, June 12, 1815, *Works,* XI, 477; to Tench Coxe, March 27, 1807, *Writings,* XI, 176.
[50] To Republican Citizens of Washington County, Maryland, March 31, 1809. *Writings,* XVI, 359.

that the Constitution of 1787 was to be used as a vehicle for popular self-government, as an instrument of democracy.[51] That document, viewed simply as a piece of political machinery, could be operated either in the Hamilton manner to pattern a government on the British monarchy, or in the Jeffersonian fashion as a means of effectuating the ideals of freedom. The nation's polity was fluid and uncertain until Jefferson's presidency. The conservative, anti-democratic sentiment which grew in strength during the period of the Confederation and which was influential at the Philadelphia Convention [52] could have used the Constitution as a basis for "administering the government into a monarchy," as the Jeffersonians feared might happen.[53]

But with Jefferson's victory at the polls the situation was different. The spirit of the government changed. Of this second "revolution" in American politics, as Jefferson called it,[54] he wrote soon after his election to an old friend who had shared his labors in establishing the nation's independence: "The storm through which we have passed has been tremendous indeed. The tough sides of our argosy have been thoroughly tried. Her strength has stood the waves into which she was steered, with a view to sink her. We shall put her on her republican tack, and she will now show by the beauty of her motion the skill of her builders." [55]

In other words, Jefferson infused into the Constitution the

[51] Walter Lippmann, *Public Opinion* (New York, 1922), p. 282: "It was Jefferson who taught the American people to regard the Constitution as an instrument of democracy."

[52] Edward S. Corwin, "The Progress of Constitutional Theory between the Declaration of Independence and the Meeting of the Philadelphia Convention," *American Historical Review*, XXX (April, 1925), 511–536.

[53] *Works*, I, 178 (Anas). Jefferson awaited the sunrise of democracy with confidence: "The unquestionable republicanism of the American mind will break through the mist under which it has been clouded, and will oblige its agents to reform the principles and practices of their administration." To Elbridge Gerry, January 26, 1799. *Works*, IX, 23.

[54] To Spencer Roane, September 6, 1819. *Works*, XII, 136.

[55] To John Dickinson, March 6, 1801. *Works*, IX, 201 (Cf. p. 76.).

spirit of the Declaration of Independence.[56] Thereafter, it was no longer merely a piece of ambivalent political machinery but an object of popular reverence, a cherished part of the American way of life.

The essential spirit of Jeffersonian political theory was faith in the people. "I have so much confidence in the good sense of man, and his qualification for self-government, that I am never afraid of the issue where reason is left free to exert her force." [57]

A new civilization, based on "cherishment of the people," Jefferson believed, was destined to arise in America. The doctrine of Europe (and of statesmen such as Alexander Hamilton) was that the people was "a great beast" and must be restrained by brute force. The Jeffersonian doctrine was "that man was a rational animal, endowed by nature with rights," and could be trusted to maintain law and order by means of a government of limited powers, responsible to the people, and permitting citizens "to think for themselves, and to follow reason as their guide." [58] The philosophy of human brotherhood and enlightenment for which Jefferson stood, the confident faith that America was a virgin land of hope and opportunity, became the dominant and distinctive national tradition.[59]

[56] Alexander M. Harvey, *Jefferson and the American Constitution* (1926), p. 8.

[57] To Count Diodati, August 3, 1789. Massachusetts Historical Society, Jefferson Papers.

[58] To William Johnson, June 12, 1823. *Writings*, XV, 442.

[59] Henry Adams, *History of the United States* (New York, 1889), I, 156–184. Americans are essentially life-affirmers rather than life-deniers; "they believe in tomorrow." Van Wyck Brooks, *The Confident Years* (Boston, 1952), pp. 582, 584ff.

SELECTED BIBLIOGRAPHY

Jefferson's Major Political Works

The Limits and Bounds of Louisiana. *In* Documents Relating to the Purchase and Exploration of Louisiana. Boston, 1904.

A Manual of Parliamentary Practice. For the Use of the Senate of the United States. Washington, 1801.

Notes on the State of Virginia. Paris, 1782. [Actually printed 1785.]

The Proceedings of the Government of the United States in Maintaining The Public Right to the Beach of the Missisipi, Adjacent to New-Orleans, against the Intrusion of Edward Livingston. New York, 1812.

Report of the Committee of Revisors Appointed by the General Assembly of Virginia In MDCCLXXVI. Richmond, 1784.

Reports of Cases Determined in the General Court of Virginia. From 1730 to 1740, and from 1768 to 1772. Charlottesville, Va., 1829.

A Summary View of the Rights of British America. Williamsburg, 1774.

Collected Works

Boyd, Julian P., and others, eds., *The Papers of Thomas Jefferson.* 10 vols. to date. Princeton, 1950–. (This magnificent edition surpasses all others but at present goes only to Dec. 31, 1786. Lipscomb and Bergh reprinted Washington with a small amount of additional material, and included some items not found in Ford, who is more accurate. For convenient bibliographical material on Jefferson, see Edward Dumbauld, *Thomas Jefferson: American Tourist,* Norman, Okla., 1946, pp. 241–260; and Dumas Malone, *Jefferson and His Time,* 2 vols. to date, Boston, 1948–1951, I, 456–470, II, 494–504. Malone's work is the standard modern biography of Jefferson, replacing Henry S.

Randall, *The Life of Thomas Jefferson,* 3 vols., New York, 1858.)

Foley, John P., ed., *The Jeffersonian Cyclopedia.* New York, 1900.

Ford, Paul L., ed., *The Works of Thomas Jefferson.* 12 vols. New York, 1904.

———, *The Writings of Thomas Jefferson.* 10 vols. New York, 1892–99.

Lipscomb, Andrew A., and A. Ellery Bergh, eds., *The Writings of Thomas Jefferson.* 20 vols. Washington, 1903.

Randolph, Thomas J., ed., *Memoir, Correspondence and Miscellanies, from the Papers of Thomas Jefferson.* 4 vols. Charlottesville, Va., 1829.

Washington, Henry A., ed., *The Writings of Thomas Jefferson.* 9 vols. Washington, 1853–54.

COLLATERAL READING

Adams, James Truslow, ed., *Jeffersonian Principles.* Boston, 1928.

Adams, Randolph G., *Political Ideas of the American Revolution.* Durham, N. C., 1922.

Barrett, Jay A., *Evolution of the Ordinance of 1787 with an Account of the Earlier Plans for the Government of the Northwest Territory.* New York, 1891.

Caldwell, Lynton K., *The Administrative Theories of Hamilton and Jefferson.* Chicago, 1944.

Chinard, Gilbert, ed., *The Commonplace Book of Thomas Jefferson.* Baltimore and Paris, 1926.

Davis, John W., "Thomas Jefferson, Attorney at Law," in Rosenberger, Francis C., *Jefferson Reader,* New York, 1953, pp. 117–130.

Dodd, William E., *Thomas Jeffersons Rückkehr zur Politik.* [Leipzig, 1899.]

Dumbauld, Edward, *The Declaration of Independence and What It Means Today.* Norman, 1950.

———, *Thomas Jefferson: American Tourist.* Norman, 1946.

———, "Thomas Jefferson and American Constitutional Law," *Journal of Public Law,* II (1953), 370–389.

Gilpatrick, Delbert H., *Jeffersonian Democracy in North Carolina*. New York, 1931.

Kean, Robert G., "Thomas Jefferson as a Legislator," *Virginia Law Journal*, XI (Dec., 1887), 705–724.

Koch, Adrienne, *Jefferson and Madison*. New York, 1950.

———, *The Philosophy of Thomas Jefferson*. New York, 1943.

Latané, John H., "Jefferson's Influence on American Foreign Policy," *University of Virginia Alumni Bulletin* (3rd series), XVII (July–Aug., 1924), 245–269.

Malone, Dumas, *Jefferson and His Time*. 2 vols. to date. Boston, 1948–1951. Vol. I, *Jefferson, the Virginian* (1948). Vol. II, *Jefferson and the Rights of Man* (1951).

Merriam, Charles E., *A History of American Political Theories*. New York, 1903.

———, "The Political Theory of Jefferson," *Political Science Quarterly*, XVII (March, 1902), 24–45.

Mullett, Charles F., *Fundamental Law and the American Revolution*. New York, 1923.

Nussbaum, Frederick L., "American Tobacco and French Politics 1783–1789," *Political Science Quarterly*, XL (Dec., 1925), 561–593.

Padover, Saul K., *Democracy: By Thomas Jefferson*. New York, 1939.

Patterson, Caleb Perry, *The Constitutional Principles of Thomas Jefferson*. Austin, 1953.

Randall, Henry S., *The Life of Thomas Jefferson*. 3 vols. New York, 1858.

Robinson, William A., *Jeffersonian Democracy in New England*. New Haven, 1916.

Ross, William E., "History of Virginia Codification," *Virginia Law Register*, XI (June, 1905), 79–101.

Russell, Elmer B., *Review of American Colonial Legislation by the King in Council*. New York, 1915.

Sanders, Jennings B., *Evolution of the Executive Departments of the Continental Congress 1774–1789*. Chapel Hill, 1935.

Schellenberg, T. R., "Jeffersonian Origins of the Monroe Doctrine," *The Hispanic American Historical Review*, XIV (Feb., 1934), 1–31.

Sears, Louis M., *Jefferson and the Embargo*. Durham, N. C., 1927.

Smith, Joseph H., *Appeals to the Privy Council from the American Plantations*. New York, 1950.

Sowerby, E. Millicent, *Catalogue of the Library of Thomas Jefferson*. 3 vols. to date. Washington, 1952–.

Thomas, Charles M., *American Neutrality in 1793*. New York, 1931.

Thomas, Elbert D., *Thomas Jefferson: World Citizen*. New York, 1942.

Vossler, Otto. *Die amerikanischen Revolutionsideale in ihrem Verhältnis zu den europäischen*. Munich and Berlin, 1929.

Warfield, Ethelbert D., *The Kentucky Resolutions of 1798*. New York, 1887.

Warren, Charles, "Fourth of July Myths," *William and Mary Quarterly* (3rd ser.), II (July, 1945), 237–272.

Washburne, George A., *Imperial Control of the Administration of Justice in the Thirteen American Colonies, 1684–1776*. New York, 1923.

Waterman, Julian S., "Thomas Jefferson and Blackstone's Commentaries," *Illinois Law Review*, XXVII (Feb., 1933), 629–659.

Wayland, John W., *The Political Opinions of Thomas Jefferson*. New York, 1907.

White, Leonard D., *The Jeffersonians: A Study in Administrative History 1801–1829*. New York, 1951.

Williams, John Sharp, *Thomas Jefferson: His Permanent Influence on American Institutions*. New York, 1913.

Wiltse, Charles M., *The Jeffersonian Tradition in American Democracy*. Chapel Hill, 1935.

Wolfe, John H., *Jeffersonian Democracy in South Carolina*. Chapel Hill, 1940.

Woolery, William K., *The Relation of Thomas Jefferson to American Foreign Policy 1783–1793*. Baltimore, 1927.

Wright, Benjamin F., Jr., *American Interpretations of Natural Law*. Cambridge, Mass., 1931.

NOTE ON THE TEXT

The faithful presentation of Jefferson's political thought being the chief criterion of selection, the material included in this volume has been gathered from several sources. Some items were transcribed directly from hitherto unpublished manuscripts in the Library of Congress. In general, the text follows the published versions as found in the editions of Ford, Washington, and Lipscomb and Bergh. Where the text on its face appeared questionable, the passage in the source being used was compared, when possible, with the other editions named or preferably with Boyd's edition now in progress at Princeton, and in some instances with the Stockdale edition of Jefferson's *Notes on Virginia.* To have verified throughout this book the accuracy of the published versions used as sources would have been an unwarranted effort, duplicating the magnificent editorial task being performed by Boyd and his staff in the definitive edition of Jefferson's papers. The text here printed is believed to be an accurate version of what Jefferson wrote, although no attempt has been made to reproduce his peculiarities of style: he seldom began a sentence with a capital letter, but would capitalize an important word in the middle of a sentence; he usually wrote "recieve," "knolege," and employed contractions such as "agst" for "against," and the like.

For the convenience of the reader the editor has provided a set of notes divided into Headnotes, Footnotes, Appendix Notes, and a Biographical Index. The Appendix Notes are marked by a superior figure in the text. The Biographical Index is organized in alphabetical order. With the exception of the Declaration of Independence, punctuation, capitalization, and spelling of the text have been modified to conform to modern American usage.

In the case of the Declaration of Independence, on account of the importance of this document, the exact text as engrossed on parchment has been reproduced as faithfully as the limitations of print and the fallibility of human eyesight and judgment permit. Through the courtesy of the Library of Congress, the editor established the present text by careful collation of the following standards: (1) the glass negative taken by Levin C. Handy April 23, 1903, and a screened print derived therefrom; (2) a photograph by Truman Stone taken May 16, 1942, 21¾ by 18½ inches; (3) the screened photograph appearing as an illustration in John H. Hazelton, *The Declaration of Independence: Its History* (1906), opposite page 218; and (4) over half a dozen other photographs examined to verify particular readings. The original parchment, which was transferred from the Library of Congress to the National Archives on December 13, 1952, has become faded and difficult to decipher especially in the center portion. This condition may have resulted from exposure to light in former years and also from the wet process used by W. J. Stone (in 1823 under the direction of John Quincy Adams, then Secretary of State) in making the copper-plate facsimile from which the reproductions commonly seen are derived.

The varied size and shape of the engrosser's ornate lettering can convey shades of emphasis not indicated by ordinary printing. Thus the enlarged lower-case *p* and *d* sometimes employed might reasonably be read as capital letters, *e.g.* in "depository of their public Records," or "do . . . publish and declare." One would also be justified, on the basis of the ocular evidence, in placing a colon after "frontiers" and a period after "humble terms." But the initial letter in "lives of our people" lacks the curve and loop characteristic of the capital *L* elsewhere; and there is no doubt that "united States of America," though in emphatic and distinctive script, does not begin with a capital *U*. In matters of typographical style the engrossed Declaration differs from the other two official texts: the broadside printed at Philadelphia on the night of July 4, 1776, by John Dunlap, and the version contained in the Corrected Journal of Congress.

E. D.

The Political Writings of
THOMAS JEFFERSON

CHAPTER ONE

FUNDAMENTALS OF RIGHTFUL GOVERNMENT

I. THE DECLARATION OF INDEPENDENCE

The Declaration of Independence is Jefferson's best known state paper. It contains, too, one of the most forceful statements of his basic political principles.[a] That Jefferson spoke of "pursuit of happiness" and did not mention "property" is due to the fact that he was referring only to "natural rights" in the Declaration, and that he considered property rights as a product of civil society rather than as something existing in the "state of nature."

When in the Course of human events it becomes necessary for one people to dissolve the political bands which have connected them with another, and to assume among the powers of the earth, the separate and equal station to which the Laws of Nature and of Nature's God entitle them, a decent respect to the opinions of mankind requires that they should declare the causes which impel them to the separation.

We hold these truths to be self-evident, that all men are created equal, that they are endowed by their Creator with certain unalienable Rights, that among these are Life, Liberty and the pursuit of Happiness.—That to secure these rights, Governments are instituted among Men, deriving their just powers from the consent of the governed.—That whenever any Form of Government becomes destructive of these ends, it is the Right of the People to alter or to abolish it, and to institute new Government, laying its foundation on such principles, and organizing its powers in such form, as to them shall seem most likely to effect their

---

[a] For detailed comments on the Declaration of Independence see the editor's *The Declaration of Independence and What It Means Today.* (Norman, Okla., 1950).

Safety and Happiness. Prudence, indeed, will dictate that Governments long established should not be changed for light and transient causes; and accordingly all experience hath shewn, that mankind are more disposed to suffer, while evils are sufferable, than to right themselves by abolishing the forms to which they are accustomed. But when a long train of abuses and usurpations, pursuing invariably the same Object, evinces a design to reduce them under absolute Despotism, it is their right, it is their duty, to throw off such Government, and to provide new Guards for their future security.—Such has been the patient sufferance of these Colonies; and such is now the necessity which constrains them to alter their former Systems of Government. The history of the present King of Great Britain is a history of repeated injuries and usurpations, all having in direct object the establishment of an absolute Tyranny over these States. To prove this, let Facts be submitted to a candid world.

He has refused his Assent to Laws, the most wholesome and necessary for the public good.

He has forbidden his Governors to pass Laws of immediate and pressing importance, unless suspended in their operation till his Assent should be obtained; and when so suspended, he has utterly neglected to attend to them.

He has refused to pass other Laws for the accommodation of large districts of people, unless those people would relinquish the right of Representation in the Legislature, a right inestimable to them and formidable to tyrants only.

He has called together legislative bodies at places unusual, uncomfortable, and distant from the depository of their public Records, for the sole purpose of fatiguing them into compliance with his measures.

He has dissolved Representative Houses repeatedly, for opposing with manly firmness his invasions on the rights of the people.

He has refused for a long time, after such dissolutions, to cause others to be elected; whereby the Legislative powers, incapable of Annihilation, have returned to the People at large for their exercise; the State remaining in the mean time exposed to all the dangers of invasion from without, and convulsions within.

He has endeavoured to prevent the population of these States; for that purpose obstructing the Laws for Naturalization of Foreigners; refusing to pass others to encourage their migrations hither, and raising the conditions of new Appropriations of Lands.

He has obstructed the Administration of Justice, by refusing his Assent to Laws for establishing Judiciary powers.

He has made Judges dependent on his Will alone, for the tenure of their offices, and the amount and payment of their salaries.

He has erected a multitude of New Offices, and sent hither swarms of Officers to harrass our people, and eat out their substance.

He has kept among us, in times of peace, Standing Armies without the Consent of our legislatures.

He has affected to render the Military independent of and superior to the Civil power.

He has combined with others to subject us to a jurisdiction foreign to our constitution, and unacknowledged by our laws; giving his Assent to their Acts of pretended Legislation:

For quartering large bodies of armed troops among us:

For protecting them, by a mock Trial, from punishment for any Murders which they should commit on the Inhabitants of these States:

For cutting off our Trade with all parts of the world:

For imposing Taxes on us without our Consent:

For depriving us in many cases, of the benefits of Trial by Jury:

For transporting us beyond Seas to be tried for pretended offences:

For abolishing the free System of English Laws in a neighbouring Province, establishing therein an Arbitrary government, and enlarging its Boundaries so as to render it at once an example and fit instrument for introducing the same absolute rule into these Colonies:

For taking away our Charters, abolishing our most valuable Laws, and altering fundamentally the Forms of our Governments:

For suspending our own Legislatures, and declaring themselves invested with power to legislate for us in all cases whatsoever.

He has abdicated Government here, by declaring us out of his Protection and waging War against us.

He has plundered our seas, ravaged our Coasts, burnt our towns, and destroyed the lives of our people.

He is at this time transporting large Armies of foreign Mercenaries to compleat the works of death, desolation and tyranny, already begun with circumstances of Cruelty & perfidy scarcely paralleled in the most barbarous ages, and totally unworthy the Head of a civilized nation.

He has constrained our fellow Citizens taken Captive on the high Seas to bear Arms against their Country, to become the executioners of their friends and Brethren, or to fall themselves by their Hands.

He has excited domestic insurrections amongst us, and has endeavoured to bring on the inhabitants of our frontiers; the merciless Indian Savages, whose known rule of warfare, is an undistinguished destruction of all ages, sexes and conditions.

In every stage of these Oppressions We have Petitioned for Redress in the most humble terms: Our repeated Petitions have been answered only by repeated injury. A Prince, whose character is thus marked by every act which may define a Tyrant, is unfit to be the ruler of a free people.

Nor have We been wanting in attentions to our Brittish brethren. We have warned them from time to time of attempts by their legislature to extend an unwarrantable jurisdiction over us. We have reminded them of the circumstances of our emigration and settlement here. We have appealed to their native justice and magnanimity, and we have conjured them by the ties of our common kindred to disavow these usurpations, which would inevitably interrupt our connections and correspondence. They too have been deaf to the voice of justice and of consanguinity. We must, therefore, acquiesce in the necessity, which denounces our Separation, and hold them, as we hold the rest of mankind, Enemies in War, in Peace Friends.

We, therefore, the Representatives of the united States of

America, in General Congress, Assembled, appealing to the Supreme Judge of the world for the rectitude of our intentions, do, in the Name, and by Authority of the good People of these Colonies solemnly publish and declare, That these United Colonies are, and of Right ought to be Free and Independent States; that they are Absolved from all Allegiance to the British Crown, and that all political connection between them and the State of Great Britain, is and ought to be totally dissolved; and that as Free and Independent States, they have full Power to levy War, conclude Peace, contract Alliances, establish Commerce, and to do all other Acts and Things which Independent States may of right do.

And for the support of this Declaration, with a firm reliance on the protection of divine Providence, we mutually pledge to each other our Lives, our Fortunes and our sacred Honor.

Circumstances of Adoption of Declaration

Timothy Pickering, a New England Federalist, in a Fourth of July address in 1823 sought to minimize the importance of Jefferson's contribution to the Declaration. This incident elicited comment by Jefferson regarding the circumstances of its adoption.

Pickering's observations, and Mr. Adams' in addition, "that it contained no new ideas, that it is a commonplace compilation, its sentiments hackneyed in Congress for two years before, and its essence contained in Otis' pamphlet," may all be true. Of that I am not to be the judge. Richard Henry Lee charged it as copied from Locke's treatise on government. Otis' pamphlet I never saw, and whether I had gathered my ideas from reading or reflection I do not know. I know only that I turned to neither book nor pamphlet while writing it. I did not consider it as any part of my charge to invent new ideas altogether and to offer no sentiment which had ever been expressed before. Had Mr.

Adams been so restrained, Congress would have lost the benefit of his bold and impressive advocations of the rights of Revolution. . . . This, however, I will say for Mr. Adams, that he supported the Declaration with zeal and ability, fighting fearlessly for every word of it. As to myself, I thought it a duty to be, on that occasion, a passive auditor of the opinions of others, more impartial judges than I could be of its merits or demerits. . . .

Timothy thinks the instrument the better for having a fourth of it expunged. He would have thought it still better had the other three fourths gone out also, all but the single sentiment (the only one he approves), which recommends friendship to his dear England, whenever she is willing to be at peace with us. . . . In opposition, however, to Mr. Pickering I pray God that these principles may be eternal.

To James Madison, Monticello, August 30, 1823.

With respect to our rights and the acts of the British government contravening those rights, there was but one opinion on this side of the water. All American Whigs thought alike on these subjects. When forced, therefore, to resort to arms for redress, an appeal to the tribunal of the world was deemed proper for our justification. This was the object of the Declaration of Independence. Not to find out new principles or new arguments never before thought of, not merely to say things which had never been said before, but to place before mankind the common sense of the subject in terms so plain and firm as to command their assent, and to justify ourselves in the independent stand we are compelled to take. Neither aiming at originality of principle or sentiment, nor yet copied from any particular and previous writing, it was intended to be an expression of the American mind, and to give to that expression the proper tone and spirit called for by the occasion. All its authority rests then on the harmonizing sentiments of the day, whether expressed in conversation, in letters, printed essays, or in the elementary books of public right, as Aristotle, Cicero, Locke, Sidney, etc.[1]

To Henry Lee, Monticello, May 8, 1825.

The kind invitation I receive from you on the part of the citizens of the city of Washington, to be present with them at their celebration on the fiftieth anniversary of American Independence, as one of the surviving signers of an instrument pregnant with our own and the fate of the world, is most flattering to myself and heightened by the honorable accompaniment proposed for the comfort of such a journey. It adds sensibly to the sufferings of sickness to be deprived by it of a personal participation in the rejoicings of that day. But acquiescence is a duty under circumstances not placed among those we are permitted to control. I should indeed, with peculiar delight, have met and exchanged there congratulations personally with the small band, the remnant of that host of worthies who joined with us on that day in the bold and doubtful election we were to make for our country between submission or the sword, and to have enjoyed with them the consolatory fact that our fellow citizens, after half a century of experience and prosperity, continue to approve the choice we made. May it be to the world what I believe it will be (to some parts sooner, to others later, but finally to all), the signal of arousing men to burst the chains under which monkish ignorance and superstition had persuaded them to bind themselves and to assume the blessings and security of self-government. That form which we have substituted restores the free right to the unbounded exercise of reason and freedom of opinion. All eyes are opened, or opening, to the rights of man. The general spread of the light of science has already laid open to every view the palpable truth that the mass of mankind has not been born with saddles on their backs, nor a favored few booted and spurred, ready to ride them legitimately, by the grace of God. These are grounds of hope for others. For ourselves, let the annual return of this day forever refresh our recollections of these rights and an undiminished devotion to them.

To Roger C. Weightman, Monticello, June 24, 1826.

II. JEFFERSON'S DRAFT CONSTITUTION FOR VIRGINIA

Though Jefferson states that he "turned to neither book nor pamphlet" while writing the Declaration, it is obvious that besides the influence of Locke and the English Bill of Rights he drew upon his own draft of a constitution for Virginia, which he had completed by the middle of June, 1776.

A Bill for new-modeling the form of Government and for establishing the fundamental principles thereof in future.

Whereas George Guelf, king of Great Britain and Ireland and Elector of Hanover, heretofore entrusted with the exercise of the kingly office in this government, has endeavored to pervert the same into a detestable and insupportable tyranny by putting his negative on laws the most wholesome and necessary for ye public good;

by denying to his governors permission to pass laws of immediate and pressing importance, unless suspended in their operation for his assent, and when so suspended, neglecting to attend to them for many years;

by refusing to pass certain other laws, unless the persons to be benefited by them would relinquish the inestimable right of representation in the legislature;

by dissolving legislative assemblies repeatedly and continually for opposing with manly firmness his invasions on the rights of the people;

when dissolved, by refusing to call others for a long space of time, thereby leaving the political system without any legislative head;

by endeavoring to prevent the population of our country, and for that purpose obstructing the laws for the naturalization of foreigners and raising the conditions of new appropriations of lands;

by keeping among us, in times of peace, standing armies and ships of war;

by affecting to render the military independent of and superior to the civil power;

by combining with others to subject us to a foreign jurisdiction, giving his assent to their pretended acts of legislation

for quartering large bodies of troops among us;

for cutting off our trade with all parts of the world;

for imposing taxes on us without our consent;

for depriving us of the benefits of trial by jury;

for transporting us beyond seas to be tried for pretended offenses; and

for suspending our own legislatures and declaring themselves invested with power to legislate for us in all cases whatsoever;

by plundering our seas, ravaging our coasts, burning our towns, and destroying the lives of our people;

by inciting insurrections of our fellow subjects with the allurements of forfeiture and confiscation;

by prompting our negroes to rise in arms among us—those very negroes whom by an inhuman use of his negative he has refused us permission to exclude by law;

by endeavoring to bring on the inhabitants of our frontiers the merciless Indian savages, whose known rule of warfare is an undistinguished destruction of all ages, sexes, and conditions of existence;

by transporting at this time a large army of foreign mercenaries to complete the works of death, desolation, and tyranny already begun with circumstances of cruelty and perfidy so unworthy the head of a civilized nation;

by answering our repeated petitions for redress with a repetition of injuries;

and finally by abandoning the helm of government and declaring us out of his allegiance and protection;

by which several acts of misrule the said George Guelf has forfeited the kingly office and has rendered it necessary for the preservation of the people that he should be immediately deposed from the same and divested of all its privileges, powers, and prerogatives:

And forasmuch as the public liberty may be more certainly secured by abolishing an office which all experience has shown to be inveterately inimical thereto and it will thereupon become further necessary to re-establish such ancient principles as are friendly to the rights of the people and to declare certain others which may co-operate with and fortify the same in future.

Be it therefore enacted by the authority of the people that the said George Guelf be, and he hereby is, deposed from the kingly office within this government and absolutely divested of all its rights, powers, and prerogatives; and that he and his descendants and all persons claiming by or through him, and all other persons whatsoever shall be and forever remain incapable of the same; and that the said office shall henceforth cease and never more either in name or substance be re-established within this colony.

And be it further enacted by the authority aforesaid that the following fundamental laws and principles of government shall henceforth be established:

The Legislative, Executive, and Judiciary offices shall be kept forever separate and no person exercising the one shall be capable of appointment to the others, or to either of them.

I. Legislative

Legislation shall be exercised by two separate houses, to wit, a house of Representatives and a house of Senators, which shall be called the General Assembly of Virginia.

The said house of Representatives shall be composed of persons chosen by the people annually. . . .

All male persons of full age and sane mind having a freehold estate in one fourth of an acre of land in any town or in 25 acres of land in the country, and all persons resident in the colony who shall have paid scot and lot [2] to government the last two years shall have right to give their vote in the election of their respective representatives. . . .

The Judges of the General Court and of the High Court of

Chancery shall have session and deliberative voice, but not suffrage, in the house of Senators.

The Senate and the house of Representatives shall each of them have power to originate and amend bills; save only that bills for levying money shall be originated and amended by the Representatives only: the assent of both houses shall be requisite to pass a law.

The General Assembly shall have no power to pass any law inflicting death for any crime excepting murder, and those offenses in the military service for which they shall think punishment by death absolutely necessary; and all capital punishments in other cases are hereby abolished. Nor shall they have power to prescribe torture in any case whatever; nor shall there be power anywhere to pardon crimes or to remit fines or punishments; nor shall any law for levying money be in force longer than ten years from the time of its commencement.

Two thirds of the members of either house shall be a Quorum to proceed to business.

II. Executive

The executive powers shall be exercised in manner following:

One person to be called the Administrator shall be annually appointed by the house of Representatives on the second day of their first session, who after having acted one year shall be incapable of being again appointed to that office until he shall have been out of the same three years. . . .

The Administrator shall possess the powers formerly held by the king, save only that:

he shall be bound by acts of legislature though not expressly named;

he shall have no negative on the bills of the legislature;

he shall be liable to action, though not to personal restraint, for private duties or wrongs;

he shall not possess the prerogatives

of dissolving, proroguing, or adjourning either house of Assembly;

of declaring war or concluding peace;

of issuing letters of marque or reprisal;

of raising or introducing armed forces, building armed vessels, forts, or strongholds;

of coining monies or regulating their value;

of regulating weights and measures;

of erecting courts, offices, boroughs, corporations, fairs, markets, ports, beacons, lighthouses, seamarks;

of laying embargoes, or prohibiting the exportation of any commodity for a longer space than 40 days;

of retaining or recalling a member of the state but by legal process *pro delicto vel contractu;*

of making denizens;

of creating dignities or granting rights of precedence; but these powers shall be exercised by the legislature alone. And excepting also those powers which by these fundamentals are given to others, or abolished. . . .

III. Judiciary

The Judiciary powers shall be exercised

First, by County Courts and other inferior jurisdictions;

Secondly, by a General Court and a High Court of Chancery;

Thirdly, by a Court of Appeals. . . .

All facts in causes, whether of Chancery, Common, Ecclesiastical, or Marine law, shall be tried by a jury upon evidence given *viva voce* in open court; but where witnesses are out of the colony or unable to attend through sickness or other invincible necessity, their depositions may be submitted to the credit of the jury.

All Fines and Amercements shall be assessed, and Terms of imprisonment for Contempts and Misdemeanors shall be fixed by the verdict of a jury.

IV. Rights Private and Public

Every person of full age neither owning nor having owned fifty acres of land shall be entitled to an appropriation of fifty acres or to so much as shall make up what he owns or has owned fifty acres in full and absolute dominion, and no other person shall be capable of taking an appropriation.

Lands heretofore holden of the crown in fee simple, and those hereafter to be appropriated, shall be holden in full and absolute dominion, of no superior whatever.

No lands shall be appropriated until purchased of the Indian native proprietors; nor shall any purchases be made of them but on behalf of the public, by authority of acts of the General Assembly to be passed for every purchase specially. . . .

Descents shall go according to the laws of gavelkind,[3] save only that females shall have equal rights with males.

No person hereafter coming into this country shall be held within the same in slavery under any pretext whatever. . . .

All persons shall have full and free liberty of religious opinion; nor shall any be compelled to frequent or maintain any religious institution.

No freeman shall be debarred the use of arms within his own lands or tenements.

There shall be no standing army but in time of actual war.

Printing presses shall be free, except so far as by commission of private injury cause may be given of private action. . . .

None of these fundamental laws and principles of government shall be repealed or altered, but by the personal consent of the people on summons to meet in their respective counties on one and the same day by an act of Legislature to be passed for every special occasion; and if in such county meetings the people of two thirds of the counties shall give their suffrage for any particular alteration or repeal referred to them by the said act, the same shall be accordingly repealed or altered, and such repeal or alteration shall take its place among these fundamentals and stand on the same footing with them, in lieu of the article repealed or altered.

The laws heretofore in force in this colony shall remain in force, except so far as they are altered by the foregoing fundamental laws or so far as they may be hereafter altered by acts of the Legislature.

III. A SUMMARY VIEW OF THE RIGHTS OF BRITISH AMERICA

Another significant document which influenced the Declaration was the *Summary View,* Jefferson's first published book. The proposed instructions to Virginia delegates in the Continental Congress which he had prepared to be presented to the Virginia Convention of 1774 were too far in advance of public sentiment to be adopted, but they were thought worthy of publication.

RESOLVED, That it be an instruction to the said deputies, when assembled in General Congress with the deputies from the other states of British America, to propose to the said Congress that an humble and dutiful address be presented to his Majesty, begging leave to lay before him as Chief Magistrate of the British empire the united complaints of his Majesty's subjects in America; complaints which are excited by many unwarrantable encroachments and usurpations, attempted to be made by the legislature of one part of the empire upon the rights which God and the laws have given equally and independently to all. To represent to his Majesty that these his States have often individually made humble application to his imperial Throne, to obtain, through its intervention, some redress of their injured rights, to none of which was ever even an answer condescended; humbly to hope that this, their joint address, penned in the language of truth and divested of those expressions of servility which would persuade his Majesty that we are asking favors and not rights, shall obtain from his Majesty a more respectful acceptance; and this his Majesty will think we have reason to expect, when he reflects that he is no more than the chief officer of the people, appointed by the laws, and circumscribed with definite powers, to assist in working the great machine of government erected for their use and consequently subject to their superintendence. And in order that these our rights, as well as the invasions of them, may be laid more fully before his Majesty, to take a view of them from the origin and first settlement of these countries.

To,remind him that our ancestors, before their emigration to America, were the free inhabitants of the British dominions in Europe and possessed a right which nature has given to all men of departing from the country in which chance, not choice, has placed them, of going in quest of new habitations, and of there establishing new societies under such laws and regulations as, to them, shall seem most likely to promote public happiness. That their Saxon ancestors had, under this universal law, in like manner left their native wilds and woods in the north of Europe, had possessed themselves of the Island of Britain, then less charged with inhabitants, and had established there that system of laws which has so long been the glory and protection of that country. Nor was ever any claim of superiority or dependence asserted over them by that mother country from which they had migrated, and were such a claim made, it is believed his Majesty's subjects in Great Britain have too firm a feeling of the rights derived to them from their ancestors to bow down the sovereignty of their state before such visionary pretensions. And it is thought that no circumstance has occurred to distinguish, materially, the British from the Saxon emigration. America was conquered and her settlements made and firmly established at the expense of individuals, and not of the British public. Their own blood was spilt in acquiring lands for their settlement, their own fortunes expended in making that settlement effectual. For themselves they fought, for themselves they conquered, and for themselves alone they have right to hold. No shilling was ever issued from the public treasures of his Majesty, or his ancestors, for their assistance till of very late times, after the colonies had become established on a firm and permanent footing. That then, indeed, having become valuable to Great Britain for her commercial purposes, his Parliament was pleased to lend them assistance against an enemy who would fain have drawn to herself the benefits of their commerce, to the great aggrandizement of herself and danger of Great Britain. Such assistance, and in such circumstances, they had often before given to Portugal and other allied states with whom they carry on a commercial intercourse. Yet these states never supposed that, by calling in her aid, they thereby submitted themselves to her sovereignty. Had such terms been proposed, they would have rejected them with disdain and trusted for better to the moderation of their enemies or to a vigorous exertion of their own force. We do not, however, mean to underrate those aids, which, to us, were doubtless valuable, on whatever principles granted; but we would show that they cannot give a title to that authority which the British Parliament would arrogate over us, and that they may amply be repaid by our giving to the inhabitants of Great Britain such exclusive privileges in trade as may be advantageous to them and, at the same time, not too restrictive to ourselves. That settlement having been thus effected in the wilds of America, the emigrants thought proper to adopt that system of laws under which they had hitherto lived in the mother country, and to continue their union with her by submitting themselves to the same common sovereign, who was thereby made the central link connecting the several parts of the empire thus newly multiplied.[b]

But that not long were they permitted, however far they thought themselves removed from the hand of oppression, to hold undisturbed the rights thus acquired at the hazard of their lives and loss of their fortunes. A family of princes was then on the British throne whose treasonable crimes against their people brought on them afterwards the exertion of those sacred and sovereign rights of punishment reserved in the hands of the people for cases of extreme necessity and judged by the constitution unsafe to be delegated to any other judicature. While every day brought forth some new and unjustifiable exertion of power over their subjects on that side of the water, it was not to be expected that those here, much less able at that time to oppose the designs of despotism, should be exempted from injury.

[b] The same concept of connection through a common king was expressed by John Adams in 1775, as well as by Jefferson on various subsequent occasions. George A. Peek, Jr., ed., *The Political Writings of John Adams*, "The American Heritage Series," No. 8 (New York: The Liberal Arts Press), p. 45; Dumbauld, *The Declaration of Independence and What It Means Today*, pp. 33, 121, 151.

Accordingly that country which had been acquired by the lives, the labors, and the fortunes of individual adventurers was by these princes several times parted out and distributed among the favorites and followers of their fortunes, and, by an assumed right of the Crown alone, were erected into distinct and independent governments—a measure which it is believed his Majesty's prudence and understanding would prevent him from imitating at this day, as no exercise of such power, of dividing and dismembering a country, has ever occurred in his Majesty's realm of England, though now of very ancient standing; nor could it be justified or acquiesced under there or in any part of his Majesty's empire.

That the exercise of a free trade with all parts of the world, possessed by the American colonists as of natural right, and which no law of their own had taken away or abridged, was next the object of unjust encroachment. Some of the colonies having thought proper to continue the administration of their government in the name and under the authority of his Majesty, King Charles the First, whom notwithstanding his late deposition by the Commonwealth of England they continued in the sovereignty of their State, the Parliament, for the Commonwealth, took the same in high offense and assumed upon themselves the power of prohibiting their trade with all other parts of the world, except the Island of Great Britain. This arbitrary act, however, they soon recalled, and by solemn treaty, entered into on the 12th day of March, 1651, between the said Commonwealth, by their Commissioners, and the colony of Virginia, by their House of Burgesses, it was expressly stipulated by the eighth article of the said treaty that they should have "free trade as the people of England do enjoy to all places and with all nations, according to the laws of that Commonwealth." But that, upon the restoration of his Majesty, King Charles the Second, their rights of free commerce fell once more a victim to arbitrary power; and by several acts of his reign, as well as of some of his successors, the trade of the colonies was laid under such restrictions as show what hopes they might form from the justice of a British Parliament were its uncontrolled power admitted over these States. History has informed us that bodies of men as well as individuals are susceptible of the spirit of tyranny. A view of these acts of Parliament for regulation, as it has been affectedly called, of the American trade, if all other evidences were removed out of the case, would undeniably evince the truth of this observation. Besides the duties they impose on our articles of export and import, they prohibit our going to any markets northward of Cape Finisterre in the kingdom of Spain for the sale of commodities which Great Britain will not take from us, and for the purchase of others with which she cannot supply us; and that for no other than the arbitrary purpose of purchasing for themselves, by a sacrifice of our rights and interests, certain privileges in their commerce with an allied state, who, in confidence that their exclusive trade with America will be continued while the principles and power of the British Parliament be the same, have indulged themselves in every exorbitance which their avarice could dictate or our necessity extort; have raised their commodities called for in America to the double and treble of what they sold for before such exclusive privileges were given them, and of what better commodities of the same kind would cost us elsewhere; and, at the same time, give us much less for what we carry thither than might be had at more convenient ports. That these acts prohibit us from carrying, in quest of other purchasers, the surplus of our tobaccos remaining after the consumption of Great Britain is supplied; so that we must leave them with the British merchant for whatever he will please to allow us, to be by him reshipped to foreign markets, where he will reap the benefits of making sale of them for full value. That, to heighten still the idea of Parliamentary justice and to show with what moderation they are like to exercise power where themselves are to feel no part of its weight, we take leave to mention to his Majesty certain other acts of the British Parliament by which they would prohibit us from manufacturing, for our own use, the articles we raise on our own lands with our own labor. By an act passed in the fifth year of the reign of his late Majesty, King George the Second, an American subject is forbidden to make a hat for himself of the fur which he has taken, perhaps, on his own soil—an instance of despotism to which no parallel can be produced in the most arbitrary ages of British history. By one other act, passed in the twenty-third year of the same reign, the iron which we make we are forbidden to manufacture, and, heavy as that article is and necessary in every branch of husbandry, besides commission and insurance, we are to pay freight for it to Great Britain and freight for it back again, for the purpose of supporting not men but machines in the island of Great Britain. In the same spirit of equal and impartial legislation is to be viewed the act of Parliament, passed in the fifth year of the same reign, by which American lands are made subject to the demands of British creditors, while their own lands were still continued unanswerable for their debts; from which one of these conclusions must necessarily follow—either that justice is not the same thing in America as in Britain, or else that the British Parliament pay less regard to it here than there. But that we do not point out to his Majesty the injustice of these acts with intent to rest on that principle the cause of their nullity, but to show that experience confirms the propriety of those political principles which exempt us from the jurisdiction of the British Parliament. The true ground on which we declare these acts void is that the British Parliament has no right to exercise authority over us.

That these exercises of usurped power have not been confined to instances alone in which themselves were interested, but they have also intermeddled with the regulation of the internal affairs of the colonies. The act of the 9th of Anne for establishing a post office in America seems to have had little connection with British convenience, except that of accommodating his Majesty's ministers and favorites with the sale of a lucrative and easy office.

That thus have we hastened through the reigns which preceded his Majesty's, during which the violations of our rights were less alarming, because repeated at more distant intervals, than that rapid and bold succession of injuries which is likely to distinguish the present from all other periods of American history. Scarcely have our minds been able to emerge from the astonishment into which one stroke of Parliamentary thunder has involved us, before another more heavy and more alarming is fallen on us. Single acts of tyranny may be ascribed to the accidental opinion of a day; but a series of oppressions, begun at a distinguished period and pursued unalterably through every change of ministers, too plainly prove a deliberate, systematical plan of reducing us to slavery.

That the act passed in the fourth year of his Majesty's reign, entitled "An act for granting certain duties in the British colonies and plantations in America, etc."

One other act passed in the fifth year of his reign, entitled "An act for granting and applying certain stamp duties and other duties in the British colonies and plantations in America, etc."

One other act passed in the sixth year of his reign, entitled "An act for the better securing the dependency of his Majesty's dominions in America upon the crown and parliament of Great Britain"; and one other act passed in the seventh year of his reign, entitled "An act for granting duties on paper, tea, etc." form that connected chain of parliamentary usurpation which has already been the subject of frequent applications to his Majesty and the Houses of Lords and Commons of Great Britain; and, no answers having yet been condescended to any of these, we shall not trouble his Majesty with a repetition of the matters they contained.

But that one other act passed in the same seventh year of his reign, having been a peculiar attempt, must ever require peculiar mention; it is entitled "An act for suspending the legislature of New York."

One free and independent legislature hereby takes upon itself to suspend the powers of another, free and independent as itself, thus exhibiting a phenomenon unknown in nature, the creator and creature of its own power. Not only the principles of common sense but the common feelings of human nature must be surrendered up before his Majesty's subjects here can be persuaded to believe that they hold their political existence at the will of a British Parliament. Shall these governments be dissolved, their property annihilated, and their people reduced to a state of nature, at the imperious breath of a body of men whom they never saw, in whom they never confided, and over whom they have no powers of punishment or removal, let their crimes against the American public be ever so great? Can any one reason be assigned why one hundred and sixty thousand electors in the island of Great Britain should give law to four millions in the States of America, every individual of whom is equal to every individual of them in virtue, in understanding, and in bodily strength? Were this to be admitted, instead of being a free people, as we have hitherto supposed and mean to continue ourselves, we should suddenly be found the slaves not of one but of one hundred and sixty thousand tyrants; distinguished, too, from all others by this singular circumstance, that they are removed from the reach of fear, the only restraining motive which may hold the hand of a tyrant.

That by "an act to discontinue, in such manner and for such time as are therein mentioned, the landing and discharging, lading or shipping of goods, wares and merchandise at the town and within the harbor of Boston, in the province of Massachusetts Bay, in North America," which was passed at the last session of the British Parliament, a large and populous town whose trade was their sole subsistence was deprived of that trade and involved in utter ruin. Let us for a while suppose the question of right suspended in order to examine this act on principles of justice. An act of Parliament had been passed imposing duties on teas, to be paid in America, against which act the Americans had protested as inauthoritative. The East India Company, who till that time had never sent a pound of tea to America on their own account, step forth on that occasion the asserters of Parliamentary right, and send hither many ship loads of that obnoxious commodity. The masters of their several vessels, however, on their arrival in America, wisely attended to admonition and returned with their cargoes. In the province of New England alone the remonstrances of the people were disregarded and a compliance, after being many days waited for, was flatly refused. Whether in this the master of the vessel was governed by his obstinacy or his instructions, let those who know say. There are extraordinary situations which require extraordinary interposition. An exasperated people, who feel that they possess power, are not easily restrained within limits strictly regular. A number of them assembled in the town of Boston, threw the tea into the ocean, and dispersed without doing any other act of violence. If in this they did wrong, they were known and were amenable to the laws of the land; against which it could not be objected that they had ever, in any instance, been obstructed or diverted from the regular course in favor of popular offenders. They should, therefore, not have been distrusted on this occasion. But that ill-fated colony had formerly been bold in their enmities against the House of Stuart, and were now devoted to ruin by that unseen hand which governs the momentous affairs of this great empire. On the partial representations of a few worthless ministerial dependents, whose constant office it has been to keep that government embroiled and who, by their treacheries, hope to obtain the dignity of British knighthood, without calling for a party accused, without asking a proof, without attempting a distinction between the guilty and the innocent, the whole of that ancient and wealthy town is in a moment reduced from opulence to beggary. Men who had spent their lives in extending the British commerce, who had invested in that place the wealth their honest endeavors had merited, found themselves and their families thrown at once on the world for subsistence by its charities. Not the hundredth part of the inhabitants of that town had been concerned in the act complained of; many of them were in Great Britain and in other parts beyond sea; yet all were involved in one indiscriminate ruin, by a new executive power unheard of till then, that of a British Parliament. A property of the value of many millions of money was sacrificed to revenge, not repay, the loss of a few thousands. This is administering justice with a heavy hand indeed! And when is this tempest to be arrested in its course? Two wharves are to be opened again when his Majesty shall think proper; the residue, which lined the extensive shores of the bay of Boston, are forever interdicted the exercise of commerce. This little exception seems to have been thrown in for no other purpose than that of setting a precedent for investing his Majesty with legislative powers. If the pulse of his people shall beat calmly under this experiment, another and another will be tried till the measure of despotism be filled up. It would be an insult on common sense to pretend that this exception was made in order to restore its commerce to that great town. The trade, which cannot be received at two wharves alone, must of necessity be transferred to some other place; to which it will soon be followed by that of the two wharves. Considered in this light, it would be an insolent and cruel mockery at the annihilation of the town of Boston. By the act for the suppression of riots and tumults in the town of Boston, passed also in the last session of Parliament, a murder committed there is, if the Governor pleases, to be tried in the court of King's Bench, in the island of Great Britain, by a jury of Middlesex. The witnesses, too, on receipt of such a sum as the Governor shall think it reasonable for them to expend, are to enter into recognizance to appear at the trial. This is, in other words, taxing them to the amount of their recognizance, and that amount may be whatever a Governor pleases. For who does his Majesty think can be prevailed on to cross the Atlantic for the sole purpose of bearing evidence to a fact? His expenses are to be borne, indeed, as they shall be estimated by a Governor; but who are to feed the wife and children whom he leaves behind and who have had no other subsistence but his daily labor? Those epidemical disorders, too, so terrible in a foreign climate, is the cure of them to be estimated among the articles of expense and their danger to be warded off by the almighty power of a Parliament? And the wretched criminal, if he happens to have offended on the American side, stripped of his privilege of trial by peers of his vicinage, removed from the place where alone full evidence could be obtained, without money, without counsel, without friends, without exculpatory proof, is tried before judges predetermined to condemn. The cowards who would suffer a countryman to be torn from the bowels of their society, in order to be thus offered a sacrifice to Parliamentary tyranny, would merit that everlasting infamy now fixed on the authors of the act! A clause for a similar purpose had been introduced into an act passed in the twelfth year of his Majesty's reign, entitled "An act for the better securing and preserving his Majesty's dock-yards, magazines, ships, ammunition, and stores," against which, as meriting the same censures, the several colonies have already protested.

That these are the acts of power assumed by a body of men foreign to our constitutions and unacknowledged by our laws, against which we do, on behalf of the inhabitants of British America, enter this our solemn and determined protest. And we do earnestly entreat his Majesty, as yet the only mediatory power between the several States of the British empire, to recommend to his Parliament of Great Britain the total revocation of these acts, which, however nugatory they be, may yet prove the cause of further discontents and jealousies among us.

That we next proceed to consider the conduct of his Majesty, as holding the executive powers of the laws of these States, and mark out his deviations from the line of duty. By the constitution of Great Britain as well as of the several American States, his Majesty possesses the power of refusing to pass into a law any bill which has already passed the other two branches of the legislature. His Majesty, however, and his ancestors, conscious of the impropriety of opposing their single opinion to the united wisdom of two Houses of Parliament, while their proceedings were unbiased by interested principles, for several ages past have modestly declined the exercise of this power in that part of his empire called Great Britain. But, by change of circumstances. other principles than those of justice simply have obtained an influence on their determinations. The addition of new States to the British Empire has produced an addition of new and sometimes opposite interests. It is now, therefore, the great office of his Majesty to resume the exercise of his negative power and to prevent the passage of laws by any one legislature of the empire which might bear injuriously on the rights and interests of another. Yet this will not excuse the wanton exercise of this power which we have seen his Majesty practice on the laws of the American legislatures. For the most trifling reasons, and sometimes for no conceivable reason at all, his Majesty has rejected laws of the most salutary tendency. The abolition of domestic slavery is the great object of desire in those colonies where it was, unhappily, introduced in their infant state. But previous to the enfranchisement of the slaves we have, it is necessary to exclude all further importations from Africa. Yet our repeated attempts to effect this, by prohibitions and by imposing duties which might amount to a prohibition, have been hitherto defeated by his Majesty's negative, thus preferring the immediate advantages of a few British corsairs to the lasting interests of the American States and to the rights of human nature, deeply wounded by this infamous practice. Nay, the single interposition of an interested individual against a law was scarcely ever known to fail of success, though in the opposite scale were placed the interests of a whole country. That this is so shameful an abuse of a power trusted with his Majesty for other purposes as, if not reformed, would call for some legal restrictions.

With equal inattention to the necessities of his people here has his Majesty permitted our laws to lie neglected in England for years, neither confirming them by his assent, nor annulling them by his negative, so that such of them as have no suspending clause we hold on the most precarious of all tenures—his Majesty's will; and such of them as suspend themselves till his Majesty's assent be obtained we have feared might be called into existence at some future and distant period when time and change of circumstances shall have rendered them destructive to his people here. And, to render this grievance still more oppressive, his Majesty, by his instructions, has laid his Governors under such restrictions that they can pass no law of any moment unless it have such suspending clause, so that, however immediate may be the call for legislative interposition, the law cannot be executed till it has twice crossed the Atlantic, by which time the evil may have spent its whole force.

But in what terms reconcilable to majesty and at the same time to truth shall we speak of a late instruction to his Majesty's Governor of the colony of Virginia, by which he is forbidden to assent to any law for the division of a county unless the new county will consent to have no representative in Assembly? That colony has as yet affixed no boundary to the westward. Their western counties, therefore, are of an indefinite extent. Some of them are actually seated many hundred miles from their eastern limits. Is it possible, then, that his Majesty can have bestowed a single thought on the situation of those people who, in order to obtain justice for injuries, however great or small, must, by the laws of that colony, attend their county court at such a distance, with all their witnesses, monthly, till their litigation be determined? Or does his Majesty seriously wish, and publish it to the world, that his subjects should give up the glorious right of representation, with all the benefits derived from that, and submit themselves the absolute slaves of his sovereign will? Or is it rather meant to confine the legislative body to their present numbers, that they may be the cheaper bargain whenever they shall become worth a purchase?

One of the articles of impeachment against Tresilian and the other judges of Westminster Hall in the reign of Richard the Second, for which they suffered death as traitors to their country, was that they had advised the King that he might dissolve his Parliament at any time; and succeeding kings have adopted the opinion of these unjust judges. Since the establishment, however, of the British constitution, at the Glorious Revolution, on its free and ancient principles, neither his Majesty nor his ancestors have exercised such a power of dissolution in the island of Great Britain; and when his Majesty was petitioned, by the united voice of his people there, to dissolve the present Parliament, who had become obnoxious to them, his Ministers were heard to declare, in open Parliament, that his Majesty possessed no such power by the constitution. But how different their language and his practice here! To declare, as their duty required, the known rights of their country, to oppose the usurpation of every foreign judicature, to disregard the imperious mandates of a Minister or Governor, have been the avowed causes of dissolving Houses of Representatives in America. But if such powers be really vested in his Majesty, can he suppose they are there placed to awe the members from such purposes as these? When the representative body have lost the confidence of their constituents, when they have notoriously made sale of their most valuable rights, when they have assumed to themselves powers which the people never put into their hands, then, indeed, their continuing in office becomes dangerous to the State and calls for an exercise of the power of dissolution. Such being the causes for which the representative body should, and should not, be dissolved, will it not appear strange to an unbiased observer that that of Great Britain was not dissolved, while those of the colonies have repeatedly incurred that sentence?

But your Majesty, or your Governors, have carried this power beyond every limit known or provided for by the laws. After dissolving one House of Representatives, they have refused to call another, so that, for a great length of time, the legislature provided by the laws has been out of existence. From the nature of things, every society must at all times possess within itself the sovereign powers of legislation. The feelings of human nature revolt against the supposition of a state so situated as that it may not in any emergency provide against dangers which perhaps threaten immediate ruin. While those bodies are in existence to whom the people have delegated the powers of legislation, they alone possess and may exercise those powers; but when they are dissolved, by the lopping off one or more of their branches, the power reverts to the people, who may exercise it to unlimited extent, either assembling together in person, sending deputies, or in any other way they may think proper. We forbear to trace consequences further; the dangers are conspicuous with which this practice is replete.

That we shall at this time also take notice of an error in the nature of our land holdings which crept in at a very early period of our settlement. The introduction of the feudal tenures into the kingdom of England, though ancient, is well enough understood to set this matter in a proper light. In the earlier ages of the Saxon settlement, feudal holdings were certainly altogether unknown and very few, if any, had been introduced at the time of the Norman conquest. Our Saxon ancestors held their lands, as they did their personal property, in absolute dominion, disencumbered with any superior, answering nearly to the nature of those possessions which the feudalists term allodial.[4] William the Norman first introduced that system generally. The lands which had belonged to those who fell in the battle of Hastings, and in the subsequent insurrections of his reign, formed a considerable proportion of the lands of the whole kingdom. These he granted out, subject to feudal duties, as did he also those of a great number of his new subjects, who, by persuasions or threats, were induced to surrender them for that purpose. But still much was left in the hands of his Saxon subjects, held of no superior and not subject to feudal conditions. These, therefore, by express laws, enacted to render uniform the system of military defense, were made liable to the same military duties as if they had been feuds; and the Norman lawyers soon found means to saddle them also with all the other feudal burdens. But still they had not been surrendered to the King, they were not derived from his grant, and therefore they were not holden of him. A general principle, indeed, was introduced, that "all lands in England were held either mediately or immediately of the Crown," but this was borrowed from those holdings which were truly feudal and only applied to others for the purposes of illustration. Feudal holdings were, therefore, but exceptions out of the Saxon laws of possession, under which all lands were held in absolute right. These, therefore, still form the basis or groundwork of the common law, to prevail wheresoever the exceptions have not taken place. America was not conquered by William the Norman, nor its lands surrendered to him or any of his successors. Possessions there are undoubtedly of the allodial nature. Our ancestors, however, who migrated hither, were laborers, not lawyers. The fictitious principle that all lands belong originally to the King they were early persuaded to believe real, and accordingly took grants of their own lands from the Crown. And, while the Crown continued to grant for small sums and on reasonable rents, there was no inducement to arrest the error and lay it open to public view. But his Majesty has lately taken on him to advance the terms of purchase and of holding to the double of what they were, by which means the acquisition of lands being rendered difficult, the population of our country is likely to be checked. It is time, therefore, for us to lay this matter before his Majesty and to declare that he has no right to grant lands of himself. From the nature and purpose of civil institutions, all the lands within the limits which any particular society has circumscribed around itself are assumed by that society and subject to their allotment only. This may be done by themselves assembled collectively, or by their legislature to whom they may have delegated sovereign authority; and, if they are allotted in neither of these ways, each individual of the society may appropriate to himself such lands as he finds vacant, and occupancy will give him title.

That, in order to enforce the arbitrary measures before complained of, his Majesty has from time to time sent among us large bodies of armed forces not made up of the people here, nor raised by the authority of our laws. Did his Majesty possess such a right as this, it might swallow up all our other rights whenever he should think proper. But his Majesty has no right to land a single armed man on our shores, and those whom he sends here are liable to our laws for the suppression and punishment of riots, routs, and unlawful assemblies, or are hostile bodies invading us in defiance of law. When, in the course of the late war, it became expedient that a body of Hanoverian troops should be brought over for the defense of Great Britain, his Majesty's grandfather, our late sovereign, did not pretend to introduce them under any authority he possessed. Such a measure would have given just alarm to his subjects in Great Britain, whose liberties would not be safe if armed men of another country, and of another spirit, might be brought into the realm at any time without the consent of their legislature. He therefore applied to Parliament, who passed an act for that purpose, limiting the number to be brought in and the time they were to continue. In like manner is his Majesty restrained in every part of the empire. He possesses indeed the executive power of the laws in every State, but they are the laws of the particular State which he is to administer within that State, and not those of any one within the limits of another. Every State must judge for itself the number of armed men which they may safely trust among them, of whom they are to consist, and under what restrictions they are to be laid.

To render these proceedings still more criminal against our laws, instead of subjecting the military to the civil power, his Majesty has expressly made the civil subordinate to the military.

But can his Majesty thus put down all law under his feet? Can he erect a power superior to that which erected himself? He has done it indeed by force, but let him remember that force cannot give right.

That these are our grievances which we have thus laid before his Majesty with that freedom of language and sentiment which becomes a free people claiming their rights as derived from the laws of nature, and not as the gift of their chief magistrate. Let those flatter who fear; it is not an American art. To give praise where it is not due might be well from the venal, but would ill beseem those who are asserting the rights of human nature. They know, and will therefore say, that Kings are the servants, not the proprietors of the people. Open your breast, Sire, to liberal and expanded thought. Let not the name of George the Third be a blot on the page of history. You are surrounded by British counselors, but remember that they are parties. You have no ministers for American affairs because you have none taken from among us nor amenable to the laws on which they are to give you advice. It behooves you, therefore, to think and to act for yourself and your people. The great principles of right and wrong are legible to every reader; to pursue them requires not the aid of many counselors. The whole art of government consists in the art of being honest. Only aim to do your duty, and mankind will give you credit where you fail. No longer persevere in sacrificing the rights of one part of the empire to the inordinate desires of another, but deal out to all equal and impartial right. Let no act be passed by any one legislature which may infringe on the rights and liberties of another. This is the important post in which fortune has placed you, holding the balance of a great if a well-poised empire. This, Sire, is the advice of your great American council, on the observance of which may perhaps depend your felicity and future fame and the preservation of that harmony which alone can continue, both to Great Britain and America, the reciprocal advantages of their connection. It is neither our wish nor our interest to separate from her. We are willing, on our part, to sacrifice everything which reason can ask to the restoration of that tranquility for which all must wish. On their part, let them be ready to establish union on a generous plan. Let them name their terms, but let them be just. Accept of every commercial preference it is in our power to give, for such things as we can raise for their use or they make for ours. But let them not think to exclude us from going to other markets to dispose of those commodities which they cannot use, or to supply those wants which they cannot supply. Still less let it be proposed that our properties within our own territories shall be taxed or regulated by any power on earth but our own. The God who gave us life gave us liberty at the same time; the hand of force may destroy but cannot disjoin them. This, Sire, is our last, our determined resolution. And that you will be pleased to interpose, with that efficacy which your earnest endeavors may insure, to procure redress of these our great grievances, to quiet the minds of your subjects in British America against any apprehensions of future encroachment, to establish fraternal love and harmony through the whole empire, and that these may continue to the latest ages of time is the fervent prayer of all British America.

IV. FREEDOM OF RELIGION

Along with the Declaration of Independence, Jefferson regarded the Statute of Virginia for Religious Freedom as one of his most important writings. It was printed as Bill No. 82 in the *Report of the Committee of Revisors* and, with slight changes, became law in 1786, largely through the efforts of James Madison, while Jefferson was in France as American minister. Jefferson's *Notes on Virginia,* published at Paris in 1785, contain similar expressions of his views on freedom of religion.

1. *Statute of Virginia for Religious Freedom as Drafted by Jefferson*

Well aware that the opinions and belief of men depend not on their own will but follow involuntarily the evidence proposed to their minds; that Almighty God has created the mind free, and manifested His supreme will that free it shall remain by making it altogether insusceptible of restraint; that all attempts to influence it by temporal punishments, or burdens, or by civil incapacitations tend only to beget habits of hypocrisy and meanness and are a departure from the plan of the holy Author of our religion, who being Lord both of body and mind, yet chose not to propagate it by coercions on either, as was in His almighty power to do, but to extend it by its influence on reason alone; that the impious presumption of legislators and rulers, civil as well as ecclesiastical, who, being themselves but fallible and uninspired men, have assumed dominion over the faith of others, setting up their own opinions and modes of thinking as the only true and infallible, and as such endeavoring to impose them on others, has established and maintained false religions over the greatest part of the world and through all time; that to compel a man to furnish contributions of money for the propagation of opinions which he disbelieves and abhors is sinful and tyrannical; that even the forcing him to support this or that teacher of his own religious persuasion is depriving him of the comfortable liberty of giving his contributions to the particular pastor whose morals he would make his pattern and whose powers he feels most persuasive to righteousness, and is withdrawing from the ministry those temporal rewards which, proceeding from an approbation of their personal conduct, are an additional incitement to earnest and unremitting labors for the instruction of mankind; that our civil rights have no dependence on our religious opinions any more than our opinions in physics or geometry; that therefore the proscribing any citizen as unworthy the public confidence by laying upon him an incapacity of being called to offices of trust and emolument unless he profess or renounce this or that religious opinion is depriving him injuriously of those privileges and advantages to which, in common with his fellow citizens, he has a natural right; that it tends also to corrupt the principles of that very religion it is meant to encourage, by bribing with a monopoly of worldly honors and emoluments those who will externally profess and conform to it; that though indeed these are criminal who do not withstand such temptation, yet neither are those innocent who lay the bait in their way; that the opinions of men are not the object of civil government, nor under its jurisdiction; that to suffer the civil magistrate to intrude his powers into the field of opinion and to restrain the profession or propagation of principles on supposition of their ill tendency is a dangerous fallacy which at once destroys all religious liberty, because he, being of course judge of that tendency, will make his opinions the rule of judgment and approve or condemn the sentiments of others only as they shall square with or differ from his own; that it is time enough, for the rightful purposes of civil government, for its officers to interfere when principles break out into overt acts against peace and good order; and, finally, that truth is great and will prevail if left to herself; that she is the proper and sufficient antagonist to error and has nothing to fear from the conflict unless by human interposition disarmed of her natural weapons, free argument and debate; errors ceasing to be dangerous when it is permitted freely to contradict them.

We, the General Assembly of Virginia, do enact that no man shall be compelled to frequent or support any religious worship, place, or ministry whatsoever, nor shall be enforced, restrained, molested, or burdened in his body or goods, nor shall otherwise suffer on account of his religious opinions or belief; but that all men shall be free to profess, and by argument to maintain, their opinions in matters of religion, and that the same shall in no wise diminish, enlarge, or affect their civil capacities.

And though we well know that this Assembly, elected by the people for the ordinary purposes of legislation only, have no power to restrain the acts of succeeding Assemblies constituted with powers equal to our own, and that therefore to declare this act irrevocable would be of no effect in law; yet we are free to declare, and do declare, that the rights hereby asserted are of the natural rights of mankind, and that, if any act shall be hereafter passed to repeal the present resolution or to narrow its operation, such act will be an infringement of natural right.

2. *Jefferson's Views on Freedom of Religion*

The error seems not sufficiently eradicated that the operations of the mind, as well as the acts of the body, are subject to the coercion of the laws. But our rulers can have authority over such natural rights only as we have submitted to them. The rights of conscience we never submitted, we could not submit. We are answerable for them to our God. The legitimate powers of government extend to such acts only as are injurious to others. But it does me no injury for my neighbor to say there are twenty gods, or no God. It neither picks my pocket nor breaks my leg. If it be said his testimony in a court of justice cannot be relied on, reject it then, and be the stigma on him. Constraint may make him worse by making him a hypocrite, but it will never make him a truer man. It may fix him obstinately in his errors but will not cure them. Reason and free inquiry are the only effectual agents against error. Give a loose rein to them, they will support the true religion by bringing every false one to their tribunal, to the test of their investigation. They are the natural enemies of error, and of error only. Had not the Roman government permitted free inquiry, Christianity could never have been introduced. Had not free inquiry been indulged at the era of the Reformation, the corruptions of Christianity could not have been purged away. If it be restrained now, the present corruptions will be protected and new ones encouraged. Were the government to prescribe to us our medicine and diet, our bodies would be in such keeping as our souls are now. Thus in France the emetic was once forbidden as a medicine, and the potato as an article of food. Government is just as infallible, too, when it fixes systems in physics. Galileo was sent to the Inquisition for affirming that the earth was a sphere; the government had declared it to be as flat as a trencher, and Galileo was obliged to abjure his error. This error, however, at length prevailed; the earth became a globe, and Descartes declared it was whirled round its axis by a vortex. The government in which he lived

was wise enough to see that this was no question of civil jurisdiction, or we should all have been involved by authority in
vortices. In fact, the vortices have been exploded, and the New-
tonian principle of gravitation is now more firmly established,
on the basis of reason, than it would be were the government
to step in and to make it an article of necessary faith. Reason
and experiment have been indulged, and error has fled before
them. It is error alone which needs the support of government.
Truth can stand by itself. Subject opinion to coercion: whom
will you make your inquisitors? Fallible men; men governed by
bad passions, by private as well as public reasons. And why subject it to coercion? To produce uniformity. But is uniformity of
opinion desirable? No more than of face and stature. Introduce
the bed of Procrustes then; and, as there is danger that the large
men may beat the small, make us all of a size by lopping the
former and stretching the latter. Difference of opinion is advantageous in religion. The several sects perform the office of *censor
morum* over each other. Is uniformity attainable? Millions of
innocent men, women, and children, since the introduction of
Christianity, have been burned, tortured, fined, imprisoned; yet
we have not advanced one inch toward uniformity. What has
been the effect of coercion? To make one half the world fools
and the other half hypocrites; to support roguery and error all
over the earth. Let us reflect that it is inhabited by a thousand
millions of people; that these profess probably a thousand different systems of religion; that ours is but one of that thousand;
that if there be but one right, and ours that one, we should wish
to see the nine hundred and ninety-nine wandering sects
gathered into the fold of truth. But against such a majority we
cannot effect this by force. Reason and persuasion are the only
practicable instruments. To make way for these, free inquiry
must be indulged; and how can we wish others to indulge it
while we refuse it ourselves? But every state, says an inquisitor,
has established some religion. No two, say I, have established
the same. Is this a proof of the infallibility of establishments?
Our sister States of Pennsylvania and New York, however, have
long subsisted without any establishment at all. The experiment

was new and doubtful when they made it. It has answered beyond conception. They flourish infinitely. Religion is well supported; of various kinds, indeed, but all good enough; all sufficient to preserve peace and order; or if a sect arises whose tenets would subvert morals, good sense has fair play, and reasons and laughs it out of doors without suffering the state to be troubled with it. They do not hang more malefactors than we do. They are not more disturbed with religious dissensions. On the contrary, their harmony is unparalleled and can be ascribed to nothing but their unbounded tolerance, because there is no other circumstance in which they differ from every nation on earth. They have made the happy discovery that the way to silence religious disputes is to take no notice of them. Let us too give this experiment fair play and get rid, while we may, of those tyrannical laws. It is true we are as yet secured against them by the spirit of the times. I doubt whether the people of this country would suffer an execution for heresy, or a three years' imprisonment for not comprehending the mysteries of the Trinity. But is the spirit of the people an infallible, a permanent reliance? Is it government? Is this the kind of protection we receive in return for the rights we give up? Besides, the spirit of the times may alter, will alter. Our rulers will become corrupt, our people careless. A single zealot may commence persecutor, and better men be his victims. It can never be too often repeated that the time for fixing every essential right on a legal basis is while our rulers are honest and ourselves united. From the conclusion of this war we shall be going downhill. It will not then be necessary to resort every moment to the people for support. They will be forgotten, therefore, and their rights disregarded. They will forget themselves but in the sole faculty of making money, and will never think of uniting to effect a due respect for their rights. The shackles, therefore, which shall not be knocked off at the conclusion of this war will remain on us long, will be made heavier and heavier, till our rights shall revive or expire in a convulsion.

Notes on Virginia, Query XVII.

V. ORDINANCE OF 1784 AS REPORTED BY JEFFERSON

Another of Jefferson's significant state papers was the Ordinance of April 23, 1784, adopted by the Continental Congress for temporary government of the Northwestern Territory. Jefferson's proposal to abolish slavery was lost by one vote. With "the fate of millions unborn hanging on the tongue of one man," Jefferson exclaimed, "heaven was silent in that awful moment!" Congress amplified these regulations in the better-known Ordinance of 1787.

The Committee to whom was recommitted the report of a plan for a temporary government of the Western territory have agreed to the following resolutions:

Resolved, That so much of the territory ceded or to be ceded by individual States to the United States as is already purchased or shall be purchased of the Indian inhabitants and offered for sale by Congress, shall be divided into distinct states. . . .

That the settlers on any territory so purchased and offered for sale shall, either on their own petition or on the order of Congress, receive authority from them with appointments of time and place for their free males of full age within the limits of their state to meet together for the purpose of establishing a temporary government, to adopt the constitution and laws of any one of the original States, so that such laws nevertheless shall be subject to alteration by their ordinary legislature; and to erect, subject to a like alteration, counties or townships for the election of members for their legislature.

That such temporary government shall only continue in force in any state until it shall have acquired 20,000 free inhabitants when, giving due proof thereof to Congress, they shall receive from them authority with appointment of time and place to call a convention of representatives to establish a permanent constitution and government for themselves; provided that both the temporary and permanent governments be established on these principles as their basis: 1. That they shall forever remain a part of this confederacy of the United States of America. 2. That in their persons, property, and territory they shall be subject to the government of the United States in Congress assembled and to the Articles of Confederation in all those cases in which the original States shall be so subject. 3. That they shall be subject to pay a part of the federal debts contracted or to be contracted, to be apportioned on them by Congress, according to the same common rule and measure by which apportionments thereof shall be made on the other States. 4. That their respective governments shall be in republican forms and shall admit no person to be a citizen who holds any hereditary title. 5. That, after the year 1800 of the Christian era, there shall be neither slavery or involuntary servitude in any of the said states otherwise than in punishment of crimes whereof the party shall have been convicted to have been personally guilty.

That whensoever any of the said states shall have, of free inhabitants, as many as shall then be in any one the least numerous of the thirteen original States, such state shall be admitted by its delegates into the Congress of the United States on an equal footing with the said original States; provided nine States agree to such admission according to the reservation of the 11th of the Articles of Confederation. And, in order to adapt the said Articles of Confederation to the state of Congress when its numbers shall be thus increased, it shall be proposed to the legislatures of the States originally parties thereto, to require the assent of two thirds of the United States in Congress assembled in all those cases wherein by the said Articles the assent of nine States is now required; which, being agreed to by them, shall be binding on the new states. Until such admission of their delegates into Congress, any of the said states, after the establishment of their temporary government, shall have authority to keep a sitting member in Congress with a right of debating but not of voting.

That the preceding articles shall be formed into a charter of compact, shall be duly executed by the President of the United States in Congress assembled, under his hand and the seal of the

United States, shall be promulgated and shall stand as fundamental constitutions between the thirteen original States and
each of the several states now newly described, unalterable but
by the joint consent of the United States in Congress assembled,
and of the particular state within which such alteration is proposed to be made.

VI. FIRST INAUGURAL ADDRESS

A concise and comprehensive outline of Jefferson's political
beliefs is contained in the conciliatory address which he delivered on March 4, 1801, when he became President of the
United States.

Friends and Fellow Citizens:

Called upon to undertake the duties of the first executive
office of our country, I avail myself of the presence of that portion
of my fellow citizens which is here assembled to express my
grateful thanks for the favor with which they have been pleased
to look toward me, to declare a sincere consciousness that the
task is above my talents, and that I approach it with those anxious
and awful presentiments which the greatness of the charge and
the weakness of my powers so justly inspire. A rising nation,
spread over a wide and fruitful land, traversing all the seas with
the rich productions of their industry, engaged in commerce with
nations who feel power and forget right, advancing rapidly to
destinies beyond the reach of mortal eye—when I contemplate
these transcendent objects and see the honor, the happiness, and
the hopes of this beloved country committed to the issue and
the auspices of this day, I shrink from the contemplation and
humble myself before the magnitude of the undertaking. Utterly
indeed should I despair did not the presence of many whom
I here see remind me that in the other high authorities provided
by our Constitution I shall find resources of wisdom, of virtue,
and of zeal on which to rely under all difficulties. To you then,

gentlemen, who are charged with the sovereign functions of legislation, and to those associated with you, I look with encouragement for that guidance and support which may enable us to steer with safety the vessel in which we are all embarked amidst the conflicting elements of a troubled world.

During the contest of opinion through which we have passed, the animation of discussions and of exertions has sometimes worn an aspect which might impose on strangers unused to think freely and to speak and to write what they think. But this being now decided by the voice of the nation, enounced according to the rules of the Constitution, all will of course arrange themselves under the will of the law and unite in common efforts for the common good. All, too, will bear in mind this sacred principle that, though the will of the majority is in all cases to prevail, that will, to be rightful, must be reasonable; that the minority possess their equal rights, which equal laws must protect and to violate which would be oppression. Let us then, fellow citizens, unite with one heart and one mind; let us restore to social intercourse that harmony and affection without which liberty, and even life itself, are but dreary things. And let us reflect that, having banished from our land that religious intolerance under which mankind so long bled and suffered, we have yet gained little if we countenance a political intolerance as despotic, as wicked, and capable of as bitter and bloody persecutions. During the throes and convulsions of the ancient world, during the agonizing spasms of infuriated man, seeking through blood and slaughter his long-lost liberty, it was not wonderful that the agitation of the billows should reach even this distant and peaceful shore, that this should be more felt and feared by some and less by others, and should divide opinions as to measures of safety.

But every difference of opinion is not a difference of principle. We have called by different names brethren of the same principle. We are all republicans; we are all federalists. If there be any among us who would wish to dissolve this Union or to change its republican form, let them stand undisturbed as monuments of the safety with which error of opinion may be tolerated, where reason is left free to combat it. I know, indeed, that some honest men fear that a republican government cannot be strong; that this government is not strong enough. But would the honest patriot, in the full tide of successful experiment, abandon a government which has so far kept us free and firm, on the theoretic and visionary fear that this government, the world's best hope, may by possibility want energy to preserve itself? I trust not. I believe this, on the contrary, the strongest government on earth. I believe it the only one where every man, at the call of the law, would fly to the standard of the law and would meet invasions of the public order as his own personal concern. Sometimes it is said that man cannot be trusted with the government of himself. Can he then be trusted with the government of others? Or have we found angels, in the form of kings, to govern him? Let history answer this question.

Let us then, with courage and confidence, pursue our own federal and republican principles, our attachment to Union and representative government. Kindly separated by nature and a wide ocean from the exterminating havoc of one quarter of the globe; too high-minded to endure the degradations of the others; possessing a chosen country, with room enough for our descendants to the thousandth and thousandth generation; entertaining a due sense of our equal right to the use of our own faculties, to the acquisitions of our own industry, to honor and confidence from our fellow citizens, resulting not from birth but from our actions and their sense of them; enlightened by a benign religion, professed indeed and practiced in various forms, yet all of them including honesty, truth, temperance, gratitude, and the love of man; acknowledging and adoring an overruling Providence which, by all its dispensations, proves that It delights in the happiness of man here and his greater happiness hereafter; with all these blessings, what more is necessary to make us a happy and a prosperous people? Still one thing more, fellow citizens— a wise and frugal government which shall restrain men from injuring one another, shall leave them otherwise free to regulate their own pursuits of industry and improvement, and shall not take from the mouth of labor the bread it has earned. This is the sum of good government, and this is necessary to close the circle of our felicities.

About to enter, fellow citizens, on the exercise of duties which comprehend everything dear and valuable to you, it is proper you should understand what I deem the essential principles of our government and, consequently, those which ought to shape its administration. I will compress them within the narrowest compass they will bear, stating the general principle but not all its limitations: Equal and exact justice to all men, of whatever state or persuasion, religious or political; peace, commerce, and honest friendship with all nations, entangling alliances with none; the support of the State governments in all their rights, as the most competent administrations for our domestic concerns and the surest bulwarks against anti-republican tendencies; the preservation of the general government in its whole constitutional vigor, as the sheet anchor of our peace at home and safety abroad; a jealous care of the right of election by the people, a mild and safe corrective of abuses which are lopped by the sword of revolution where peaceable remedies are unprovided; absolute acquiescence in the decisions of the majority, the vital principle of republics from which there is no appeal but to force, the vital principle and immediate parent of despotism; a well-disciplined militia, our best reliance in peace and for the first moments of war till regulars may relieve them; the supremacy of the civil over the military authority; economy in the public expense, that labor may be lightly burdened; the honest payment of our debts and sacred preservation of the public faith; encouragement of agriculture, and of commerce as its handmaid; the diffusion of information, and arraignment of all abuses at the bar of the public reason; freedom of religion; freedom of the press; freedom of person, under the protection of the habeas corpus; and trial by juries, impartially selected. These principles form the bright constellation which has gone before us and guided our steps through an age of revolution and reformation. The wisdom of our sages and blood of our heroes have been devoted to their attainment; they should be the creed of our political faith, the text of civic instruction, the touchstone by which to try the services of those we trust; and should we wander from them in moments of error or of alarm, let us hasten to retrace our steps and to regain the road which alone leads to peace, liberty, and safety.

I repair then, fellow citizens, to the post you have assigned me. With experience enough in subordinate offices to have seen the difficulties of this, the greatest of all, I have learned to expect that it will rarely fall to the lot of imperfect man to retire from this station with the reputation and the favor which bring him into it. Without pretensions to that high confidence you reposed in our first and great revolutionary character, whose pre-eminent services had entitled him to the first place in his country's love and destined for him the fairest page in the volume of faithful history, I ask so much confidence only as may give firmness and effect to the legal administration of your affairs. I shall often go wrong through defect of judgment. When right, I shall often be thought wrong by those whose positions will not command a view of the whole ground. I ask your indulgence for my own errors, which will never be intentional, and your support against the errors of others who may condemn what they would not if seen in all its parts. The approbation implied by your suffrage is a great consolation to me for the past, and my future solicitude will be to retain the good opinion of those who have bestowed it in advance, to conciliate that of others by doing them all the good in my power, and to be instrumental to the happiness and freedom of all.

Relying then on the patronage of your good will, I advance with obedience to the work, ready to retire from it whenever you become sensible how much better choice it is in your power to make. And may that Infinite Power which rules the destinies of the universe lead our councils to what is best and give them a favorable issue for your peace and prosperity.

VII. FOUR SIGNIFICANT LETTERS

Important statements of Jefferson's principles were formulated in letters written at different times during his career.

You say that I have been dished up to you as an anti-Federalist and ask me if it be just. My opinion was never worthy enough of notice to merit citing, but since you ask it, I will tell it to you. I am not a Federalist [5] because I never submitted the whole system of my opinions to the creed of any party of men whatever, in religion, in philosophy, in politics, or in anything else, where I was capable of thinking for myself. Such an addiction is the last degradation of a free and moral agent. If I could not go to heaven but with a party, I would not go there at all. Therefore, I am not of the party of Federalists. But I am much farther from that of the anti-Federalists. I approved, from the first moment, of the great mass of what is in the new Constitution: the consolidation of the government; the organization into executive, legislative, and judiciary; the subdivision of the legislative; the happy compromise of interests between the great and little States by the different manner of voting in the different Houses; the voting by persons instead of States; the qualified negative on laws given to the executive, which, however, I should have liked better if associated with the judiciary also, as in New York; and the power of taxation. I thought at first that the latter might have been limited. A little reflection soon convinced me it ought not to be. What I disapproved from the first moment, also, was the want of a bill of rights to guard liberty against the legislative as well as the executive branches of the government; that is to say, to secure freedom in religion, freedom of the press, freedom from monopolies, freedom from unlawful imprisonment, freedom from a permanent military, and a trial by jury in all cases determinable by the laws of the land. I disapproved, also, the perpetual re-eligibility of the President.

To Francis Hopkinson, Paris, March 13, 1789.

I do then, with sincere zeal, wish an inviolable preservation of our present federal Constitution, according to the true sense in which it was adopted by the States, that in which it was advocated by its friends, and not that which its enemies apprehended, who therefore became its enemies; and I am opposed to the monarchizing its features by the forms of its administration with a view to conciliate a first transition to a President and Senate for life and from that to a hereditary tenure of these offices, and thus to worm out the elective principle. I am for preserving to the States the powers not yielded by them to the Union, and to the legislature of the Union its constitutional share in the division of powers, and I am not for transferring all the powers of the States to the General Government and all those of that government to the executive branch. I am for a government rigorously frugal and simple, applying all the possible savings of the public revenue to the discharge of the national debt, and not for a multiplication of officers and salaries merely to make partisans, and for increasing, by every device, the public debt on the principle of its being a public blessing. I am for relying, for internal defense, on our militia solely till actual invasion and for such a naval force only as may protect our coasts and harbors from such depredations as we have experienced, and not for a standing army in time of peace, which may overawe the public sentiment; nor for a navy which, by its own expenses and the eternal wars in which it will implicate us, will grind us with public burdens and sink us under them. I am for free commerce with all nations, political connection with none, and little or no diplomatic establishment. And I am not for linking ourselves by new treaties with the quarrels of Europe, entering that field of slaughter to preserve their balance, or joining in the confederacy of kings to war against the principles of liberty. I am for freedom of religion and against all maneuvers to bring about a legal ascendancy of one sect over another; for freedom of the press and against all violations of the Constitution to silence by force and not by reason the complaints or criticisms, just or unjust, of our citizens against the conduct of their agents. And I am for encouraging the progress of science in all its branches; and not for raising a hue and cry against the sacred name of philosophy; for awing the human mind by stories of raw head and bloody bones to a distrust of its own vision and to repose implicitly on that of others; to go backward instead of forward to look for improvement; to believe that government, religion, morality, and every other science were in the highest perfection in ages of the darkest ignorance, and that nothing can ever be devised more perfect than what was established by our forefathers. To these I will add that I was a sincere well-wisher to the success of the French Revolution and still wish it may end in the establishment of a free and well-ordered republic; but I have not been insensible under the atrocious depredations they have committed on our commerce. The first object of my heart is my own country. In that is embarked my family, my fortune, and my own existence. I have not one farthing of interest, nor one fiber of attachment out of it, nor a single motive of preference of any one nation to another but in proportion as they are more or less friendly to us.

To Elbridge Gerry, Philadelphia, January 26, 1799.

I received, my dear friend, your letter covering the constitution for your Equinoctial republics. . . . I suppose it well-formed for those for whom it was intended, and the excellence of every government is its adaptation to the state of those to be governed by it. For us it would not do. Distinguishing between the structure of the government and the moral principles on which you prescribe its administration, with the latter we concur cordially, with the former we should not. We of the United States, you know, are constitutionally and conscientiously democrats. We consider society as one of the natural wants with which man has been created; that he has been endowed with faculties and qualities to effect its satisfaction by concurrence of others having the same want; that when, by the exercise of these faculties, he has procured a state of society, it is one of his acquisitions which he has a right to regulate and control, jointly indeed with all those who have concurred in the procurement, whom he cannot exclude from its use or direction more than they him. We think experience has proved it safer, for the mass of individuals composing the society, to reserve to themselves personally the exercise of all rightful powers to which they are competent, and to delegate those to which they are not competent to deputies named, and removable for unfaithful conduct by themselves immediately. Hence, with us, the people (by which is meant the mass of individuals composing the society) being competent to judge of the facts occurring in ordinary life, they have retained the functions of judges of facts under the name of jurors; but being unqualified for the management of affairs requiring intelligence above the common level, yet competent judges of human character, they chose, for their management, representatives, some by themselves immediately, others by electors chosen by themselves. . . .

But when we come to the moral principles on which the government is to be administered, we come to what is proper for all conditions of society. I meet you there in all the benevolence and rectitude of your native character, and I love myself always most where I concur most with you. Liberty, truth, probity, honor are declared to be the four cardinal principles of your society. I believe with you that morality, compassion, generosity are innate elements of the human constitution; that there exists a right independent of force; that a right to property is founded in our natural wants, in the means with which we are endowed to satisfy these wants, and the right to what we acquire by those means without violating the similar rights of other sensible beings; that no one has a right to obstruct another exercising his faculties innocently for the relief of sensibilities made a part of his nature; that justice is the fundamental law of society; that the majority, oppressing an individual, is guilty of a crime, abuses its strength, and by acting on the law of the strongest breaks up the foundations of society; that action by the citizens in person, in affairs within their reach and competence, and in all others by representatives, chosen immediately and removable by themselves, constitutes the essence of a republic; that all governments are more or less republican in proportion as this principle enters more or less into their composition; and that a government by representation is capable of extension over a greater surface of country than one of any other form.[c] These, my friend, are the essentials in which you and I agree; however, in our zeal for their maintenance we may be perplexed and divaricate as to the structure of society most likely to secure them.

In the constitution of Spain, as proposed by the late Cortes, there was a principle entirely new to me and not noticed in yours, that no person born after that day should ever acquire the rights of citizenship until he could read and write. It is impossible sufficiently to estimate the wisdom of this provision. Of all those which have been thought of for securing fidelity in the administration of the government, constant ralliance to the principles of the constitution, and progressive amendments with the progressive advances of the human mind or changes in human affairs, it is the most effectual. Enlighten the people generally, and tyranny and oppressions of body and mind will vanish like evil spirits at the dawn of day. Although I do not with some enthusiasts believe that the human condition will ever advance to such a state of perfection as that there shall no longer be pain or vice in the world, yet I believe it susceptible of much improvement, and most of all in matters of government and religion, and that the diffusion of knowledge among the people is to be the instrument by which it is to be effected.

To Pierre Samuel Dupont de Nemours, Poplar Forest, April 24, 1816.

Besides much other good matter [in your *Enquiry into the Principles of Our Government*], it settles unanswerably the right of instructing representatives and their duty to obey. The system of banking we have both equally and ever reprobated. I contemplate it as a blot left in all our constitutions, which, if not covered, will end in their destruction, which is already hit by the gamblers in corruption and is sweeping away in

[c] National expansion, Jefferson believed, would produce "such an empire for liberty as she has never surveyed since the creation; and I am persuaded no constitution was ever before so well calculated as ours for extensive empire and self-government." To James Madison, Monticello, April 27, 1809. *Writings*, XII, 277.

its progress the fortunes and morals of our citizens. Funding I consider as limited, rightfully, to a redemption of the debt within the lives of a majority of the generation contracting it; every generation coming equally, by the laws of the Creator of the world, to the free possession of the earth he made for their subsistence, unencumbered by their predecessors, who, like them, were but tenants for life. You have successfully and completely pulverized Mr. Adams' system of orders and his opening the mantle of republicanism to every government of laws, whether consistent or not with natural right.[6] Indeed, it must be acknowledged that the term "republic" is of very vague application in every language. Witness the self-styled republics of Holland, Switzerland, Genoa, Venice, Poland. Were I to assign to this term a precise and definite idea, I would say purely and simply it means a government by its citizens in mass, acting directly and personally, according to rules established by the majority, and that every other government is more or less republican in proportion as it has in its composition more or less of this ingredient of the direct action of the citizens. Such a government is evidently restrained to very narrow limits of space and population. I doubt if it would be practicable beyond the extent of a New England township.[d] . . . Other shades of republicanism may be found in other forms of government where the executive, judiciary, and legislative functions, and the different branches of the latter, are chosen by the people more or less directly for longer terms of years, or for life, or made hereditary; or where there are mixtures of authorities, some dependent on, and others independent of, the people. The further the departure from direct and constant control by the citizens, the less has the government of the ingredient of republicanism; evidently none where the authorities are hereditary, as in France, Venice, etc., or self-chosen, as in Holland, and little, where for life, in proportion as the life continues in being after the act of election.

The purest republican feature in the government of our own State is the House of Representatives. The Senate is equally

[d] See pp. 55, 114–118.

so the first year, less the second, and so on. The Executive still less, because not chosen by the people directly. The Judiciary seriously anti-republican, because for life, and the national arm wielded, as you observe, by military leaders irresponsible but to themselves. Add to this the vicious constitution of our county courts (to whom the justice, the executive administration, the taxation, police, the military appointments of the county, and nearly all our daily concerns are confided), self-appointed, self-continued, holding their authorities for life, and with an impossibility of breaking in on the perpetual succession of any faction once possessed of the bench. They are in truth the executive, the judiciary, and the military of their respective counties, and the sum of the counties makes the State. And add also that one half of our brethren who fight and pay taxes are excluded like helots from the rights of representation, as if society were instituted for the soil and not for the men inhabiting it, or one half of these could dispose of the rights and the will of the other half without their consent.

> What constitutes a State?
> Not high-raised battlements, or labor'd mound,
>   Thick wall, or moated gate;
> Not cities proud, with spires and turrets crown'd;
>   No! men, high-minded men;
>   Men, who their duties know;
> But know their rights; and knowing, dare maintain;
>   These constitute a State.

In the General Government, the House of Representatives is mainly republican; the Senate scarcely so at all, as not elected by the people directly and so long secured even against those who do elect them; the Executive more republican than the Senate, from its shorter term, its election by the people in *practice*, (for they vote for A only on an assurance that he will vote for B), and because, *in practice also*, a principle of rotation seems to be in a course of establishment; the judiciary independent of the nation, their coercion by impeachment being found nugatory.

If, then, the control of the people over the organs of their government be the measure of its republicanism, and I confess I know no other measure, it must be agreed that our governments have much less of republicanism than ought to have been expected; in other words, that the people have less regular control over their agents than their rights and their interests require. And this I ascribe, not to any want of republican dispositions in those who formed these constitutions, but to a submission of true principle to European authorities, to speculators on government, whose fears of the people have been inspired by the populace of their own great cities and were unjustly entertained against the independent, the happy, and therefore orderly citizens of the United States. . . .

On this view of the import of the term "republic," instead of saying, as has been said, "that it may mean anything or nothing," we may say with truth and meaning that governments are more or less republican as they have more or less of the element of popular election and control in their composition; and believing as I do that the mass of the citizens is the safest depository of their own rights, and especially that the evils flowing from the duperies of the people are less injurious than those from the egoism of their agents, I am a friend to that composition of government which has in it the most of this ingredient. And I sincerely believe with you that banking establishments are more dangerous than standing armies, and that the principle of spending money to be paid by posterity, under the name of funding, is but swindling futurity on a large scale.

To John Taylor, Monticello, May 28, 1816.

CHAPTER TWO

THE BLESSINGS OF A FREE GOVERNMENT

I. OBJECT OF GOVERNMENT: TO PROTECT NATURAL RIGHTS AND PROMOTE HAPPINESS OF THE PEOPLE

As stated in the Declaration of Independence, Jefferson regarded government as an instrument for protecting and safeguarding the natural rights of the people. It should be so fashioned as best to "effect their safety and happiness."

1. Natural Rights in General

Should our Convention propose to establish now a form of government, perhaps it might be agreeable to recall for a short time their delegates. It is a work of the most interesting nature and such as every individual would wish to have his voice in. In truth it is the whole object of the present controversy, for should a bad government be instituted for us in future, it had been as well to have accepted at first the bad one offered to us from beyond the water without the risk and expense of contest.

To Thomas Nelson, Philadelphia, May 16, 1776.

I suspect that the doctrine that small States alone are fitted to be republics will be exploded by experience, with some other brilliant fallacies accredited by Montesquieu[1] and other political writers. Perhaps it will be found that to obtain a just republic (and it is to secure our just rights that we resort to government at all) it must be so extensive as that local egoisms may never reach its greater part; that on every particular question a majority may be found in its councils free from particular interests and giving, therefore, a uniform prevalence to the principles of justice.

To François d'Ivernois, Monticello, February 6, 1795.

I will . . . essay . . . definitions . . . of the terms "Liberty" and "Republic," aware however that they have been so multifariously applied as to convey no precise idea to the mind. Of liberty then I would say that, in the whole plenitude of its extent, it is unobstructed action according to our will, but rightful liberty is unobstructed action according to our will within limits drawn around us by the equal rights of others. I do not add "within the limits of the law," because law is often but the tyrant's will, and always so when it violates the right of an individual. I will add, secondly, that a pure republic is a state of society in which every member of mature and sound mind has an equal right of participation, personally, in the direction of the affairs of the society. Such a regimen is obviously impracticable beyond the limits of an encampment or of a small village. When numbers, distance, or force oblige them to act by deputy, then their government continues republican in proportion only as the functions they still exercise in person are more or fewer and, as in those exercised by deputy, the right of appointing their deputy is *pro hac vice* only, or for more or fewer purposes, or for shorter or longer terms.

To Isaac H. Tiffany, Monticello, April 4, 1819.

Our legislators are not sufficiently apprised of the rightful limits of their power: that their true office is to declare and enforce only our natural rights and duties and to take none of them from us. No man has a natural right to commit aggression on the equal rights of another, and this is all from which the laws ought to restrain him; every man is under the natural duty of contributing to the necessities of the society, and this is all the laws should enforce on him; and, no man having a natural right to be the judge between himself and another, it is his natural duty to submit to the umpirage of an impartial third. When the laws have declared and enforced all this, they have fulfilled their functions; and the idea is quite unfounded that on entering into society we give up any natural right. The trial of every law by one of these texts would lessen much the labors of our legislators and lighten equally our municipal codes.

To Francis W. Gilmer, Monticello, June 7, 1816.

It is not only vain but wicked in a legislator to frame laws in opposition to the laws of nature, and to arm them with the terrors of death. . . . The law of nature impels everyone to escape from confinement; it should not therefore be subjected to punishment. Let the legislator restrain his criminal by walls, not by parchment.

Note to Bill for Proportioning Crimes and Punishments in
Cases Heretofore Capital.

The sentiment that *ex post facto* laws are against natural right is so strong in the United States that few, if any, of the State constitutions have failed to proscribe them. . . . Laws, moreover, abridging the natural right of the citizen should be restrained by rigorous constructions within their narrowest limits.

It has been pretended by some (and in England especially) that inventors have a natural and exclusive right to their inventions and not merely for their own lives but inheritable to their heirs. But while it is a moot question whether the origin of any kind of property is derived from nature at all, it would be singular to admit a natural and even a hereditary right to inventors. It is agreed by those who have seriously considered the subject that no individual has, of natural right, a separate property in an acre of land, for instance. By a universal law, indeed, whatever, whether fixed or movable, belongs to all men equally and in common is the property for the moment of him who occupies it, but when he relinquishes the occupation, the property goes with it. Stable ownership is the gift of social law and is given late in the progress of society. It would be curious then if an idea, the fugitive fermentation of an individual brain, could, of natural right, be claimed in exclusive and stable property. If nature has made any one thing less susceptible than all others of exclusive property, it is the action of the thinking power called an idea.

To Isaac McPherson, Monticello, August 13, 1813.

Where there are in any country uncultivated lands and unemployed poor, it is clear that the laws of property have been so far extended as to violate natural right.

To the Rev. James Madison, Fontainebleau, October 28, 1785.

Charged with the care of the general interests of the nation, and among these with the preservation of their lands from intrusion, I exercised on their behalf a right given by nature to all men, individual or associated: that of rescuing their own property wrongfully taken.

To W. C. C. Claiborne, Monticello, May 3, 1810.

Neither natural right nor reason subjects the body of a man to restraint for debt.

To George Hammond, Philadelphia, May 29, 1792.

It had become a universal and almost uncontroverted position in the several States that the purposes of society do not require a surrender of all our rights to our ordinary governors; that there are certain portions of right not necessary to enable them to carry on an effective government and which experience has nevertheless proved they will be constantly encroaching on if submitted to them; that there are also certain fences which experience has proved peculiarly efficacious against wrong and rarely obstructive of right which yet the governing powers have ever shown a disposition to weaken and remove. Of the first kind, for instance, is freedom of religion; of the second, trial by jury, habeas corpus laws, free presses.

To Noah Webster, Philadelphia, December 4, 1790.

There are rights which it is useless to surrender to the government and which governments have yet always been found to invade. These are the rights of thinking and publishing our thoughts by speaking or writing; the right of free commerce; the right of personal freedom. There are instruments for administering the government so peculiarly trustworthy that we should never leave the legislature at liberty to change them. The new Constitution has secured these in the executive and legislative department, but not in the judiciary. It should have established trials by the people themselves, that is to say, by jury. There are instruments so dangerous to the rights of the nation and which place them so totally at the mercy of their governors that those governors, whether legislative or executive, should be restrained from keeping such instruments on foot but in well-defined cases. Such an instrument is a standing army.

To David Humphreys, Paris, March 18, 1789.

The care of human life and happiness, and not their destruction, is the first and only legitimate object of good government.

To Republican Citizens of Washington County, Maryland,
Monticello, March 31, 1809.

A part of my occupation, and by no means the least pleasing, is the direction of the studies of such young men as ask it. They place themselves in the neighboring village, and have the use of my library and counsel, and make a part of my society. In advising the course of their reading, I endeavor to keep their attention fixed on the main objects of all science, the freedom and happiness of man, so that, coming to bear a share in the councils and government of their country, they will keep ever in view the sole objects of all legitimate government.

To Thaddeus Kosciusko, Monticello, February 26, 1810.

Civil government being the sole object of forming societies, its administration must be conducted by common consent. Every species of government has its specific principles. Ours perhaps are more peculiar than those of any other in the universe. It is a composition of the freest principles of the English constitution with others derived from natural right and natural reason.

Notes on Virginia, Query VIII.

The only orthodox object of the institution of government is to secure the greatest degree of happiness possible to the general mass of those associated under it.

To Francis A. Vanderkemp, Monticello, March 22, 1812.

I confess I look to this duplication of area [by the Louisiana Purchase] for the extending a government so free and economical as ours as a great achievement to the mass of happiness which is to ensue.[a] Whether we remain in one confederacy or form into Atlantic and Mississippi confederacies, I believe not very important to the happiness of either part.

To Joseph Priestley, Washington, January 29, 1804.

With respect to the new States, were the question to stand simply in this form: how may the ultramontane territory be disposed of so as to produce the greatest and most immediate benefit to the inhabitants of the maritime States of the Union, the plan would be more plausible of laying it off into two or three States only. Even on this view, however, there would still be something to be said against it which might render it at least doubtful. But that is a question which good faith forbids us to receive into discussion. This requires us to state the question in its just form: how may the territories of the Union be disposed of so as to produce the greatest degree of happiness to their inhabitants? . . . They will not only be happier in States of moderate size, but it is the only way in which they can exist as a regular society.

To James Monroe, Paris, July 9, 1786.

The king [Louis XVI in 1789] would then have yielded by convention freedom of religion, freedom of the press, trial by jury, habeas corpus, and a representative legislature. These I consider as the essentials constituting free government, and that the organization of the executive is interesting as it may insure wisdom and integrity in the first place, but next as it may favor or endanger the preservation of these fundamentals.

To Pierre Samuel Dupont de Nemours, Monticello, February 28, 1815.

Possessing ourselves the combined blessing of liberty and order, we wish the same to other countries and to none more than yours [Greece], which the first of civilized nations presented examples of what man should be. Not, indeed, that the forms of govern-

[a] Cf. to William H. Crawford, Monticello, June 20, 1816. *Works*, XI, 538. See also to William Short, Monticello, January 18, 1826 (Library of Congress, Jefferson Papers).

ment adapted to their age and country are practicable or to be imitated in our day, although prejudices in their favor would be natural enough to your people. The circumstances of the world are too much changed for that. . . . The equal rights of man and the happiness of every individual are now acknowledged to be the only legitimate objects of government. Modern times have the signal advantage, too, of having discovered the only device by which these rights can be secured, to wit: government by the people, acting not in person but by representatives chosen by themselves—that is to say, by every man of ripe years and sane mind who either contributes by his purse or person to the support of his country.

To Adamantios Coray, Monticello, October 31, 1823.

2. Slavery a Violation of Natural Rights

Nothing could be a greater violation of the natural right to liberty and pursuit of happiness than the institution of slavery. Throughout his life Jefferson was a tireless advocate of the abolition of that system of bondage. A philippic against slavery was eliminated by Congress from Jefferson's draft of the Declaration of Independence. His plan of legislative reform in Virginia included a provision that all persons born after a certain date should be free. His proposal to prohibit slavery in the Northwest Territory failed in Congress by one vote. His hesitancy to publish his *Notes on Virginia* was due to fears that the strictures on slavery it contained would arouse antagonism which might prolong the life of the South's "peculiar institution."

The whole commerce between master and slave is a perpetual exercise of the most boisterous passions, the most unremitting despotism on the one part and degrading submissions on the other. . . . The man must be a prodigy who can retain his manners and morals undepraved by such circumstances. And with what execration should the statesman be loaded who, permitting one half the citizens thus to trample on the rights of the other, transforms those into despots and these into enemies, destroys the morals of the one part and the *amor patriae* of the other! For if a slave can have a country in this world, it must be any other in preference to that in which he is born to live and labor for another; . . . And can the liberties of a nation be thought secure when we have removed their only firm basis, a conviction in the minds of the people that these liberties are of the gift of God—that they are not to be violated but with His wrath? Indeed I tremble for my country when I reflect that God is just; that His justice cannot sleep forever; that, considering numbers, nature, and natural means only, a revolution of the wheel of fortune, an exchange of situation is among possible events; that it may become probable by supernatural interference! The Almighty has no attribute which can take side with us in such a contest.

Notes on Virginia, Query XVIII.

I had for a long time ceased to read newspapers or pay any attention to public affairs, confident they were in good hands and content to be a passenger in our bark to the shore from which I am not distant. But this momentous question [Missouri],[2] like a fire bell in the night, awakened and filled me with terror. I considered it at once as the knell of the Union. It is hushed, indeed, for the moment. But this is a reprieve only, not a final sentence. A geographical line, coinciding with a marked principle, moral and political, once conceived and held up to the angry passions of men, will never be obliterated, and every new irritation will mark it deeper and deeper. I can say, with conscious truth, that there is not a man on earth who would sacrifice more than I would to relieve us from this heavy reproach in any *practicable* way. The cession of that kind of property (for so it is misnamed) is a bagatelle which would not cost me a second thought if, in that way, a general emancipation and *expatriation* could be effected; and gradually and with due sacrifices, I think it might be. But as it is, we have the wolf by the ears, and we can neither hold him nor safely let him go. Justice is in one scale and self-preservation in the other. . . .

I regret that I am now to die in the belief that the useless sacrifice of themselves by the generation of 1776, to acquire self-government and happiness to their country, is to be thrown away by the unwise and unworthy passions of their sons; and that my only consolation is to be that I live not to weep over it. If they would but dispassionately weigh the blessings they will throw away against an abstract principle more likely to be effected by union than by scission, they would pause before they would perpetrate this act of suicide on themselves and of treason against the hopes of the world.

To John Holmes, Monticello, April 22, 1820.

The subject [slavery] . . . is one on which I do not permit myself to express an opinion but when time, place, and occasion may give it some favorable effect. A good cause is often injured more by ill-timed efforts of its friends than by the arguments of its enemies. Persuasion, perseverance, and patience are the best advocates on questions depending on the will of others. The revolution in public opinion which this case requires is not to be expected in a day, or perhaps in an age. But time, which outlives all things, will outlive this evil also. My sentiments have been forty years before the public. Had I repeated them forty times, they would only have become the more stale and thread-bare. Although I shall not live to see them consummated, they will not die with me. But, living or dying, they will ever be in my most fervent prayers.

To James Heaton, Monticello, May 20, 1826.

II. EFFECT OF THE FORM OF GOVERNMENT ON THE HAPPINESS OF THE PEOPLE

1. The Evils of Hereditary Government and the Advantages of Republican Government

Comparison of conditions in America with those in Europe confirmed Jefferson's convictions regarding the superior virtues of republican government as a means of effecting the happi-

THE BLESSINGS OF A FREE GOVERNMENT 63

ness of the people. He noted the evils of hereditary and oppressive governments which provoked the people to rebellion. The remedy for such uprisings, he insisted, was to correct the grievances suffered by the people, or to inform and educate them if the revolt was caused by a supposed grievance which did not in fact exist. Punishment for such resistance to government should not be so severe as to encourage acquiescence by the people in violation of their rights.

Indeed, it is difficult to conceive how so good a people, with so good a King, so well-disposed rulers in general, so genial a climate, so fertile a soil, should be rendered so ineffectual for producing human happiness by one single curse—that of a bad form of government. But it is a fact. In spite of the mildness of their governors, the people are ground to powder by the vices of the form of government. Of twenty millions of people supposed to be in France, I am of opinion there are nineteen millions more wretched, more accursed in every circumstance of human existence than the most conspicuously wretched individual of the whole United States.

To Mrs. Elizabeth Trist, Paris, August 18, 1785.

What a crowd of lessons do the present miseries of Holland teach us?—Never to have an hereditary officer of any sort; never to let a citizen ally himself with kings; never to call in foreign nations to settle domestic differences; never to suppose that any nation will expose itself to war for us, etc.

To John Adams, Paris, September 28, 1787.

What a cruel reflection, that a rich country cannot long be a free one.

Travel Notes (March, 1788).

I have never heard a person in Europe, learned or unlearned, express his thoughts on this institution [the Cincinnati [3]] who did not consider it as dishonorable and destructive to our governments, and that every writing which has come out since my arrival here in which it is mentioned considers it, even as now reformed, as the germ whose development is one day to destroy the fabric we have reared. I did not apprehend this while I had American ideas only. But I confess that what I have seen in Europe has brought me over to that opinion, and that though the day may be at some distance, beyond the reach of our lives perhaps, yet it will certainly come when a single fiber left of this institution will produce a hereditary aristocracy which will change the form of our governments from the best to the worst in the world. To know the mass of evil which flows from this fatal source a person must be in France; he must see the finest soil, the finest climate, the most compact state, the most benevolent character of people, and every earthly advantage combined insufficient to prevent this scourge from rendering existence a curse to twenty-four out of twenty-five parts of the inhabitants of this country.

To George Washington, Paris, November 14, 1786.

Our Act for Freedom of Religion [b] is extremely applauded. The ambassadors and ministers of the several nations of Europe resident at this court have asked of me copies of it to send to their sovereigns, and it is inserted at full length in several books now in the press—among others, in the new Encyclopédie. I think it will produce considerable good even in these countries where ignorance, superstition, poverty, and oppression of body and mind in every form are so firmly settled on the mass of the people that their redemption from them can never be hoped. If all the sovereigns of Europe were to set themselves to work to emancipate the minds of their subjects from their present ignorance and prejudices, and that as zealously as they now endeavor the contrary, a thousand years would not place them on that high ground on which our common people are now setting out. Ours could not have been so fairly placed under the control of the common sense of the people had they not been separated from their parent stock and kept from contamination, either from them or the other people of the old world, by the intervention of so wide an ocean. To know the worth of this, one must see

[b] Statute of Virginia for Religious Freedom, 1786 (Cf. pp. 33ff.).

the want of it here. I think by far the most important bill in our whole code is that for the diffusion of knowledge among the people. No other sure foundation can be devised for the preservation of freedom and happiness. If anybody thinks that kings, nobles, or priests are good conservators of the public happiness, send him here. It is the best school in the universe to cure him of that folly. He will see here with his own eyes that these descriptions of men are an abandoned confederacy against the happiness of the mass of the people. The omnipotence of their effect cannot be better proved than in this country particularly, where, notwithstanding the finest soil upon earth, the finest climate under heaven, and a people of the most benevolent, the most gay and amiable character of which the human form is susceptible—where such a people, I say, surrounded by so many blessings from nature, are loaded with misery, by kings, nobles, and priests, and by them alone. Preach, my dear Sir, a crusade against ignorance. Establish and improve the law for educating the common people. Let our countrymen know that the people alone can protect us against these evils, and that the tax which will be paid for this purpose is not more than the thousandth part of what will be paid to kings, priests, and nobles, who will rise up among us if we leave the people in ignorance.

To George Wythe, Paris, August 13, 1786.

I am convinced that those societies (as the Indians) which live without government enjoy in their general mass an infinitely greater degree of happiness than those who live under the European governments. Among the former public opinion is in the place of law and restrains morals as powerfully as laws ever did anywhere. Among the latter, under pretence of governing they have divided their nations into two classes, wolves and sheep. I do not exaggerate. This is a true picture of Europe. Cherish, therefore, the spirit of our people, and keep alive their attention. Do not be too severe upon their errors, but reclaim them by enlightening them. If once they become inattentive to the public affairs, you and I, and Congress and Assemblies, Judges and Governors, shall all become wolves. It seems to be the law of our general nature, in spite of individual exceptions, and experience declares that man is the only animal which devours his own kind; for I can apply no milder term to the governments of Europe and to the general prey of the rich on the poor.

To Edward Carrington, Paris, January 16, 1787.

I am impatient to learn your sentiments on the late troubles in the eastern States. So far as I have yet seen they do not appear to threaten serious consequences. Those States have suffered by the stoppage of the channels of their commerce, which have not yet found other issues. This must render money scarce and make the people uneasy. This uneasiness has produced acts absolutely unjustifiable, but I hope they will provoke no severities from their governments. A consciousness of those in power that their administration of the public affairs has been honest may, perhaps, produce too great a degree of indignation, and those characters wherein fear predominates over hope may apprehend too much from these instances of irregularity. They may conclude too hastily that nature has formed man insusceptible of any other government than that of force, a conclusion not founded in truth nor experience. Societies exist under three forms, sufficiently distinguishable: (1) without government, as among our Indians; (2) under governments wherein the will of everyone has a just influence, as is the case in England in a slight degree and in our States in a great one; (3) under governments of force, as is the case in all other monarchies and in most of the other republics. To have an idea of the curse of existence under these last, they must be seen. It is a government of wolves over sheep. It is a problem, not clear in my mind, that the first condition is not the best. But I believe it to be inconsistent with any great degree of population. The second state has a great deal of good in it. The mass of mankind under that enjoys a precious degree of liberty and happiness. It has its evils, too, the principal of which is the turbulence to which it is subject. But weigh this against the oppressions of monarchy and it becomes nothing. *Malo periculosam libertatem quam quietam servitutem.*[4] Even this evil is productive of good. It prevents the degeneracy of government and nourishes a general attention to the public affairs. I hold it that a little rebellion now and then is a good thing, and as necessary in the political world as storms in the physical. Unsuccessful rebellions, indeed, generally establish the encroachments on the rights of the people which have produced them. An observation of this truth should render honest republican governors so mild in their punishment of rebellions as not to discourage them too much. It is a medicine necessary for the sound health of government.

To James Madison, Paris, January 30, 1787.

It has been said, too, that our governments, both federal and particular, want energy; that it is difficult to restrain both individuals and States from committing wrong. This is true, and it is an inconvenience. On the other hand, that energy which absolute governments derive from an armed force, which is the effect of the bayonet constantly held at the breast of every citizen and which resembles very much the stillness of the grave, must be admitted also to have its inconveniences. We weigh the two together and like best to submit to the former. Compare the number of wrongs committed with impunity by citizens among us with those committed by the sovereign in other countries, and the last will be found most numerous, most oppressive on the mind, and most degrading of the dignity of man.

To Jean Nicolas Démeunier, Paris, January 24, 1786.

I own I am not a friend to a very energetic government. It is always oppressive. It places the governors indeed more at their ease at the expense of the people. The late rebellion in Massachusetts [5] has given more alarm than I think it should have done. Calculate that one rebellion in thirteen States in the course of eleven years is but one for each State in a century and a half. No country should be so long without one. Nor will any degree of power in the hands of government prevent insurrections. In England, where the hand of power is heavier than with us, there are seldom half a dozen years without an insurrection. In France, where it is still heavier but less despotic, as Montesquieu supposes, than in some other countries and where there are always two or three hundred thousand men ready to crush insurrections, there have been three in the course of the three years I have been here, in every one of which greater numbers were engaged than in Massachusetts and a great deal more blood was spilt. In Turkey, where the sole nod of the despot is death, insurrections are the events of every day. Compare again the ferocious depredations of their insurgents with the order, the moderation, and the almost self-extinguishment of ours. And say, finally, whether peace is best preserved by giving energy to the government or information to the people. This last is the most certain and the most legitimate engine of government. Educate and inform the whole mass of the people. Enable them to see that it is their interest to preserve peace and order, and they will preserve them. And it requires no very high degree of education to convince them of this. They are the only sure reliance for the preservation of our liberty.

To James Madison, Paris, December 20, 1787.

The commotions that have taken place in America, as far as they are yet known to me, offer nothing threatening. They are a proof that the people have liberty enough, and I could not wish them less than they have. If the happiness of the mass of the people can be secured at the expense of a little tempest now and then, or even of a little blood, it will be a precious purchase.

To Ezra Stiles, Paris, December 24, 1786.

God forbid we should ever be twenty years without such a rebellion [Shays's Rebellion]. The people cannot be all, and always, well-informed. The part which is wrong will be discontented in proportion to the importance of the facts they misconceive. If they remain quiet under such misconceptions, it is a lethargy, the forerunner of death to the public liberty. We have had thirteen States independent for eleven years. There has been one rebellion. That comes to one rebellion in a century and a half for each State. What country before ever existed a century and a half without a rebellion? And what country can preserve its liberties if its rulers are not warned from time to time that this people preserve the spirit of resistance? Let them take arms. The remedy is to set them right as to facts, pardon and pacify them. What signify a few lives lost in a century or two? The tree of liberty must be refreshed from time to time with the blood of patriots and tyrants. It is its natural manure. Our convention has been too much impressed by the insurrection of Massachusetts, and on the spur of the moment they are setting up a kite to keep the hen yard in order.

To William S. Smith, Paris, November 13, 1787.

2. On the Evils of Monarchies

If all the evils which can arise among us from the republican form of government, from this day to the day of judgment, could be put into a scale against what this country suffers from its monarchical form in a week, or England in a month, the latter would preponderate. . . . No race of kings has ever presented above one man of common sense in twenty generations.

To Benjamin Hawkins, Paris, August 4, 1787.

The practice of kings marrying only in the families of kings has been that of Europe for some centuries. Now, take any race of animals, confine them in idleness and inaction, whether in a stye, a stable, or a stateroom, pamper them with high diet, gratify all their sexual appetites, immerse them in sensualities, nourish their passions, let everything bend before them, and banish whatever might lead them to think, and in a few generations they become all body and no mind; and this, too, by a law of nature, by that very law by which we are in the constant practice of changing the characters and propensities of the animals we raise for our own purposes. Such is the regimen in raising kings, and in this way they have gone on for centuries.[c]

To John Langdon, Monticello, March 5, 1810.

[c] See also to John Jay, Paris, January 11, 1789. *Works*, V, 441–43.

So much for the blessings of having kings, and magistrates who would be kings. From these events, our young republic may learn useful lessons: never to call on foreign powers to settle their differences; to guard against hereditary magistrates; to prevent their citizens from becoming so established in wealth and power as to be thought worthy of alliance by marriage with the nieces, sisters, etc., of kings; and, in short, to besiege the throne of heaven with eternal prayers, to extirpate from creation this class of human lions, tigers, and mammoths called kings, from whom let him perish who does not say "good Lord deliver us."

To David Humphreys, Paris, August 14, 1787.

I was much an enemy to monarchies before I came to Europe. I am ten thousand times more so since I have seen what they are. There is scarcely an evil known in these countries which may not be traced to their king as its source, nor a good which is not derived from the small fibers of republicanism existing among them. I can further say, with safety, there is not a crowned head in Europe whose talents or merits would entitle him to be elected a vestryman by the people of any parish in America.

To George Washington, Paris, May 2, 1788.

With all the defects of our constitutions, whether general or particular, the comparison of our governments with those of Europe is like a comparison of heaven and hell. England, like the earth, may be allowed to take the intermediate station. And yet I hear there are people among you who think the experience of our governments has already proved that republican governments will not answer. Send those gentry here to count the blessings of monarchy.

To Joseph Jones, Paris, August 14, 1787.

We may say with confidence that the worst of the American constitutions is better than the best which ever existed before in any other country.

To Thomas M. Randolph, Jr., Paris, July 6, 1787.

I am sensible that there are defects in our federal government, yet they are so much lighter than those of monarchies that I view them with much indulgence. I rely, too, on the good sense of the people for remedy, whereas the evils of monarchical government are beyond remedy. If any of our countrymen wish for a king, give them Aesop's fable of the frogs who asked for a king; if this does not cure them, send them to Europe. They will go back good republicans.

To David Ramsay, Paris, August 4, 1787.

I sincerely wish you may find it convenient to come here; the pleasure of the trip will be less than you expect, but the utility greater. It will make you adore your own country—its soil, its climate, its equality, liberty, laws, people, and manners. My God! how little do my countrymen know what precious blessings they are in possession of and which no other people on earth enjoy. I confess I had no idea of it myself. While we shall see multiplied instances of Europeans going to live in America, I will venture to say no man now living will ever see an instance of an American removing to settle in Europe and continuing there. Come, then, and see the proofs of this, and on your return add your testimony to that of every thinking American in order to satisfy our countrymen how much it is their interest to preserve, uninfected by contagion, those peculiarities in their government and manners to which they are indebted for those blessings.

To James Monroe, Paris, June 17, 1785.

III. AN AMERICAN SYSTEM

Instead of the everlasting warfare and oppression, typical of governments in the Old World, Jefferson aimed at the establishment in America of a new system based on "cherishment of the people," where peace and productivity could flourish, under a polity which would demonstrate to the world "that a government of reason is better than one of force."

Nothing is so important as that America shall separate herself from the systems of Europe and establish one of her own. Our circumstances, our pursuits, our interests are distinct; the principles of our policy should be so also. All entanglements with that quarter of the globe should be avoided if we mean that peace and justice shall be the polar stars of the American societies.

To Joseph Correa de Serra, Monticello, October 24, 1820.

. . . I often doubt whether I should trouble Congress or my friends with these details of European politics. I know they do not excite that interest in America of which it is impossible for one to divest himself here. I know, too, that it is a maxim with us, and I think it a wise one, not to entangle ourselves with the affairs of Europe.[d] Still, I think we should know them. The Turks have practiced the same maxim of not meddling in the complicated wrangles of this continent. But they have unwisely chosen to be ignorant of them also.

To Edward Carrington, Paris, December 21, 1789.

Separated by a wide ocean from the nations of Europe and from the political interests which entangle them together, with productions and wants which render our commerce and friendship useful to them and theirs to us, it cannot be the interest of any to assail us, nor ours to disturb them. We should be most unwise, indeed, were we to cast away the singular blessings of the position in which nature has placed us, the opportunity she has endowed us with of pursuing, at a distance from foreign contentions, the paths of industry, peace, and happiness; of cultivating general friendship, and of bringing collisions of interest to the umpirage of reason rather than of force.

Third Annual Message, October 17, 1803.

Mr. Correa[6] is here, on his farewell visit to us. . . . From many conversations with him, I hope he sees, and will promote in his new situation, the advantages of a cordial fraternization among all the American nations, and the importance of their coalescing

d See also pp. 44, 183.

in an American system of policy totally independent of and unconnected with that of Europe. The day is not distant when we may formally require a meridian of partition through the ocean which separates the two hemispheres, on the hither side of which no European gun shall ever be heard, nor an American on the other; and when, during the rage of the eternal wars of Europe, the lion and the lamb within our regions shall lie down together in peace. The excess of population in Europe and want of room render war, in their opinion, necessary to keep down that excess of numbers. Here room is abundant, population scanty, and peace the necessary means for producing men to whom the redundant soil is offering the means of life and happiness. The principles of society there and here, then, are radically different, and I hope no American patriot will ever lose sight of the essential policy of interdicting in the seas and territories of both Americas the ferocious and sanguinary contests of Europe. I wish to see this coalition begun.

To William Short, Monticello, August 4, 1820.

The matter which now embroils Europe,[7] the presumption of dictating to an independent nation the form of its government, is so arrogant, so atrocious, that indignation, as well as moral sentiment, enlists all our partialities and prayers in favor of one and our equal execrations against the other. I do not know, indeed, whether all nations do not owe to one another a bold and open declaration of their sympathies with the one party and their detestation of the conduct of the other. But farther than this we are not bound to go; and, indeed, for the sake of the world, we ought not to increase the jealousies or draw on ourselves the power of this formidable confederacy. I have ever deemed it fundamental for the United States never to take active part in the quarrels of Europe. Their political interests are entirely distinct from ours. Their mutual jealousies, their balance of power, their complicated alliances, their forms and principles of government are all foreign to us. They are nations of eternal war. All their energies are expended in the destruction of the labor, property, and lives of their people. On our part never had a people so favorable a chance of trying the opposite system of peace and fraternity with mankind and the direction of all our means and faculties to the purposes of improvement instead of destruction.

To James Monroe, Monticello, June 11, 1823.

The question presented by the letters you have sent me is the most momentous which has ever been offered to my contemplation since that of Independence. That made us a nation, this sets our compass and points the course which we are to steer through the ocean of time opening on us. And never could we embark on it under circumstances more auspicious. Our first and fundamental maxim should be never to entangle ourselves in the broils of Europe, our second never to suffer Europe to intermeddle with cis-Atlantic affairs. America, North and South, has a set of interests distinct from those of Europe and peculiarly her own. She should therefore have a system of her own, separate and apart from that of Europe. While the last is laboring to become the domicile of despotism, our endeavor should surely be to make our hemisphere that of freedom.[e]

To James Monroe, Monticello, October 24, 1823.

The doctrines of Europe were that men in numerous associations cannot be restrained within the limits of order and justice but by forces physical and moral wielded over them by authorities independent of their will—hence their organization of kings, hereditary nobles, and priests. Still further, to constrain the brute force of the people, they deem it necessary to keep them down by hard labor, poverty, and ignorance; and to take from them, as from bees, so much of their earnings as that unremitting labor shall be necessary to obtain a sufficient surplus barely to sustain a scanty and miserable life. And these earnings they apply to maintain their privileged orders in splendor and idleness, to fascinate the eyes of the people, and excite in them a humble adoration and submission, as to an order of superior beings.

[e] In this letter Jefferson urges the President to proclaim the Monroe Doctrine.

Although few among us had gone all these lengths of opinion, yet many had advanced, some more, some less, on the way. And in the convention which formed our government, they endeavored to draw the cords of power as tight as they could obtain them, to lessen the dependence of the general functionaries on their constituents, to subject to them those of the States, and to weaken their means of maintaining the steady equilibrium which the majority of the convention had deemed salutary for both branches, general and local. To recover, therefore, in practice, the powers which the nation had refused, and to warp to their own wishes those actually given, was the steady object of the federal party. Ours, on the contrary, was to maintain the will of the majority of the convention and of the people themselves. We believed . . . that man was a rational animal, endowed by nature with rights, and with an innate sense of justice; and that he could be restrained from wrong and protected in right by moderate powers confided to persons of his own choice and held to their duties by dependence on his own will. We believed that the complicated organization of kings, nobles, and priests was not the wisest nor best to effect the happiness of associated man, that wisdom and virtue were not hereditary, that the trappings of such a machinery consumed by their expense those earnings of industry they were meant to protect and by the inequalities they produced exposed liberty to sufferance. We believed that men, enjoying in ease and security the full fruits of their own industry, enlisted by all their interests on the side of law and order, habituated to think for themselves and to follow their reason as their guide, would be more easily and safely governed than with minds nourished in error and vitiated and debased, as in Europe, by ignorance, indigence, and oppression. The cherishment [8] of the people then was our principle, the fear and distrust of them that of the other party.

To William Johnson, Monticello, June 12, 1823.

I consider the establishment and success of their [French] government as necessary to stay up our own, and to prevent it from falling back to that kind of a halfway house, the English constitution. It cannot be denied that we have among us a sect who believe that [constitution] to contain whatever is perfect in human institutions; that the members of this sect have, many of them, names and offices which stand high in the estimation of our countrymen. I still rely that the great mass of our community is untainted with these heresies as is its head. On this I build my hope that we have not labored in vain, and that our experiment will still prove that men can be governed by reason.

To George Mason, Philadelphia, February 4, 1791.

I have sworn upon the altar of God eternal hostility against every form of tyranny over the mind of man.

To Benjamin Rush, Monticello, September 23, 1800.

This institution [the University of Virginia] will be based on the illimitable freedom of the human mind. For here we are not afraid to follow truth wherever it may lead, nor to tolerate any error so long as reason is left free to combat it.

To William Roscoe, Monticello, December 27, 1820.

The storm through which we have passed has been tremendous indeed. The tough sides of our argosy have been thoroughly tried. Her strength has stood the waves into which she was steered with a view to sink her. We shall put her on her republican tack, and she will now show by the beauty of her motion the skill of her builders. Figure apart, our fellow citizens have been led hoodwinked from their principles by a most extraordinary combination of circumstances. But the band is removed, and they now see for themselves. I hope to see shortly a perfect consolidation, to effect which nothing shall be spared on my part short of the abandonment of the principles of our revolution. A just and solid republican government maintained here will be a standing monument and example for the aim and imitation of the people of other countries, and I join with you in the hope and belief that they will see, from our example, that a free government is of all others the most energetic, that the inquiry which has been excited among the mass of mankind by our revolution and its consequences will ameliorate the condition of man over a great portion of the globe.[†] What a satisfaction have we in the contemplation of the benevolent effects of our efforts, compared with those of the leaders on the other side, who have discountenanced all advances in science as dangerous innovations, have endeavored to render philosophy and republicanism terms of reproach, to persuade us that man cannot be governed but by the rod, etc. I shall have the happiness of living and dying in the contrary hope.

To John Dickinson, Washington, March 6, 1801.

In the great work which has been effected in America, no individual has a right to take any great share to himself. Our people in a body are wise because they are under the unrestrained and unperverted operation of their own understandings. Those whom we have assigned to the direction of their affairs have stood with a pretty even front. If any one of them was withdrawn, many others entirely equal have been ready to fill his place with as good abilities. A nation composed of such materials and free in all its members from distressing wants furnishes hopeful implements for the interesting experiment of self-government, and we feel that we are acting under obligations not confined to the limits of our own society. It is impossible not to be sensible that we are acting for all mankind; that circumstances denied to others but indulged to us have imposed on us the duty of proving what is the degree of freedom and self-government in which a society may venture to leave its individual members.

To Joseph Priestley, Washington, June 19, 1802.

I have no fear but that the result of our experiment will be that men may be trusted to govern themselves without a master. Could the contrary of this be proved, I should conclude either that there is no God or that he is a malevolent being.

To David Hartley, Paris, July 2, 1787.

[†] The importance of the experiment of self-government in America as an example to other nations is also eloquently expressed in the following: to Governor Hall, Washington, July 6, 1802, *Works*, IX, 378; to John Hollins, Monticello, May 5, 1811, *Writings*, XIII, 58.

We exist and are quoted as standing proofs that a government so modeled as to rest continually on the will of the whole society is a practicable government. Were we to break to pieces, it would damp the hopes and the efforts of the good and give triumph to those of the bad through the whole enslaved world. As members, therefore, of the universal society of mankind and standing in high and responsible relation with them, it is our sacred duty to suppress passion among ourselves and not to blast the confidence we have inspired of proof that a government of reason is better than one of force.

To Richard Rush, Monticello, October 20, 1820.

Convinced that the republican is the only form of government which is not eternally at open or secret war with the rights of mankind, my prayers and efforts shall be cordially distributed to the support of that we have so happily established. It is indeed an animating thought that, while we are securing the rights of ourselves and our posterity, we are pointing out the way to struggling nations who wish like us to emerge from their tyrannies also. Heaven help their struggles and lead them, as it has done us, triumphantly through them.

To William Hunter, Alexandria, March 11, 1790.

The spirit of 1776 is not dead. It has only been slumbering. The body of the American people is substantially republican.

To Thomas Lomax, Monticello, March 12, 1799.

CHAPTER THREE

GOVERNMENT FOUNDED ON THE WILL OF THE PEOPLE

That, as stated in the Declaration of Independence, all "just powers" exercised by a government are derived from and founded upon the consent of the people governed is a basic and constantly recurring theme in Jefferson's political thinking.

I. THE PEOPLE AS SOURCE OF ALL AUTHORITY

The rightful basis of any government, in Jefferson's opinion, must be found in "the will of the nation, substantially declared." The forms and agencies of government may be modified or reorganized by the people at any time or to any extent.

I consider the people who constitute a society or nation as the source of all authority in that nation; as free to transact their common concerns by any agents they think proper; to change these agents individually or the organization of them in form or function whenever they please; that all the acts done by these agents under the authority of the nation are the acts of the nation, are obligatory on them and enure to their use, and can in no wise be annulled or affected by any change in the form of the government, or of the persons administering it.

Cabinet Opinion, April 28, 1793.

In every country where man is free to think and to speak, differences of opinion will arise from difference of perception and the imperfection of reason; but these differences, when permitted, as in this happy country, to purify themselves by free discussion, are but as passing clouds overspreading our land transiently and leaving our horizon more bright and serene. That love of order and obedience to the laws, which so remarkably characterize the citizens of the United States, are sure pledges of internal tranquility; and the elective franchise, if guarded as the ark of our safety, will peaceably dissipate all combinations to subvert a Constitution dictated by the wisdom and resting on the will of the people. That will is the only legitimate foundation of any government, and to protect its free expression should be our first object.

To Benjamin Waring, Washington, March 23, 1801.

The government of a nation may be usurped by the forcible intrusion of an individual into the throne. But to conquer its will so as to rest the right on that, the only legitimate basis, requires long acquiescence and cessation of all opposition.

To George W. Lewis, Monticello, October 25, 1825.

It accords with our principles to acknowledge any government to be rightful which is formed by the will of the nation substantially declared. The late government was of this kind and was accordingly acknowledged by all the branches of ours. So any alteration of it, which shall be made by the will of the nation substantially declared, will doubtless be acknowledged in like manner.

To Gouverneur Morris, Philadelphia, November 7, 1792.

We surely cannot deny to any nation that right whereon our own government is founded, that every one may govern itself according to whatever form it pleases and change these forms at its own will; and that it may transact its business with foreign nations through whatever organ it thinks proper, whether king, convention, assembly, committee, president, or anything else it may choose. The will of the nation is the only thing essential to be regarded.

To Gouverneur Morris, Philadelphia, March 12, 1793.

I consider the source of authority with us to be the nation. Their will, declared through its proper organ, is valid till revoked by their will declared through its proper organ again also. Between 1776 and 1789, the proper organ for pronouncing their will, whether legislative or executive, was a Congress formed in a particular manner. Since 1789 it is a Congress formed in a different manner, for laws, and a President elected in a particular way, for making appointments and doing other executive acts. The laws and appointments of the ancient Congress were as valid and permanent in their nature as the laws of the new Congress or appointments of the new Executive, these laws and appointments in both cases deriving equally their source from the will of the nation; and when a question arises whether any particular law or appointment is still in force, we are to examine not whether it was pronounced by the ancient or present organ but whether it has been at any time revoked by the authority of the nation, expressed by the organ competent at the time.

To George Washington, Philadelphia, February 4, 1792.

The whole body of the nation is the sovereign legislative, judiciary, and executive power for itself. The inconvenience of meeting to exercise these powers in person and their inaptitude to exercise them induce them to appoint special organs to declare their legislative will, to judge and to execute it. It is the will of the nation which makes the law obligatory; it is their will which creates or annihilates the organ which is to declare and announce it. They may do it by a single person, as an emperor of Russia (constituting his declarations evidence of their will), or by a few persons, as the aristocracy of Venice, or by a complication of councils, as in our former regal government or our present republican one. The law, being law because it is the will of the nation, is not changed by their changing the organ through which they choose to announce their future will; no more than the acts I have done by one attorney lose their obligation by my changing or discontinuing that attorney. . . . Before the revolution the nation of Virginia had, by the organs they then thought proper to constitute, established a system of laws, which they divided into three denominations of: 1. common law; 2. statute law; 3. chancery; or, if you please, into two only, of: 1. common law; 2. chancery. When by the Declaration of Independence they chose to abolish their former organs of declaring their will, the acts of will already formally and constitutionally declared remained untouched. For the nation was not dissolved, was not annihilated; its will, therefore, remained in full vigor, and on the establishing the new organs, first of a convention and afterwards a more complicated legislature, the old acts of national will continued in force until the nation should by its new organs declare its will changed. The common law, therefore, which was not in force when we landed here nor till we had formed ourselves into a nation and had manifested by the organs we constituted that the common law was to be our law, continued to be our law because the nation continued in being and because, though it changed the organs for the future declarations of its will, yet it did not change its former declarations that the common law was its law. Apply these principles to the present case. Before the revolution there existed no such nation as the United States; they then first associated as a nation, but for special purposes only. They had all their laws to make, as Virginia had on her first establishment as a nation. But they did not, as Virginia had done, proceed to adopt a whole system of laws ready made to their hand. As their association as a nation was only for special purposes—to wit, for the management of their concerns with one another and with foreign nations—and the States composing the association chose to give it powers for those purposes and no others, they could not adopt any general system because it would have embraced objects on which this association had no right to form or declare a will. It was not the organ for declaring a national will in these cases. In the cases confided to them they were free to declare the will of the nation, the law; but till it was declared there could be no law. So that the common law did not become, *ipso facto,* law on the new association; it could only become so by a positive adoption, and so far only as they were authorized to adopt.

To Edmund Randolph, Monticello, August 18, 1799.

II. THE RIGHT OF SELF-GOVERNMENT

It was Jefferson's wish that "every man and every body of men on earth" might enjoy and exercise "the blessings of self-government."

Every man, and every body of men on earth, possesses the right of self-government. They receive it with their being from the hand of nature. Individuals exercise it by their single will—collections of men by that of their majority; for the law of the *majority* is the natural law of every society of men. When a certain description of men are to transact together a particular business, the times and places of their meeting and separating depend on their own will; they make a part of the natural right of self-government. This, like all other natural rights, may be abridged or modified in its exercise by their own consent or by the law of those who depute them, if they meet in the right of others; but, as far as it is not abridged or modified, they retain it as a natural right and may exercise it in what form they please, either exclusively by themselves or in association with others or by others altogether, as they shall agree.

Each house of Congress possesses this natural right of governing itself and, consequently, of fixing its own times and places of meeting, so far as it has not been abridged by the law of those who employ them, that is to say, by the Constitution.

Cabinet Opinion, July 15, 1790.

The present generation has the same right of self-government which the past one has exercised for itself.

To John H. Pleasants, Monticello, April 19, 1824.

The first principle of republicanism is that the *lex majoris partis* is the fundamental law of every society of individuals of equal rights; to consider the will of the society enounced by the majority of a single vote as sacred as if unanimous is the first of all lessons in importance, yet the last which is thoroughly learnt. This law once disregarded, no other remains but that of force, which ends necessarily in military despotism.

To Alexander Humboldt, Monticello, June 13, 1817.

On the late revolution the changes which their new form of government rendered necessary were easily made. It was only necessary to say that the powers of legislation, the judiciary, and the executive powers, heretofore exercised by persons of such and such description, shall henceforth be exercised by persons to be appointed in such and such manners. This was what their constitutions did.

To Jean Nicolas Démeunier, Paris, January 24, 1786.

With respect to the State of Virginia in particular, the people seem to have laid aside the monarchical and taken up the republican government with as much ease as would have attended their throwing off an old and putting on a new suit of clothes.

To Benjamin Franklin, Virginia, August 13, 1777.

The several States now comprising the United States of America were, from their first establishment, separate and distinct societies, dependent on no other society of men whatever. They continued at the head of their respective governments the executive magistrate who presided over the one they had left, and thereby secured in effect a constant amity with that nation. . . . The part which our chief magistrate [King George III] took in a war waged against us by the nation among whom he resided obliged us to discontinue him and to name one within every State.

Report on Negotiations with Spain, March 18, 1792.

That we should wish to see the people of other countries free is as natural and at least as justifiable as that one king should wish to see the kings of other countries maintained in their despotism.

To Albert Gallatin, Monticello, June 16, 1817.

I wish I could give better hopes of our southern brethren. The achievement of their independence of Spain is no longer a question. But it is a very serious one: What will then become of them? . . . No one, I hope, can doubt my wish to see them and all mankind exercising self-government and capable of exercising it. But the question is not what we wish, but what is practicable? [1]

To Lafayette, Monticello, May 14, 1817.

Surely it is our duty to wish them [the Latin American states] independence and self-government because they wish it themselves, and they have the right, and we none, to choose for themselves.

To John Adams, Monticello, May 17, 1818.

Although we have no right to intermeddle with the form of government of other nations, yet it is lawful to wish to see no emperors nor king in our hemisphere.

To James Monroe, Monticello, December 1, 1822.

As far as we can judge from appearances, Bonaparte, from being a mere military usurper, seems to have become the choice of his nation, and the allies, in their turn, the usurpers and spoliators of the European world. The right of nations to self-government being my polar star, my partialities are steered by it without asking whether it is a Bonaparte or an Alexander toward whom the helm is directed.

To Joseph Correa de Serra, Monticello, June 28, 1815.

At length Bonaparte has got on the right side of a question. . . . At least he is defending the cause of his nation and that of all mankind, the rights of every people to independence and self-government. He and the allies have now changed sides. They are parceling out among themselves Poland, Belgium, Saxony, Italy, dictating a ruler and government to France, and looking askance at our republic, the splendid libel on their governments, and he is fighting for the principles of national independence, of which his whole life hitherto has been a continued violation.

To John Adams, Monticello, August 10, 1815.

The subjugation of England would be a general calamity. But happily it is impossible. Should it end in her being only republicanized, I know not on what principle a true republican of our country could lament it, whether he considers it as extending the blessings of a purer government to other portions of mankind or strengthening the cause of liberty in our own country by the influence of that example. I do not indeed wish to see any nation have a form of government forced on them, but if it is to be done, I should rejoice at its being a freer one.

To Peregrine Fitzhugh, Philadelphia, February 23, 1798.

The French have been guilty of great errors in their conduct toward other nations, not only insulting uselessly all crowned heads but endeavoring to force liberty on their neighbors in their own form.

To Thomas Mann Randolph, Philadelphia, June 24, 1793.

I learn with pleasure that republican principles are predominant in your State, because I conscientiously believe that governments founded in these are more friendly to the happiness of the people at large and especially of a people so capable of self-government as ours. I have been ever opposed to the party so falsely called Federalists, because I believe them desirous of introducing into our government authorities hereditary or otherwise independent of the national will. These always consume the public contributions and oppress the people with labor and poverty.

To David Howell, Monticello, December 15, 1810.

I . . . proceeded to New York in March, 1790, to enter on the office of Secretary of State. . . . The President received me cordially and my colleagues and the circle of principal citizens apparently with welcome. The courtesies of dinner parties given me as a stranger newly arrived among them placed me at once in their familiar society. But I cannot describe the wonder and mortification with which the table conversations filled me. Politics were the chief topic, and a preference of kingly over republican government was evidently the favorite sentiment. An apostate I could not be nor yet a hypocrite, and I found myself, for the most part, the only advocate on the republican side of the question unless among the guests there chanced to be some member of that party from the legislative Houses.

Anas, February 4, 1818.

But so different was the style of society then and with those people [the ancient Greeks] from what it is now and with us that I think little edification can be obtained from their writings on the subject of government. They had just ideas of the value of personal liberty, but none at all of the structure of government best calculated to preserve it. They knew no medium between a democracy (the only pure republic, but impracticable beyond the limits of a town) and an abandonment of themselves to an aristocracy or a tyranny independent of the people. It seems not to have occurred that where the citizens cannot meet to transact their business in person, they alone have the right to choose the agents who shall transact it; and that in this way a republican or popular government of the second grade of purity may be exercised over any extent of country. The full experiment of a government democratical but representative was and is still reserved for us. The idea (taken, indeed, from the little specimen formerly existing in the English constitution but now lost) has been carried by us more or less into all our legislative and executive departments; but it has not yet by any of us been pushed into all the ramifications of the system, so far as to leave no authority existing not responsible to the people, whose rights, however, to the exercise and fruits of their own industry can never be protected against the selfishness of rulers not subject to their control at short periods. The introduction of this new principle of representative democracy has rendered useless almost everything written before on the structure of government, and in a great measure relieves our regret if the political writings of

Aristotle or of any other ancient have been lost or are unfaithfully rendered or explained to us. My most earnest wish is to see the republican element of popular control pushed to the maximum of its practicable exercise. I shall then believe that our government may be pure and perpetual.

To Isaac H. Tiffany, Monticello, August 26, 1816.

The friendship which has subsisted between us now half a century and the harmony of our political principles and pursuits have been sources of constant happiness to me through that long period. And if I remove beyond the reach of attentions to the University, or beyond the bourne of life itself, as I soon must, it is a comfort to leave that institution under your care, and an assurance that it will not be wanting. It has also been a great solace to me to believe that you are engaged in vindicating to posterity the course we have pursued for preserving to them, in all their purity, the blessings of self-government, which we had assisted too in acquiring for them. If ever the earth has beheld a system of administration conducted with a single and steadfast eye to the general interest and happiness of those committed to it—one which, protected by truth, can never know reproach—it is that to which our lives have been devoted. To myself you have been a pillar of support through life. Take care of me when dead, and be assured that I shall leave with you my last affections.

To James Madison, Monticello, February 17, 1826.

III. PARTICIPATION BY THE PEOPLE IN EVERY BRANCH OF GOVERNMENT

Effective self-government required, in Jefferson's opinion, that the people participate in every feature of the political process. Hence he valued highly the jury system, believing that: "The execution of the laws is more important than the making of them."

We think, in America, that it is necessary to introduce the people into every department of government as far as they are capable of exercising it, and that this is the only way to insure a long continued and honest administration of its powers.

1. They are not qualified to exercise themselves the executive department, but they are qualified to name the person who shall exercise it. With us, therefore, they choose this officer every four years. 2. They are not qualified to legislate. With us, therefore, they only choose the legislators. 3. They are not qualified to judge questions of *law*, but they are very capable of judging questions of *fact*. In the form of juries, therefore, they determine all matters of fact, leaving to the permanent judges to decide the law resulting from those facts. But we all know that permanent judges acquire an *esprit de corps;* that, being known, they are liable to be tempted by bribery; that they are misled by favor, by relationship, by a spirit of party, by a devotion to the executive or legislative power; that it is better to leave a cause to the decision of cross and pile than to that of a judge biased to one side; and that the opinion of twelve honest jurymen gives still a better hope of right than cross and pile does. It is left, therefore, to the juries, if they think the permanent judges are under any bias whatever in any cause, to take on themselves to judge the law as well as the fact. They never exercise this power but when they suspect partiality in the judges, and by the exercise of this power they have been the firmest bulwarks of English liberty. Were I called upon to decide whether the people had best be omitted in the legislative or judiciary department, I would say it is better to leave them out of the legislature. The execution of the laws is more important than the making of them. However, it is best to have the people in all the three departments, where that is possible.

To the Abbé Arnoux, Paris, July 19, 1789.

With us, all the branches of the government are elective by the people themselves, except the judiciary, of whose science and qualifications they are not competent judges. Yet even in that department we call in a jury of the people to decide all controverted matters of fact because to that investigation they are entirely competent, leaving thus as little as possible, merely the law of the case, to the decision of the judges. And true it is that the people, especially when moderately instructed, are the only safe, because the only honest, depositories of the public rights and should therefore be introduced into the administration of them in every function to which they are sufficient. They will err sometimes and accidentally but never designedly and with a systematic and persevering purpose of overthrowing the free principles of the government. Hereditary bodies, on the contrary, always existing, always on the watch for their own aggrandizement, profit of every opportunity of advancing the privileges of their order and encroaching on the rights of the people.

To Adamantios Coray, Monticello, October 31, 1823.

The constitutions of most of our States assert that all power is inherent in the people; that they may exercise it by themselves in all cases to which they think themselves competent (as in electing their functionaries, executive and legislative, and deciding by a jury of themselves in all judiciary cases in which any fact is involved), or they may act by representatives freely and equally chosen; that it is their right and duty to be at all times armed; that they are entitled to freedom of person, freedom of religion, freedom of property, and freedom of the press. In the structure of our legislatures we think experience has proved the benefit of subjecting questions to two separate bodies of deliberants; but in constituting these, natural right has been mistaken, some making one of these bodies and some both, the representatives of property instead of persons; whereas the double deliberation might be as well obtained without any violation of true principle, either by requiring a greater age in one of the bodies or by electing a proper number of representatives of persons, dividing them by lots into two chambers and renewing the division at frequent intervals in order to break up all cabals.[a]

To John Cartwright, Monticello, June 5, 1824.

a Cf. p. 103.

I agree with you that there is a natural aristocracy among men. The grounds of this are virtue and talents. Formerly, bodily powers gave place among the *aristoi*. But since the invention of gunpowder has armed the weak as well as the strong with missile death, bodily strength like beauty, good humor, politeness, and other accomplishments has become but an auxiliary ground of distinction. There is also an artificial aristocracy, founded on wealth and birth, without either virtue or talents; for with these it would belong to the first class. The natural aristocracy I consider as the most precious gift of nature for the instruction, the trusts, and government of society. And, indeed, it would have been inconsistent in creation to have formed man for the social state and not to have provided virtue and wisdom enough to manage the concerns of the society. May we not even say that that form of government is the best which provides the most effectually for a pure selection of these natural *aristoi* into the offices of government? The artificial aristocracy is a mischievous ingredient in government, and provision should be made to prevent its ascendency. On the question what is the best provision, you and I differ, but we differ as rational friends, using the free exercise of our own reason and mutually indulging its errors. You think it best to put the pseudo-*aristoi* into a separate chamber of legislation, where they may be hindered from doing mischief by their co-ordinate branches and where, also, they may be a protection to wealth against the agrarian and plundering enterprises of the majority of the people. I think that to give them power in order to prevent them from doing mischief is arming them for it and increasing instead of remedying the evil.

To John Adams, Monticello, October 28, 1813.

But of the views of this law [for the diffusion of knowledge] none is more important, none more legitimate than that of rendering the people the safe, as they are the ultimate, guardians of their own liberty. . . . History, by apprising them of the past, will enable them to judge of the future; it will avail them of the experience of other times and other nations; it will qualify them as judges of the actions and designs of men; it will enable them to know ambition under every disguise it may assume; and, knowing it, to defeat its views. In every government on earth is some trace of human weakness, some germ of corruption and degeneracy, which cunning will discover and wickedness insensibly open, cultivate, and improve. Every government degenerates when trusted to the rulers of the people alone. The people themselves therefore are its only safe depositories. And to render even them safe, their minds must be improved to a certain degree. This indeed is not all that is necessary, though it be essentially necessary. An amendment of our constitution must here come in aid of the public education. The influence over government must be shared among all the people. If every individual which composes their mass participates of the ultimate authority, the government will be safe, because the corrupting of the whole mass will exceed any private resources of wealth, and public ones cannot be provided but by levies on the people. In this case every man would have to pay his own price.

Notes on Virginia, Query XIV.

In your present situation [after defeat of Bonaparte at Waterloo] you will effect a constitution in which the will of the nation shall have an organized control over the actions of its government and its citizens a regular protection against its oppressions.

To Lafayette, Monticello, May 17, 1816.

No government can continue good but under the control of the people.

To John Adams, Monticello, December 10, 1819.

It is a misnomer to call a government republican in which a branch of the supreme power is independent of the nation.

To James Pleasants, Monticello, December 26, 1821.

IV. ON PUBLIC EDUCATION AND A FREE PRESS

"Diffusion of knowledge" among all the people was advocated by Jefferson throughout his life as being vital to free government and national progress. Hence he regarded a comprehensive system of public education and a free press as essential features of a democratic polity.

I know of no safe depository of the ultimate powers of the society but the people themselves, and if we think them not enlightened enough to exercise their control with a wholesome discretion, the remedy is not to take it from them but to inform their discretion by education.

To William C. Jarvis, Monticello, September 28, 1820.

It is an axiom in my mind that our liberty can never be safe but in the hands of the people themselves, and that, too, of the people with a certain degree of instruction. This it is the business of the state to effect and on a general plan.

To George Washington, Paris, January 4, 1786.

If a nation expects to be ignorant and free in a state of civilization, it expects what never was and never will be. The functionaries of every government have propensities to command at will the liberty and property of their constituents. There is no safe deposit for these but with the people themselves, nor can they be safe with them without information. Where the press is free and every man able to read, all is safe.

To Charles Yancey, Monticello, January 6, 1816.

A system of general instruction which shall reach every description of our citizens, from the richest to the poorest, as it was the earliest, so will it be the latest, of all the public concerns in which I shall permit myself to take an interest.

To Joseph C. Cabell, Monticello, January 14, 1818.

The tumults in America [Shays's Rebellion] I expected would have produced in Europe an unfavorable opinion of our political state.[2] But it has not. On the contrary, the small effect of these tumults seems to have given more confidence in the firmness of our governments. The interposition of the people themselves on the side of government has had a great effect on the opinion here. I am persuaded myself that the good sense of the people will always be found to be the best army. They may be led astray for a moment but will soon correct themselves. The people are the only censors of their governors, and even their errors will tend to keep these to the true principles of their institution. To punish these errors too severely would be to suppress the only safeguard of the public liberty. The way to prevent these irregular interpositions of the people is to give them full information of their affairs through the channel of the public papers, and to contrive that those papers should penetrate the whole mass of the people. The basis of our governments being the opinion of the people, the very first object should be to keep that right; and were it left to me to decide whether we should have a government without newspapers or newspapers without a government, I should not hesitate a moment to prefer the latter. But I should mean that every man should receive those papers and be capable of reading them.

To Edward Carrington, Paris, January 16, 1787.

To your request of my opinion of the manner in which a newspaper should be conducted so as to be most useful, I should answer, "by restraining it to true facts and sound principles only." Yet I fear such a paper would find few subscribers. It is a melancholy truth that a suppression of the press could not more completely deprive the nation of its benefits than is done by its abandoned prostitution to falsehood. Nothing can now be believed which is seen in a newspaper. Truth itself becomes suspicious by being put into that polluted vehicle. The real extent of this state of misinformation is known only to those who are in situations to confront facts within their knowledge with the lies of the day. I really look with commiseration over the great body of my fellow citizens who, reading newspapers, live and die in the belief that they have known something of what has been passing in the world in their time; whereas the accounts they have read in newspapers are just as true a history of any other period of the world as of the present except that the real names of the day are affixed to their fables. General facts may indeed be collected from them—such as that Europe is now at war, that Bonaparte has been a successful warrior, that he has subjected a great portion of Europe to his will, etc., etc., but no details can be relied on. I will add that the man who never looks into a newspaper is better informed than he who reads them, inasmuch as he who knows nothing is nearer to truth than he whose mind is filled with falsehoods and errors. He who reads nothing will still learn the great facts, and the details are all false.

Perhaps an editor might begin a reformation in some such way as this: divide his paper into four chapters, heading the first, Truths, 2nd, Probabilities, 3rd, Possibilities, 4th, Lies. The first chapter would be very short, as it would contain little more than authentic papers and information from such sources as the editor would be willing to risk his own reputation for their truth. The second would contain what, from a mature consideration of all circumstances, his judgment should conclude to be probably true. This, however, should rather contain too little than too much. The third and fourth should be professedly for those readers who would rather have lies for their money than the blank paper they would occupy.

To John Norvell, Washington, June 11, 1807.

V. THE JEFFERSONIAN SYSTEM: A GRADATION OF REPUBLICS

"A gradation of authorities" is a vital feature in the structure of good government. Participation by every citizen in the conduct of public affairs is thereby assured. It is by judicious division of labor, "placing under everyone what his own eye can superintend," that government is best administered and the people protected against mismanagement. This doctrine is perhaps the most basic feature in Jefferson's political thinking, and might even be called "the Jeffersonian system."

I . . . am much comforted by the appearance of a change of opinion in your State; for though we may obtain—and I believe shall obtain—a majority in the Legislature of the United States attached to the preservation of the federal Constitution according to its obvious principles and those on which it was known to be received; attached equally to the preservation to the States of those rights unquestionably remaining with them; friends to the freedom of religion, freedom of the press, trial by jury, and to economical government; opposed to standing armies, paper systems, war, and all connection, other than commerce, with any foreign nation—in short, a majority firm in all those principles which we have espoused and the Federalists have opposed uniformly; still, should the whole body of New England continue in opposition to these principles of government, either knowingly or through delusion, our government will be a very uneasy one. It can never be harmonious and solid while so respectable a portion of its citizens support principles which go directly to a change of the federal Constitution, to sink the State governments, consolidate them into one, and to monarchize that. Our country is too large to have all its affairs directed by a single government. Public servants at such a distance and from under the eye of their constituents must, from the circumstance of distance, be unable to administer and overlook all the details necessary for the good government of the citizens, and the same circumstance, by rendering detection impossible to their constituents, will invite the public agents to corruption, plunder, and waste. And I do verily believe that if the principle were to prevail of a common law being in force in the United States (which principle possesses the General Government at once of all the powers of the State governments and reduces us to a single consolidated government), it would become the most corrupt government on the earth. You have seen the practices by which the public servants have been able to cover their conduct or, where that could not be done, delusions by which they have varnished it for the eye of their constituents. What an augmentation of the field for jobbing, speculating, plundering, office-building, and office-hunting would be produced by an assumption of all the State powers into the hands of the General Government! The true theory of our Constitution is surely the wisest and best, that the States are independent as to everything within themselves and united as to everything respecting foreign nations. Let the General Government be reduced to foreign concerns only, and let our affairs be disentangled from those of all other nations, except as to commerce which the merchants will manage the better the more they are left free to manage for themselves, and our General Government may be reduced to a very simple organization and a very inexpensive one, a few plain duties to be performed by a few servants.

To Gideon Granger, Monticello, August 13, 1800.

I meddle little or not at all with public affairs. There are two subjects, indeed, which I shall claim a right to further as long as I breathe: the public education and the subdivision of counties into wards. I consider the continuance of republican government as absolutely hanging on these two hooks.

To Joseph C. Cabell, Monticello, January 31, 1814.

The article, however, nearest my heart is the division of counties into wards. These will be pure and elementary republics, the sum of all which taken together composes the State, and will make of the whole a true democracy as to the business of the wards, which is that of nearest and daily concern. The affairs of the larger sections: of counties, of States, and of the Union, not admitting personal transaction by the people, will be delegated to agents elected by themselves, and representation will thus be substituted where personal action becomes impracticable. Yet, even over these representative organs, should they become corrupt and perverted, the division into wards, constituting the people in their wards a regularly organized power, enables them by that organization to crush, regularly and peaceably, the usurpations of their unfaithful agents, and rescues them from the dreadful necessity of doing it insurrectionally. In this way we shall be as republican as a large society can be and secure the continuance of purity in our government by the salutary, peaceable, and regular control of the people. No other depositories of power have ever yet been found which did not end in converting to their own profit the earnings of those committed to their charge. . . .

. . . I have been told that on the question of equal representation, our fellow citizens in some sections of the State claim peremptorily a right of representation for their slaves. Principle will, in this as in most other cases, open the way for us to correct conclusion. Were our State a pure democracy in which all its inhabitants should meet together to transact all their business, there would yet be excluded from their deliberations: 1. infants, until arrived at years of discretion; 2. women, who, to prevent depravation of morals and ambiguity of issue, could not mix promiscuously in the public meetings of men; 3. slaves, from whom the unfortunate state of things with us takes away the rights of will and of property. Those then who have no will could be permitted to exercise none in the popular assembly, and, of course, could delegate none to an agent in a representative assembly.

To Samuel Kercheval, Monticello, September 5, 1816.

If it is believed that these elementary schools will be better managed by the governor and council, the commissioners of the literary fund, or any other general authority of the government, than by the parents within each ward, it is a belief against all experience. Try the principle one step further and amend the bill so as to commit to the governor and council the management of all our farms, our mills, and merchants' stores. No, my friend, the way to have good and safe government is not to trust it all to one but to divide it among the many, distributing to everyone exactly the functions he is competent to. Let the national government be entrusted with the defense of the nation and its foreign and federal relations; the State governments with the civil rights, laws, police, and administration of what concerns the State generally; the counties with the local concerns of the counties, and each ward direct the interests within itself. It is by dividing and subdividing these republics from the great national one down through all its subordinations until it ends in the administration of every man's farm by himself, by placing under everyone what his own eye may superintend, that all will be done for the best.[b] What has destroyed liberty and the rights of man in every government which has ever existed under the sun? The generalizing and concentrating all cares and powers into one body, no matter whether of the autocrats of Russia or France, or of the aristocrats of a Venetian senate. And I do believe that if the Almighty has not decreed that man shall never be free (and it is a blasphemy to believe it), that the secret will be found to be in the making himself the depository of the powers respecting himself, so far as he is competent to them, and delegating only what is beyond his competence by a synthetical process to higher and higher orders of functionaries, so as to trust fewer and fewer powers in proportion as the trustees become more and more oligarchical. The elementary republics of the wards, the county republics, the State republics, and the republic of the Union would form a gradation of authorities, standing each on the basis of law, holding every one its delegated share of powers, and constituting truly a system of fundamental balances and checks for the government. Where every man is a sharer in the direction of his ward-republic, or of some of the higher ones, and feels that he is a participator in the government of affairs, not merely at an election one day in the year but every day; when there shall not be a man in the State who will not be a member of some one of its councils, great or small, he will let the heart be torn out of his body sooner than his power be wrested from him by a Caesar or a Bonaparte. How powerfully did we feel the energy of this organization in the case of embargo? . . . As Cato, then, concluded every speech with the words, "*Carthago delenda est,*" so do I every opinion with the injunction, "divide the counties into

[b] See also p. 117.

wards." Begin them only for a single purpose; they will soon show for what others they are the best instruments.

To Joseph C. Cabell, Monticello, February 2, 1816.

At the first session of our legislature after the Declaration of Independence we passed a law abolishing entails. And this was followed by one abolishing the privilege of primogeniture and dividing the lands of intestates equally among all their children or other representatives. These laws, drawn by myself, laid the axe to the foot of pseudo-aristocracy. And had another which I prepared been adopted by the legislature, our work would have been complete. It was a bill for the more general diffusion of learning. This proposed to divide every county into wards of five or six miles square, like your townships; to establish in each ward a free school for reading, writing, and common arithmetic; to provide for the annual selection of the best subjects from these schools, who might receive at the public expense a higher degree of education at a district school; and from these district schools to select a certain number of the most promising subjects to be completed t a University, where all the useful sciences should be taught. Worth and genius would thus have been sought out from every condition of life and completely prepared by education for defeating the competition of wealth and birth for public trusts. My proposition had, for a further object, to impart to these wards those portions of self-government for which they are best qualified, by confiding to them the care of their poor, their roads, police, elections, the nomination of jurors, administration of justice in small cases, elementary exercises of militia; in short, to have made them little republics with a warden at the head of each for all those concerns which, being under their eye, they would better manage than the larger republics of the county or State. A general call of ward meetings by their wardens on the same day through the State would at any time produce the genuine sense of the people on any required point and would enable the State to act in mass, as your people have so often done and with so much effect by their town meetings. The law for religious freedom, which made a part of this system, having put down the aristocracy of the clergy and restored to the citizen the freedom of the mind, and those of entails and descents nurturing an equality of condition among them, this on education would have raised the mass of the people to the high ground of moral respectability necessary to their own safety and to orderly government, and would have completed the great object of qualifying them to select the veritable *aristoi* for the trusts of government.

To John Adams, Monticello, October 28, 1813.

My own State . . . is now proposing to call a convention for amendment. Among other improvements, I hope they will adopt the subdivision of our counties into wards. The former may be estimated at an average of twenty-four miles square; the latter should be about six miles square each, and would answer to the hundreds of your Saxon Alfred. In each of these might be: 1st. an elementary school; 2nd. a company of militia with its officers; 3rd. a justice of the peace and constable; 4th. each ward should take care of their own poor; 5th. their own roads; 6th. their own police; 7th. elect within themselves one or more jurors to attend the courts of justice; and, 8th. give in at their Folkhouse their votes for all functionaries reserved to their election. Each ward would thus be a small republic within itself, and every man in the State would thus become an acting member of the common government, transacting in person a great portion of its rights and duties, subordinate indeed, yet important, and entirely within his competence. The wit of man cannot devise a more solid basis for a free, durable, and well administered republic.

To John Cartwright, Monticello, June 5, 1824.

CHAPTER FOUR

THE VALUE OF CONSTITUTIONS

I. WHAT IS A CONSTITUTION?

Only a law emanating directly from the authority of the people themselves, a law binding upon the ordinary organs of government and unchangeable by them, deserved in Jefferson's opinion to be called a constitution. The Virginia Constitution of 1776 he believed did not meet this test. Throughout his life he was anxious that it be replaced by a true fundamental law and one that embodied provisions necessary to give the government of the commonwealth a genuinely democratic character. In his *Notes on Virginia* he discussed at length the defects of the State's constitution, and appended to that book a draft for a constitution which he had prepared in 1783 when there was talk of holding a constitutional convention in Virginia.

1. Defects of the Virginia Constitution

This constitution was formed when we were new and inexperienced in the science of government. It was the first, too, which was formed in the whole United States. No wonder then that time and trial have discovered very capital defects in it.

1. The majority of the men in the State who pay and fight for its support are unrepresented in the legislature, the roll of freeholders entitled to vote not including generally the half of those on the roll of the militia or of the taxgatherers.

2. Among those who share the representation, the shares are very unequal. Thus the county of Warwick, with only one hundred fighting men, has an equal representation with the county of Loudoun, which has one thousand seven hundred and forty-six; so that every man in Warwick has as much influence in the government as seventeen men in Loudoun. . . .

3. The senate is, by its constitution, too homogeneous with

the house of delegates. Being chosen by the same electors, at the same time and out of the same subjects, the choice falls of course on men of the same description. The purpose of establishing different houses of legislation is to introduce the influence of different interests or different principles. Thus in Great Britain it is said their constitution relies on the House of Commons for honesty, and the Lords for wisdom; which would be a rational reliance if honesty were to be bought with money and if wisdom were hereditary. In some of the American States the delegates and senators are so chosen as that the first represent the persons and the second the property of the State. But with us wealth and wisdom have equal chance for admission into both houses. We do not therefore derive from the separation of our legislature into two houses those benefits which a proper complication of principles is capable of producing and those which alone can compensate the evils which may be produced by their dissensions.

4. All the powers of government, legislative, executive, and judiciary, result to the legislative body. The concentrating of these in the same hands is precisely the definition of despotic government. It will be no alleviation that these powers will be exercised by a plurality of hands and not by a single one. One hundred and seventy-three despots would surely be as oppressive as one. Let those who doubt it turn their eyes on the republic of Venice. As little will it avail us that they are chosen by ourselves. An *elective despotism* was not the government we fought for, but one which should not only be founded on free principles but in which the powers of government should be so divided and balanced among several bodies of magistracy as that no one could transcend their legal limits without being effectually checked and restrained by the others. For this reason that convention which passed the ordinance of government laid its foundation on this basis: that the legislative, executive, and judiciary departments should be separate and distinct, so that no person should exercise the powers of more than one of them at the same time. But no barrier was provided between these several powers. The judiciary and executive members were left dependent on the legislative for their subsistence in office and some of them for

their continuance in it. If, therefore, the legislature assumes executive and judiciary powers, no opposition is likely to be made; nor, if made, can it be effectual, because in that case they may put their proceedings into the form of an act of assembly which will render them obligatory on the other branches. . . .

5. That the ordinary legislature may alter the constitution itself. . . . Though this opinion seems founded on the first elements of common sense, yet is the contrary maintained by some persons. (1) Because, say they, the conventions were vested with every power necessary to make effectual opposition to Great Britain. But to complete this argument, they must go on and say further, that effectual opposition could not be made to Great Britain without establishing a form of government perpetual and unalterable by the legislature, which is not true. . . . (2) They urge that if the convention had meant that this instrument should be alterable as their other ordinances were, they would have called it an ordinance: but they have called it a "constitution," which *ex vi termini* [1] means "an act above the power of the ordinary legislature." . . . To get rid of the magic supposed to be in the word "constitution," let us translate it into its definition as given by those who think it above the power of the law; and let us suppose the convention, instead of saying, "We, the ordinary legislature, establish a *constitution*," had said, "We the ordinary legislature, establish an act *above the power of the ordinary legislature*." Does not this expose the absurdity of the attempt? (3) But, say they, the people have acquiesced, and this has given it an authority superior to the laws. It is true that the people did not rebel against it, and was that a time for the people to rise in rebellion? Should a prudent acquiescence, at a critical time, be construed into a confirmation of every illegal thing done during that period? . . . Did the acquiescence of the colonies under the various acts of power exercised by Great Britain in our infant state confirm these acts and so far invest them with the authority of the people as to render them unalterable, and our present resistance wrong? On every unauthoritative exercise of power by the legislature must the people rise in rebellion, or their silence be construed into a surrender of that power to them? . . .

6. That the assembly exercises a power of determining the quorum of their own body which may legislate for us. After the establishment of the new form they adhered to the *lex majoris partis,* founded in common law as well as common right. It is the natural law of every assembly of men whose numbers are not fixed by any other law. They continued for some time to require the presence of a majority of their whole number to pass an act. But the British parliament fixes its own quorum; our former assemblies fixed their own quorum, and one precedent in favor of power is stronger than a hundred against it. The house of delegates therefore have lately voted that, during the present dangerous invasion, forty members shall be a house to proceed to business. They have been moved to this by the fear of not being able to collect a house. But this danger could not authorize them to call that a house which was none, and if they may fix it at one number, they may at another till it loses its fundamental character of being a representative body. . . .

In enumerating the defects of the Constitution, it would be wrong to count among them what is only the error of particular persons. In December, 1776, our circumstances being much distressed, it was proposed in the house of delegates to create a Dictator, invested with every power legislative, executive, and judiciary, civil and military, of life and of death, over our persons and over our properties; and in June, 1781, again under calamity, the same proposition was repeated and wanted a few votes only of being passed.[a] One who entered into this contest from a pure love of liberty and a sense of injured rights, who determined to make every sacrifice and to meet every danger for the re-establishment of those rights on a firm basis, who did not mean to expend his blood and substance for the wretched purpose of changing this master for that, but to place the powers of governing him in a plurality of hands of his own choice so that the corrupt will of no one man might in future oppress him, must stand confounded and dismayed when he is told that a considerable por-

[a] Regarding the proposals of Patrick Henry to establish a dictatorship in Virginia, see Dumas Malone, *Jefferson and His Time,* I, 305, 361.

tion of that plurality had meditated the surrender of them into a single hand, and, in lieu of a limited monarch, to deliver him over to a despotic one! How must we find his efforts and sacrifices abused and baffled, if he may still by a single vote be laid prostrate at the feet of one man! In God's name, from whence have they derived this power? Is it from our ancient laws? None such can be produced. Is it from any principle in our new Constitution, expressed or implied? Every lineament of that, expressed or implied, is in full opposition to it. Its fundamental principle is that the State shall be governed as a commonwealth. . . . Was it from the necessity of the case? Necessities which dissolve a government do not convey its authority to an oligarchy or a monarchy. They throw back into the hands of the people the powers they had delegated and leave them as individuals to shift for themselves. . . . The very thought alone was treason against the people—was treason against mankind in general—as riveting forever the chains which bow down their necks, by giving to their oppressors a proof (which they would have trumpeted through the universe) of the imbecility of republican government in times of pressing danger to shield them from harm. . . . Searching for the foundation of this proposition, I can find none which may pretend a color of right or reason but the defect before developed: that, there being no barrier between the legislative, executive, and judiciary departments, the legislature may seize the whole; that, having seized it and possessing a right to fix their own quorum, they may reduce that quorum to one, whom they may call a chairman, speaker, dictator, or by any other name they please. Our situation is indeed perilous, and I hope my countrymen will be sensible of it and will apply at a proper season the proper remedy, which is a convention to fix the Constitution, to amend its defects, to bind up the several branches of government by certain laws which when they transgress, their acts shall become nullities, to render unnecessary an appeal to the people, or in other words a rebellion on every infraction of their rights, on the peril that their acquiescence shall be construed into an intention to surrender those rights.

Notes on Virginia, Query XIII.

In Virginia, where a great proportion of the legislature consider the constitution but as other acts of legislation, laws have been frequently passed which controlled its effects. I have not heard that in the other States they have ever infringed their constitution, and I suppose they have not done it, as the judges would consider any law as void which was contrary to the constitution. Pennsylvania is divided into two parties very nearly equal, the one desiring to change the constitution, the other opposing a change. In Virginia there is a part of the State which considers the act for organizing their government as a constitution and are content to let it remain; there is another part which considers it only as an ordinary act of the legislature, who, therefore, wish to form a real constitution, correcting some defects which have been observed in the acts now in force.

To Jean Nicolas Démeunier, Paris, January 24, 1786.

Particular instances whereby the General Assembly of Virginia have shown that they considered the ordinance, called their constitution, as every other ordinance or act of the legislature, subject to be altered by the legislature for the time being.

1. The convention which formed that constitution declared themselves to be the House of Delegates during the term for which they were originally elected, and in the autumn of the year met the Senate elected under the new constitution and did legislative business with them. At this time there were malefactors in the public jail, and there was as yet no court established for their trial. They passed a law, appointing certain members by name, who were then members of the Executive Council, to be a court for the trial of these malefactors—though the constitution had said in express words that no person should exercise the powers of more than one of the three departments, legislative, executive, and judiciary, at the same time. This proves that the very men who had made that constitution understood that it would be alterable by the General Assembly. . . .

2. There was a process depending in the ordinary courts of justice between two individuals of the names of Robinson and Fauntleroy, who were relations of different descriptions to one

Robinson, a British subject lately dead. Each party claimed a right to inherit the lands of the decedent according to the laws. Their right should by the constitution have been decided by the judiciary courts, and it was actually depending before them. One of the parties petitioned the Assembly (I think it was in the year 1782), who passed a law deciding the right in his favor. . . . These acts are occasional repeals of that part of the constitution which forbids the same person to exercise *legislative* and *judiciary* powers at the same time.

3. The Assembly is in the habitual exercise during their sessions of directing the Executive what to do. There are few pages of their journals which do not show proof of this, and consequently instances of the *legislative* and *executive* powers exercised by the same persons at the same time. These things prove that it has been the uninterrupted opinion of every Assembly, from that which passed the ordinance called the constitution down to the present day, that their acts may control that ordinance, and, of course, that the State of Virginia has no fixed constitution at all.

To Jean Nicolas Démeunier, Paris, (after January 24, 1786).

These were the settled opinions of all the States—of that of Virginia of which I was writing, as well as of the others. The others had, in consequence, delineated these unceded portions of right and these fences against wrong which they meant to exempt from the powers of their governors, in instruments called declarations of rights and constitutions, and as they did this by conventions which they appointed for the express purpose of reserving these rights and of delegating others to their ordinary legislative, executive, and judiciary bodies, none of the reserved rights can be touched without resorting to the people to appoint another convention for the express purpose of permitting it.

To Noah Webster, Philadelphia, December 4, 1790.

2. Jefferson's Draft of a Constitution for Virginia (1783)[b]

But this, like all other acts of legislation, being subject to change by subsequent legislatures, possessing equal powers with themselves, it has been thought expedient that it should receive those amendments which time and trial have suggested and be rendered permanent by a power superior to that of the ordinary legislature. The general assembly, therefore, of this State recommended it to the good people thereof to choose delegates to meet in general convention with powers to form a constitution of government for them and to declare those fundamentals to which all our laws present and future shall be subordinate, and, in compliance with this recommendation, they have thought proper to make choice of us and to vest us with powers for this purpose.

We, therefore, the delegates chosen by the said good people of this State for the purpose aforesaid and now assembled in general convention do, in execution of the authority with which we are invested, establish the following constitution and fundamentals of government for the said State of Virginia:

The said State shall forever hereafter be governed as a commonwealth.

The powers of government shall be divided into three distinct departments, each of them to be confided to a separate body of magistracy; to wit, those which are legislative to one, those which are judiciary to another, and those which are executive to another. No person, or collection of persons, being of one of these departments, shall exercise any power properly belonging to either of the others, except in the instances hereinafter expressly permitted.

The *Legislature* shall consist of two branches, the one to be called the House of Delegates, the other the Senate, and both together the General Assembly. The concurrence of both of

[b] Cf. Jefferson's earlier draft of a constitution for Virginia in 1776 (reprinted on p. 10).

these, expressed on three several readings, shall be necessary to the passage of a law. . . .

All free male citizens, of full age and sane mind, who for one year before shall have been resident in the county or shall through the whole of that time have possessed therein real property of the value of............................. or shall for the same time have been enrolled in the militia, and no others, shall have a right to vote for delegates for the said county, and for senatorial electors for the district. They shall give their votes personally and *viva voce*. . . .

A majority of either house shall be a quorum and shall be requisite for doing business, but any smaller proportion which from time to time shall be thought expedient by the respective houses shall be sufficient to call for, and to punish, their non-attending members, and to adjourn themselves for any time not exceeding one week. . . .

The General Assembly shall not have power to infringe this constitution; to abridge the civil rights of any person on account of his religious belief; to restrain him from professing and supporting that belief or to compel him to make contributions other than those he shall have personally stipulated for the support of that or any other; to ordain death for any crime but treason or murder or military offenses; to pardon, or give a power of pardoning, persons duly convicted of treason or felony, but instead thereof they may substitute one or two new trials, and no more; to pass laws for punishing actions done before the existence of such laws; to pass any bill of attainder of treason or felony; to prescribe torture in any case whatever; nor to permit the introduction of any more slaves to reside in this State, or the continuance of slavery beyond the generation which shall be living on the thirty-first day of December, One Thousand Eight Hundred—all persons born after that day being hereby declared free. . . .

The *executive* powers shall be exercised by a *Governor*, who shall be chosen by joint ballot of both houses of assembly and, when chosen, shall remain in office five years and be ineligible a second time. During his term he shall hold no other office or

emolument under this State or any other State or power whatsoever. By executive powers we mean no reference to those powers
exercised under our former government by the crown as of its
prerogative, nor that these shall be the standard of what may or
may not be deemed the rightful powers of the governor. We give
him those powers only which are necessary to execute the laws
(and administer the government) and which are not in their
nature either legislative or judiciary. The application of this idea
must be left to reason. We do however expressly deny him the
prerogative powers of erecting courts, offices, boroughs, corporations, fairs, markets, ports, beacons, lighthouses, and sea-marks;
of laying embargoes, of establishing precedence, of retaining
within the State or recalling to it any citizen thereof, and of
making denizens, except so far as he may be authorized from
time to time by the legislature to exercise any of those powers.
The powers of declaring war and concluding peace, of contracting
alliances, of issuing letters of marque and reprisal, of raising and
introducing armed forces, of building armed vessels, forts, or
strongholds, of coining money or regulating its value, of regulating weights and measures, we leave to be exercised under the
authority of the confederation; but, in all cases respecting them
which are out of the said confederation, they shall be exercised
by the governor under the regulation of such laws as the legislature may think it expedient to pass. . . .

The *judiciary* powers shall be exercised by county courts and
such other inferior courts as the legislature shall think proper to
continue or to erect, by three superior courts, to wit: a Court of
Admiralty, a General Court of Common Law, and a High Court
of Chancery, and by one Supreme Court, to be called the Court
of Appeals. . . .

The confederation is made a part of this constitution, subject
to such future alterations as shall be agreed to by the legislature
of this State and by all the other confederating States.

The delegates to Congress shall be five in number, any three
of whom and no fewer may be a representation. They shall be
appointed by joint ballot of both houses of assembly for any
term not exceeding one year, subject to be recalled at any time

within the term by joint vote of both the said houses. They may at the same time be members of the legislative or judiciary departments, but not of the executive.

The benefits of the writ of habeas corpus [2] shall be extended by the legislature to every person within this State, and without fee, and shall be so facilitated that no person may be detained in prison more than ten days after he shall have demanded and been refused such writ by the judge appointed by law; or if none be appointed, then by any judge of a superior court, nor more than ten days after such writ shall have been served on the person detaining him, and no order given, on due examination, for his remandment or discharge.

The military shall be subordinate to the civil power.

Printing presses shall be subject to no other restraint than liableness to legal prosecution for false facts printed and published.

Any two of the three branches of government concurring in opinion, each by the voices of two-thirds of their whole existing number, that a convention is necessary for altering this constitution or correcting breaches of it, they shall be authorized to issue writs to every county for the election of so many delegates as they are authorized to send to the general assembly, which elections shall be held, and writs returned, as the laws shall have provided in the case of elections of delegates to assembly, *mutatis mutandis* [the necessary changes being made], and the said delegates shall meet at the usual place of holding assemblies three months after date of such writs and shall be acknowledged to have equal powers with this present convention. The said writs shall be signed by all the members approving the same.

> Draft of a Fundamental Constitution for the
> Commonwealth of Virginia, 1783.

3. *What State Constitutions Should Contain*

That it is really important to provide a constitution for our State cannot be doubted; as little can it be doubted that the ordinance called by that name has important defects. . . .

I shall hazard my own ideas to you as hastily as my business obliges me. I wish to preserve the line drawn by the federal constitution between the general and particular governments as it stands at present and to take every prudent means of preventing either from stepping over it. Though the experiment has not yet had a long enough course to show us from which quarter encroachments are most to be feared, yet it is easy to foresee from the nature of things that the encroachments of the State governments will tend to an excess of liberty which will correct itself (as in the late instance), while those of the general government will tend to monarchy which will fortify itself from day to day, instead of working its own cure as all experience shows. I would rather be exposed to the inconveniences attending too much liberty than those attending too small a degree of it. Then it is important to strengthen the State governments, and as this cannot be done by any change in the federal constitution (for the preservation of that is all we need contend for), it must be done by the States themselves, erecting such barriers at the constitutional line as cannot be surmounted either by themselves or by the general government. The only barrier in their power is a wise government. A weak one will lose ground in every contest. To obtain a wise and an able government, I consider the following changes as important: render the legislature a desirable station by lessening the number of representatives (say to 100) and lengthening somewhat their term and proportion them equally among the electors; adopt also a better mode of appointing senators; render the Executive a more desirable post to men of abilities by making it more independent of the legislature—to wit, let him be chosen by other electors for a longer time and ineligible forever after. Responsibility is a tremendous engine in a free government. Let him feel the whole weight of it then by taking away the shelter of his executive council. Experience both ways has already established the superiority of this measure. Render the judiciary respectable by every possible means, to wit, firm tenure in office, competent salaries, and reduction of their numbers. Men of high learning and abilities are few in every country, and by taking in those who are not so the able part of the body have their hands tied by the unable.

To Archibald Stuart, Philadelphia, December 23, 1791.

The question you propose on equal representation has become a party one in which I wish to take no public share. Yet, if it be asked for your own satisfaction only and not to be quoted before the public, I have no motive to withhold it, and the less from you, as it coincides with your own. At the birth of our republic I committed that opinion to the world in the draft of a constitution annexed to the *Notes on Virginia*, in which a provision was inserted for a representation permanently equal. The infancy of the subject at that moment and our inexperience of self-government occasioned gross departures in that draft from genuine republican canons. In truth, the abuses of monarchy had so much filled all the space of political contemplation that we imagined everything republican which was not monarchy. We had not yet penetrated to the mother principle that "governments are republican only in proportion as they embody the will of their people and execute it." Hence our first constitutions had really no leading principles in them. But experience and reflection have but more and more confirmed me in the particular importance of the equal representation then proposed. . . .

But inequality of representation in both Houses of our legislature is not the only republican heresy in this first essay of our revolutionary patriots at forming a constitution. For let it be agreed that a government is republican in proportion as every member composing it has his equal voice in the direction of its concerns (not indeed in person, which would be impracticable beyond the limits of a city or small township, but by representatives chosen by himself and responsible to him at short periods), and let us bring to the test of this canon every branch of our constitution.

In the legislature, the House of Representatives is chosen by less than half the people and not at all in proportion to those who do choose. The Senate are still more disproportionate and for long terms of irresponsibility. In the Executive, the Governor is entirely independent of the choice of the people and of their control; his Council equally so and at best but a fifth wheel to a wagon. In the Judiciary, the judges of the highest courts are dependent on none but themselves. In England, where judges were named and removable at the will of a hereditary executive, from which branch most misrule was feared and has flowed, it was a great point gained by fixing them for life, to make them independent of that executive. But in a government founded on the public will, this principle operates in an opposite direction and against that will. There, too, they were still removable on a concurrence of the executive and legislative branches. But we have made them independent of the nation itself. They are irremovable but by their own body for any depravities of conduct, and even by their own body for the imbecilities of dotage. The justices of the inferior courts are self-chosen, are for life, and perpetuate their own body in succession forever, so that a faction once possessing themselves of the bench of a county can never be broken up, but hold their county in chains forever indissoluble. Yet these justices are the real executive as well as judiciary in all our minor and most ordinary concerns. They tax us at will; fill the office of sheriff—the most important of all the executive officers of the county; name nearly all our military leaders, which leaders, once named, are removable but by themselves. The juries, our judges of all fact and of law when they choose it, are not selected by the people nor amenable to them. They are chosen by an officer named by the court and executive. Chosen, did I say? Picked up by the sheriff from the loungings of the courtyard after everything respectable has retired from it. Where then is our republicanism to be found? Not in our Constitution certainly, but merely in the spirit of our people. That would oblige even a despot to govern us republicanly. Owing to this spirit and to nothing in the form of our Constitution, all things have gone well. But this fact, so triumphantly misquoted by the enemies of reformation, is not the fruit of our Constitution but has prevailed in spite of it. Our functionaries have done well, because generally honest men. If any were not so, they feared to show it.

But it will be said it is easier to find faults than to amend them. I do not think their amendment so difficult as is pretended. Only lay down true principles and adhere to them inflexibly. Do not be frightened into their surrender by the alarms of the timid or the croakings of wealth against the ascendency of the people. If experience be called for, appeal to that of our fifteen or twenty governments for forty years and show me where the people have done half the mischief in these forty years that a single despot would have done in a single year; or show half the riots and rebellions, the crimes and the punishments which have taken place in any single nation under kingly government during the same period. The true foundation of republican government is the equal right of every citizen in his person and property, and in their management. Try by this, as a tally, every provision of our Constitution and see if it hangs directly on the will of the people. Reduce your legislature to a convenient number for full but orderly discussion. Let every man who fights or pays exercise his just and equal right in their election. Submit them to approbation or rejection at short intervals. Let the executive be chosen in the same way and for the same term by those whose agent he is to be, and leave no screen of a council behind which to skulk from responsibility. It has been thought that the people are not competent electors of judges *learned in the law.* But I do not know that this is true, and if doubtful, we should follow principle. In this as in many other elections, they would be guided by reputation which would not err oftener, perhaps, than the present mode of appointment. In one State of the Union at least it has long been tried and with the most satisfactory success. The judges of Connecticut have been chosen by the people every six months, for nearly two centuries, and I believe there has hardly ever been an instance of change, so powerful is the curb of incessant responsibility. If prejudice, however, derived from a monarchical institution is still to prevail against the vital elective principle of our own, and if the existing example among ourselves of periodical election of judges by the people be still mistrusted, let us at least not adopt the evil and reject the good of the English precedent; let us retain amovability on the concurrence of the executive and legislative branches, and nomination by the executive alone. Nomination to office is an executive function. To give it to the legislature, as we do, is a violation of the principle of the separation of powers. It swerves the members from correctness by temptations to intrigue for office themselves and to a corrupt barter of votes, and destroys responsibility by dividing it among a multitude. By leaving nomination in its proper place, among executive functions, the principle of the distribution of power is preserved and responsibility weighs with its heaviest force on a single head.

The organization of our county administrations may be thought more difficult. But follow principle and the knot unties itself. Divide the counties into wards of such size as that every citizen can attend when called on and act in person. Ascribe to them the government of their wards in all things relating to themselves exclusively. A justice chosen by themselves in each, a constable, a military company, a patrol, a school, the care of their own poor, their own portion of the public roads, the choice of one or more jurors to serve in some court, and the delivery, within their own wards, of their own votes for all elective officers of higher sphere will relieve the county administration of nearly all its business, will have it better done, and, by making every citizen an acting member of the government and in the offices nearest and most interesting to him, will attach him by his strongest feelings to the independence of his country and its republican constitution. The justices thus chosen by every ward would constitute the county court, would do its judiciary business, direct roads and bridges, levy county and poor rates, and administer all the matters of common interest to the whole country. These wards, called townships in New England, are the vital principle of their governments and have proved themselves the wisest invention ever devised by the wit of man for the perfect exercise of self-government and for its preservation. We should thus marshal our government into: (1) the general federal republic, for all concerns foreign and federal; (2) that of the State, for what relates to our own citizens exclusively; (3) the county republics, for the duties and concerns of the county; and (4) the ward republics, for the small and yet numerous and interesting concerns of the neighborhood; and in government, as well as in every other business of life, it is by division and subdivision of duties alone that all matters, great and small, can be managed to perfection. And the whole is cemented by giving to every citizen, personally, a part in the administration of the public affairs.

The sum of these amendments is: (1) general suffrage, (2) equal representation in the legislature, (3) an executive chosen by the people, (4) judges elective or amovable, (5) justices, jurors, and sheriffs elective, (6) ward divisions, and (7) periodical amendments of the constitution.

I have thrown out these as loose heads of amendment for consideration and correction, and their object is to secure self-government by the republicanism of our Constitution as well as by the spirit of the people, and to nourish and perpetuate that spirit. I am not among those who fear the people. They, and not the rich, are our dependence for continued freedom. And to preserve their independence we must not let our rulers load us with perpetual debt.

To Samuel Kercheval, Monticello, July 12, 1816.

I received in due time your favor of the 12th, requesting my opinion on the proposition to call a convention for amending the constitution of the State. . . . One [improvement] which has been adopted in every subsequent constitution was to lay its foundation in the authority of the nation. To our convention no special authority had been delegated by the people to form a permanent constitution over which their successors in legislation should have no powers of alteration. They had been elected for the ordinary purposes of legislation only, and at a time when the establishment of a new government had not been proposed or contemplated. Although, therefore, they gave to this act the title of a constitution, yet it could be no more than an act of legislation subject, as their other acts were, to alteration by their successors. . . .

Another defect which has been corrected by most of the States is that the basis of our constitution is in opposition to the principle of equal political rights, refusing to all but freeholders any participation in the natural right of self-government. . . .

And even among our citizens who participate in the representative privilege, the equality of political rights is entirely prostrated by our constitution. Upon which principle of right or reason can anyone justify the giving to every citizen of Warwick as much weight in the government as to twenty-two equal citizens in Loudoun, and similar inequalities among the other counties? If these fundamental principles are of no importance in actual government, then no principles are important, and it is as well to rely on the dispositions of an administration, good or evil, as on the provisions of a constitution.

To John H. Pleasants, Monticello, April 19, 1824.

But, whatever be the constitution, great care must be taken to provide a mode of amendment when experience or change of circumstances shall have manifested that any part of it is unadapted to the good of the nation. In some of our States it requires a new authority from the whole people, acting by their representatives chosen for this express purpose and assembled in convention. This is found too difficult for remedying the imperfections which experience develops from time to time in an organization of the first impression. A greater facility of amendment is certainly requisite to maintain it in a course of action accommodated to the times and changes through which we are ever passing. In England the constitution may be altered by a single act of the legislature, which amounts to the having no constitution at all. In some of our States an act passed by two different legislatures, chosen by the people at different and successive elections, is sufficient to make a change in the constitution. As this mode may be rendered more or less easy by requiring the approbation of fewer or more successive legislatures, according to the degree of difficulty thought sufficient and yet safe, it is evidently the best principle which can be adopted for constitutional amendments.

I have stated that the constitutions of our several States vary more or less in some particulars. But there are certain principles in which all agree and which all cherish as vitally essential to the protection of the life, liberty, property, and safety of the citizen:

1. Freedom of religion, restricted only from *acts* of trespass on that of others;

2. Freedom of person, securing every one from imprisonment or other bodily restraint but by the laws of the land—this is effected by the well-known law of habeas corpus;

3. Trial by jury, the best of all safeguards for the person, the property, and the fame of every individual;

4. The exclusive right of legislation and taxation in the representatives of the people;

5. Freedom of the press, subject only to liability for personal injuries. This formidable censor of the public functionaries, by arraigning them at the tribunal of public opinion, produces reform peaceably, which must otherwise be done by revolution. It is also the best instrument for enlightening the mind of man and improving him as a rational, moral, and social being.

To Adamantios Coray, Monticello, October 31, 1823.

4. *Jefferson on the French Constitution*

Jefferson applied the same standard to efforts made to reform the government of France. Recognizing that "the excellence of every government is its adaptation to the state of those who are governed by it," he urged that progress be made cautiously and gradually. He even drafted a proposed Charter of Rights which he felt was suitable to conditions in France at the time, and would embody "the essentials constituting free government." [3]

But they hope they may be got to concur in a declaration of rights, at least, so that the nation may be acknowledged to have some fundamental rights not alterable by their ordinary legislature, and that this may form a ground work for future improvements.

To John Jay, Paris, May 23, 1788.

The internal affairs here do not yet clear up. Most of the late innovations have been much for the better. Two only must be fundamentally condemned: the abolishing, in so great a degree, of the parliaments and the substitution of so ill-composed a body as the *cour plenière*. If the king has power to do this, the government of this country is a pure despotism. I think it a pure despotism in theory but moderated in practice by the respect which the public opinion commands. But the nation repeats, after Montesquieu, that the different bodies of magistracy, of priests and nobles, are barriers between the king and the people. It would be easy to prove that these barriers can only appeal to public opinion, and that neither these bodies nor the people can oppose any legal check to the will of the monarch. But they are manifestly advancing fast to a constitution.

To John B. Cutting, Paris, July 24, 1788.

We are now to come to prophecy; for you will ask, to what will all this lead? I answer, if the States General do not stumble at the threshold . . . they will in their first session easily obtain: 1. Their future periodical convocation of the States. 2. Their exclusive right to raise and appropriate money, which includes that of establishing a civil list. 3. A participation in legislation. Probably at first it will only be a transfer to them of the portion of it now exercised by parliament, that is to say, a right to propose amendments and a negative, but it must infallibly end in a right of origination. 4. Perhaps they may make a declaration of rights. It will be attempted at least. Two other objects will be attempted, viz., a habeas corpus law and a free press. . . . They flatter themselves they shall form a better constitution than the English. I think it will be better in some points, worse in others. It will be better in the article of representation, which will be more equal. It will be worse, as their situation obliges them to keep up the dangerous machine of a standing army. I doubt, too, whether they will obtain the trial by jury, because they are not sensible of its value.

To Richard Price, Paris, January 8, 1789.

With respect to their government we are under no call to express opinions which might please or offend any party, and therefore it will be best to avoid them on all occasions, public or private. Could any circumstances require unavoidably such expressions, they would naturally be in conformity with the sentiments of the great mass of our countrymen who, having first in modern times taken the ground of government founded on the will of the people, cannot but be delighted on seeing so distinguished and so esteemed a nation [France] arrive on the same ground and plant their standard by our side.

To Gouverneur Morris, Philadelphia, January 23, 1792.

A Charter of Rights, solemnly established by the King and Nation

1. The States General shall assemble, uncalled, on the first day of November, annually, and shall remain together so long as they shall see cause. They shall regulate their own elections and proceedings, and until they shall ordain otherwise, their elections shall be in the forms observed in the present year and shall be triennial.

2. The States General alone shall levy money on the nation and shall appropriate it.

3. Laws shall be made by the States General only, with the consent of the King.

4. No person shall be restrained of his liberty but by regular process from a court of justice, authorized by a general law. (Except that a Noble may be imprisoned by order of a court of justice, on the prayer of twelve of his nearest relations.) On complaint of an unlawful imprisonment, to any judge whatever, he shall have the prisoner immediately brought before him and shall discharge him if his imprisonment be unlawful. The officer in whose custody the prisoner is shall obey the orders of the judge; and both judge and officer shall be responsible, civilly and criminally, for a failure of duty herein.

5. The military shall be subordinate to the civil authority.

6. Printers shall be liable to legal prosecution for printing

and publishing false facts, injurious to the party prosecuting, but they shall be under no other restraint.

7. All pecuniary privileges and exemptions, enjoyed by any description of persons, are abolished.

8. All debts already contracted by the King are hereby made the debts of the nation, and the faith thereof is pledged for their payment in due time.

9. Eighty millions of livres are now granted to the King, to be raised by loan and reimbursed by the nation, and the taxes heretofore paid shall continue to be paid to the end of the present year and no longer.

10. The States General shall now separate and meet again on the 1st day of November next.

Done, on behalf of the whole nation, by the King and their representatives in the States General, at Versailles, this ——— day of June, 1789.

Signed by the King, and by every member individually, and in his presence.

Jefferson's Draft of a Constitution for France, June 3, 1789.

II. CONSTITUTION MUST KEEP PACE WITH PROGRESS AND CANNOT BE PERPETUAL

1. Amendments

That the people must modify their fundamental law from time to time so that it will keep abreast of current conditions was a basic tenet of Jefferson's political philosophy. The strongest statement of this idea occurs in the letter to Samuel Kercheval of which the pertinent passages are given below.

Some men look at constitutions with sanctimonious reverence and deem them like the ark of the covenant, too sacred to be touched. They ascribe to the men of the preceding age a wisdom more than human and suppose what they did to be beyond amendment. I knew that age well; I belonged to it and labored with it. It deserved well of its country. It was very like the present but without the experience of the present, and forty years of experience in government is worth a century of book reading, and this they would say themselves were they to rise from the dead. I am certainly not an advocate for frequent and untried changes in laws and constitutions. I think moderate imperfections had better be borne with, because, when once known, we accommodate ourselves to them and find practical means of correcting their ill effects. But I know also that laws and institutions must go hand in hand with the progress of the human mind. As that becomes more developed, more enlightened, as new discoveries are made, new truths disclosed, and manners and opinions change with the change of circumstances, institutions must advance also and keep pace with the times. We might as well require a man to wear still the coat which fitted him when a boy as civilized society to remain ever under the regimen of their barbarous ancestors. It is this preposterous idea which has lately deluged Europe in blood. Their monarchs, instead of wisely yielding to the gradual change of circumstances, of favoring progressive accommodation to progressive improvement, have clung to old abuses, entrenched themselves behind steady habits, and obliged their subjects to seek through blood and violence rash and ruinous innovations, which, had they been referred to the peaceful deliberations and collected wisdom of the nation, would have been put into acceptable and salutary forms. Let us follow no such examples, nor weakly believe that one generation is not as capable as another of taking care of itself and of ordering its own affairs. . . . Each generation is as independent of the one preceding as that was of all which had gone before. It has then, like them, a right to choose for itself the form of government it believes most promotive of its own happiness, consequently, to accommodate to the circumstances in which it finds itself that received from its predecessors; and it is for the peace and good of mankind that a solemn opportunity of doing this every nineteen or twenty years should be provided by the constitution, so that it may be handed on, with periodical repairs, from generation to generation to the end of time, if anything human can so long endure. . . .

These, Sir, are my opinions of the governments we see among men and of the principles by which alone we may prevent our own from falling into the same dreadful track. I have given them at greater length than your letter called for. But I cannot say things by halves, and I confide them to your honor so to use them as to preserve me from the gridiron of the public papers.

To Samuel Kercheval, Monticello, July 12, 1816.

The real friends of the constitution in its federal form, if they wish it to be immortal, should be attentive by amendments to make it keep pace with the advance of the age in science and experience. Instead of this, the European governments have resisted reformation, until the people, seeing no other resource, undertake it themselves by force, their only weapon, and work it out through blood, desolation, and long-continued anarchy.

To Robert J. Garnett, Monticello, February 14, 1824.

2. The Right to Amend

That "the earth belongs to the living," and hence that no law or constitution can be perpetual, was a favorite theme of Jefferson's.[c] By statistical computation he sought to determine the average lifetime of a generation, and urged that no obligations should be incurred extending beyond that period or seeking to bind future generations.

You will perceive by these details that we have not yet so far perfected our constitutions as to venture to make them unchangeable. But still, in their present state, we consider them not otherwise changeable than by the authority of the people, on a special

[c] This favorite notion of Jefferson's was developed in numerous letters: to James Madison, Paris, September 6, 1789, *Works*, VI, 3; to John W. Eppes, Monticello, June 24, 1813, *Works*, XI, 298; to John W. Eppes, Poplar Forest, September 11, 1813, *Writings*, XIII, 360; to William Plumer, Monticello, July 21, 1816, *Writings*, XV, 46–47; to Thomas Earle, Monticello, September 24, 1823, *Writings*, XV, 470.

election of representatives for that purpose expressly; they are until then the *lex legum*.

But can they be made unchangeable? Can one generation bind another, and all others, in succession forever? I think not. The Creator has made the earth for the living, not the dead. Rights and powers can only belong to persons, not to things, not to mere matter unendowed with will. The dead are not even things. The particles of matter which composed their bodies make part now of the bodies of other animals, vegetables, or minerals of a thousand forms. To what then are attached the rights and powers they held while in the form of men? A generation may bind itself as long as its majority continues in life; when that has disappeared, another majority is in place, holds all the rights and powers their predecessors once held, and may change their laws and institutions to suit themselves. Nothing then is unchangeable but the inherent and unalienable rights of man.

To John Cartwright, Monticello, June 5, 1824.

III. VALUE OF A BILL OF RIGHTS

In the arguments in favor of a declaration of rights, you omit one which has great weight with me; the legal check which it puts into the hands of the judiciary. This is a body which, if rendered independent and kept strictly to their own department, merits great confidence for their learning and integrity. In fact, what degree of confidence would be too much for a body composed of such men as Wythe, Blair and Pendleton? On characters like these, the *civium ardor prava jubentium* would make no impression. I am happy to find that, on the whole, you are a friend to this amendment. The declaration of rights is, like all other human blessings, alloyed with some inconveniences and not accomplishing fully its object. But the good in this instance vastly overweighs the evil. I cannot refrain from making short answers to the objections which your letter states to have been raised. 1. *That the rights in question are reserved by the manner in which the federal powers are granted.* Answer: A constitutive act may, certainly, be so formed as to need no declaration of rights. The act itself has the force of a declaration, as far as it goes, and, if it goes to all material points, nothing more is wanting. In the draught of a constitution which I had once a thought of proposing in Virginia and printed afterwards, I endeavored to reach all the great objects of public liberty and did not mean to add a declaration of rights. Probably the object was imperfectly executed, but the deficiencies would have been supplied by others in the course of discussion. But in a constitutive act which leaves some precious articles unnoticed and raises implications against others, a declaration of rights becomes necessary by way of supplement. This is the case of our new Federal Constitution. This instrument forms us into one state as to certain objects and gives us a legislative and executive body for these objects. It should, therefore, guard us against their abuses of power within the field submitted to them. 2. *A positive declaration of some essential rights could not be obtained in the requisite latitude.* Answer: Half a loaf is better than no bread. If we cannot secure all our rights, let us secure what we can. 3. *The limited powers of the federal government and jealousy of the subordinate governments afford a security which exists in no other instance.* Answer: The first member of this seems resolvable into the first objection before stated. The jealousy of the subordinate governments is a precious reliance. But observe that those governments are only agents. They must have principles furnished them whereon to found their opposition. The declaration of rights will be the text whereby they will try all the acts of the federal government. In this view, it is necessary to the federal government also, as by the same text they may try the opposition of the subordinate governments. 4. *Experience proves the inefficacy of a bill of rights.* True. But though it is not absolutely efficacious under all circumstances, it is of great potency always and rarely inefficacious. A brace the more will often keep up the building which would have fallen with that brace the less. There is a remarkable difference between the characters of the inconveniences which attend a declaration of rights and those which attend the want of it. The inconveniences of the declaration are that it may cramp government in its useful exertions. But the evil of this is short-lived, moderate, and reparable. The inconveniences of the want of a declaration are permanent, afflicting, and irreparable. They are in constant progression from bad to worse. The executive, in our governments, is not the sole, it is scarcely the principal object of my jealousy. The tyranny of the legislatures is the most formidable dread at present and will be for many years. That of the executive will come in its turn, but it will be at a remote period. I know there are some among us who would now establish a monarchy. But they are inconsiderable in number and weight of character. The rising race are all republicans. We were educated in royalism; no wonder if some of us retain that idolatry still. Our young people are educated in republicanism; an apostasy from that to royalism is unprecedented and impossible. I am much pleased with the prospect that a declaration of rights will be added, and I hope it will be done in that way which will not endanger the whole frame of government or any essential part of it.

To James Madison, Paris, March 15, 1789.

It is still certain that though written constitutions may be violated in moments of passion or delusion, yet they furnish a text to which those who are watchful may again rally and recall the people; they fix, too, for the people the principles of their political creed.

To Joseph Priestley, Washington, June 19, 1802.

CHAPTER FIVE

THE TRUE PRINCIPLES OF THE UNITED STATES CONSTITUTION

I. DEFECTS OF THE ARTICLES OF CONFEDERATION

The weaknesses of the loose Union under the Articles of Confederation were brought home to Jefferson, perhaps more than to any other American statesman, while he was in Europe attempting to negotiate treaties of commerce and to borrow money to pay public debts and expenses. He was in a position to realize the difficulties arising from the lack of adequate federal power to regulate commerce and to raise revenue by taxation. As a member of the old Congress he was aware also of its exasperating procedural shortcomings which impeded effective action.

I am also much pleased with the proposition to the States to invest Congress with the regulation of their trade, reserving its revenue to the States. I think it a happy idea, removing the only objection which could have been justly made to the proposition. The time, too, is the present, before the admission of the western States. I am very differently affected toward the new plan of opening our land office by dividing the lands among the States and selling them at vendue. It separates still more the interests of the States, which ought to be made joint in every possible instance in order to cultivate the idea of our being one nation, and to multiply the instances in which the people shall look up to Congress as their head. And when the States get their portions, they will either fool them away or make a job of it to serve individuals. . . .

I will take the liberty of hazarding to you some thoughts on the policy of entering into treaties with the European nations, and the nature of them. I am not wedded to these ideas, and, therefore, shall relinquish them cheerfully when Congress shall adopt others, and zealously endeavor to carry theirs into effect. First, as to the policy of making treaties. Congress, by the Confederation, have no original and inherent power over the commerce of the States. But, by the 9th article, we are authorized to enter into treaties of commerce.[a] The moment these treaties are concluded, the jurisdiction of Congress over the commerce of the States springs into existence, and that of the particular States is superseded so far as the articles of the treaty may have taken up the subject. . . . Though they may exercise their other powers by resolution or ordinance, those over commerce can only be exercised by forming a treaty, and this probably by an accidental wording of our Confederation. If, therefore, it is better for the States that Congress should regulate their commerce, it is proper that they should form treaties with all nations with whom they may possibly trade. You see that my primary object in the formation of treaties is to take the commerce of the States out of the hands of the States and to place it under the superintendence of Congress, so far as the imperfect provisions of our constitutions will admit, and until the States shall by new compact make them more perfect. I would say, then, to every nation on earth, *by treaty,* your people shall trade freely with us and ours with you, paying no more than the most favored nation, in order to put an end to the right of individual States, acting by fits and starts, to interrupt our commerce or to embroil us with any nation.

To James Monroe, Paris, June 17, 1785.

The Confederation is a wonderfully perfect instrument, considering the circumstances under which it was formed. There are, however, some alterations which experience proves to be wanting. These are principally three: 1. To establish a general rule for the admission of new States into the Union. . . . 2. The Confederation, in its eighth article, decides that the quota of

[a] On the subject of commercial treaties under the Articles of Confederation, see also to David Hartley, Paris, September 5, 1785. *Works,* IV, 459–61.

money to be contributed by the several States shall be proportioned to the value of the landed property in the State. Experience has shown it impracticable to come at this value. Congress have therefore recommended to the States to agree that their quotas shall be in proportion to the number of their inhabitants, counting five slaves, however, but as equal to three free inhabitants. I believe all the States have agreed to this alteration except Rhode Island. 3. The Confederation forbids the States individually to enter into treaties of commerce or of any other nature with foreign nations, and it authorizes Congress to establish such treaties, with two reservations, however, viz., that they shall agree to no treaty which would (a) restrain the legislatures from imposing such duties on foreigners as natives are subject to, or (b) from prohibiting the exportation or importation of any species of commodities. Congress may therefore be said to have a power to regulate commerce so far as it can be effected by conventions with other nations and by conventions which do not infringe the two fundamental reservations before mentioned. But this is too imperfect. Because, till a convention be made with any particular nation, the commerce of any one of our States with that nation may be regulated by the State itself, and even when a convention is made the regulation of the commerce is taken out of the hands of the several States only so far as it is covered or provided for by that convention or treaty. But treaties . . . are very imperfect machines for regulating commerce in the detail. The principal objects in the regulation of our commerce would be: 1. to lay such duties, restrictions, or prohibitions on the goods of any particular nation as might oblige that nation to concur in just and equal arrangements of commerce; 2. to lay such uniform duties on the articles of commerce throughout all the States as may avail them of that fund for assisting to bear the burden of public expenses. Now, this cannot be done by the States separately because they will not separately pursue the same plan. . . . It is visible, therefore, that the commerce of the States cannot be regulated to the best advantage but by a single body, and no body so proper as Congress.

To Jean Nicolas Démeunier, Paris, January 24, 1786.

Perhaps it might have been better, when they were forming the federal constitution, to have assimilated it as much as possible to the particular constitutions of the States. All of these have distributed the legislative, executive, and judiciary powers into different departments. In the federal constitution the judiciary powers are separated from the others, but the legislative and executive are both exercised by Congress. A means of amending this defect has been thought of. Congress having a power to establish what committees of their own body they please and to arrange among them the distribution of their business, they might on the first day of their annual meeting appoint an executive committee consisting of a member from each State, and refer to them all executive business which should occur during their session; confining themselves to what is of a legislative nature, that is to say, to the heads described in the ninth article, as of the competence of nine States only, and to such other questions as should lead to the establishment of general rules.

To Jean Nicolas Démeunier, Paris, after January 24, 1786.

To make us one nation as to foreign concerns and keep us distinct in domestic ones gives the outline of the proper division of powers between the general and particular governments. But, to enable the federal head to exercise the powers given it to best advantage, it should be organized as the particular ones are into legislative, executive, and judiciary. The first and last are already separated. The second should be.

To James Madison, Paris, December 16, 1786.

I have read your book [b] with infinite satisfaction and improvement. It will do great good in America. Its learning and its good sense will, I hope, make it an institute for our politicians, old as well as young. There is one opinion in it, however, which I will ask you to reconsider, because it appears to me not entirely accurate and not likely to do good. Page 362, "Congress is not a legislative but a diplomatic assembly." Separating into parts the whole

[b] A Defence of the Constitutions of Government of the United States of America.

sovereignty of our States, some of these parts are yielded to Congress. Upon these I should think them both legislative and executive, and that they would have been judiciary also had not the Confederation required them for certain purposes to appoint a judiciary. It has accordingly been the decision of our courts that the Confederation is a part of the law of the land and superior in authority to the ordinary laws, because it cannot be altered by the legislature of any one State. I doubt whether they are at all a diplomatic assembly.

To John Adams, Paris, February 23, 1787.

I am anxious to hear what you have done in your federal convention. I am in hopes at least you will persuade the States to commit their commercial arrangements to Congress and to enable them to pay their debts, interest and capital. The coercive powers supposed to be wanting in the federal head I am of opinion they possess by the law of nature, which authorizes one party to an agreement to compel the other to performance. A delinquent State makes itself a party against the rest of the confederacy.

To Edmund Randolph, Paris, August 3, 1787.

My general plan would be to make the States one as to everything connected with foreign nations and several as to everything purely domestic. But with all the imperfections of our present government, it is without comparison the best existing, or that ever did exist. Its greatest defect is the imperfect manner in which matters of commerce have been provided for. It has been so often said as to be generally believed that Congress have no power by the Confederation to enforce anything, for example, contributions of money. It was not necessary to give them that power expressly; they have it by the law of nature. When two parties make a compact, there results to each a power of compelling the other to execute it.

To Edward Carrington, Paris, August 4, 1787.

You ask me in your letter what ameliorations I think necessary in our federal constitution. It is now too late to answer the question, and it would always have been presumption in me to have done it. Your own ideas, and those of the great characters who were to be concerned with you in these discussions, will give the law, as they ought to do, to us all. My own general idea was that the States should severally preserve their sovereignty in whatever concerns themselves alone, and that whatever may concern another State or any foreign nation should be made a part of the federal sovereignty; that the exercise of the federal sovereignty should be divided among three several bodies, legislative, executive, and judiciary, as the State sovereignties are; and that some peaceable means should be contrived for the federal head to force compliance on the part of the States.

To George Wythe, Paris, September 16, 1787.

The first principle of a good government is certainly a distribution of its powers into executive, judiciary, and legislative, and a subdivision of the latter into two or three branches. It is a good step gained when it is proved that the English constitution, acknowledged to be better than all which have preceded it, is only better in proportion as it has approached nearer to this distribution of powers. From this the last step is easy, to show by a comparison of our constitutions with that of England how much more perfect they are. The article of Confederations is certainly worthy of your pen. It would form a most interesting addition to show what have been the nature of the Confederations which have existed hitherto, what were their excellences, and what their defects. A comparison of ours with them would be to the advantage of ours and would increase the veneration of our countrymen for it. It is a misfortune that they do not sufficiently know the value of their constitutions, and how much happier they are rendered by them than any other people on earth by the governments under which they live.

To John Adams, Paris, September 28, 1787.

II. JEFFERSON'S ATTITUDE TOWARD THE NEW CONSTITUTION OF THE UNITED STATES

1. During the Constitutional Convention

In the Constitutional Convention at Philadelphia in 1787, James Madison repeatedly urged that the federal government should be given a veto on all acts of the State legislatures. Jefferson thought this proposal too broad: "the hole and the patch should be commensurate." He proposed judicial review instead. This was the solution adopted by the Convention and incorporated in Article VI, clause 2, of the Constitution, making the Constitution and federal laws and treaties the "supreme law of the land," binding upon State courts notwithstanding anything contained in State constitutions or laws. The federal judiciary was also given extensive jurisdiction of federal questions by Article III of the Constitution.

The idea of separating the executive business of the confederacy from Congress, as the judiciary is already in some degree, is just and necessary. I had frequently pressed on the members individually, while in Congress, the doing this by a resolution of Congress for appointing an executive committee to act during the sessions of Congress, as the committee of the States was to act during their vacations. But the referring to this committee all executive business, as it should present itself, would require a more persevering self-denial than I suppose Congress to possess. It will be much better to make that separation by a federal act. The negative, proposed to be given them on all the acts of the several legislatures, is now for the first time suggested to my mind. *Prima facie*, I do not like it. It fails in an essential character: that the hole and the patch should be commensurate. But this proposes to mend a small hole by covering the whole garment. Not more than one out of one hundred State acts concern the confederacy. This proposition, then, in order to give them one degree of power which they ought to have, gives them ninety-nine more which they ought not to have, upon a presumption that they will not exercise the ninety-nine. But upon every act there will be a preliminary question, "Does this act concern the confederacy?" And was there ever a proposition so plain as to pass Congress without a debate? Their decisions are almost always wise; they are like pure metal. But you know of how much dross this is the result. Would not an appeal from the State judicatures to a federal court in all cases where the act of Confederation controlled the question be as effectual a remedy and exactly commensurate to the defect? A British creditor, for example, sues for his debt in Virginia; the defendant pleads an act of the State excluding him from their courts; the plaintiff urges the Confederation and the treaty made under that as controlling the State law; the judges are weak enough to decide according to the views of their legislature. An appeal to a federal court sets all to rights. It will be said that this court may encroach on the jurisdiction of the State courts. It may. But there will be a power, to wit, Congress, to watch and restrain them. But place the same authority in Congress itself, and there will be no power above them to perform the same office. They will restrain within due bounds a jurisdiction exercised by others much more rigorously than if exercised by themselves.

To James Madison, Paris, June 20, 1787.

I am sorry they [the Constitutional Convention] began their deliberations by so abominable a precedent as that of tying up the tongues of their members. Nothing can justify this example but the innocence of their intentions and ignorance of the value of public discussions. I have no doubt that all their other measures will be good and wise. It is really an assembly of demigods.[c]

To John Adams, Paris, August 30, 1787.

The example of changing a constitution by assembling the wise men of the State instead of assembling armies[d] will be

[c] Shortly afterward Jefferson wrote that "a more able assembly never sat in America." To C. W. F. Dumas, Paris, September 10, 1787. *Writings,* VI, 295.

[d] Jefferson's pride in change of the Constitution without bloodshed was frequently expressed. See letters to C. W. F. Dumas, Paris, September

worth as much to the world as the former examples we had given them. The Constitution, too, which was the result of our deliberations, is unquestionably the wisest ever yet presented to men.

To David Humphreys, Paris, March 18, 1789.

2. *During Ratification*

When Jefferson saw the new Constitution, his first reaction was one of surprise. The principal defects of the document, in his mind, were the lack of a bill of rights and the perpetual re-eligibility of the President. The first objection was promptly removed by the adoption of the first ten Amendments, which went into force in 1791. (They were belatedly ratified by Connecticut, Georgia, and Massachusetts in 1939.) Jefferson's second objection was not met until the Twenty-second Amendment went into force on March 1, 1951.

How do you like our new constitution? I confess there are things in it which stagger all my dispositions to subscribe to what such an Assembly has proposed. The house of federal representatives will not be adequate to the management of affairs, either foreign or federal. Their President seems a bad edition of a Polish king.

To John Adams, Paris, November 13, 1787.

As to the new constitution, I find myself nearly a neutral. There is a great mass of good in it, in a very desirable form, but there is also, to me, a bitter pill or two.

To Edward Carrington, Paris, December 21, 1787.

I wish with all my soul that the nine first conventions may accept the new constitution, because this will secure to us the good it contains, which I think great and important. But I

10, 1787, *Writings*, VI, 295; to Ralph Izard, Paris, July 17, 1788, *Writings*, VII, 72–73; to Edward Rutledge, Paris, July 18, 1788, *Writings*, VII, 81.

equally wish that the four latest conventions, whichever they be, may refuse to accede to it till a declaration of rights be annexed. This would probably command the offer of such a declaration and thus give to the whole fabric, perhaps, as much perfection as any one of that kind ever had. By a declaration of rights, I mean one which shall stipulate freedom of religion, freedom of the press, freedom of commerce against monopolies, trial by juries in all cases, no suspensions of the habeas corpus, no standing armies. These are fetters against doing evil which no honest government should decline. There is another strong feature in the new constitution which I as strongly dislike. That is the perpetual re-eligibility of the President. e

To Alexander Donald, Paris, February 7, 1788.

I learn with great pleasure the progress of the new Constitution. Indeed I have presumed it would gain on the public mind, as I confess it has on my own. . . . My first wish was that nine States would adopt it in order to ensure what was good in it, and that the others might by holding off produce the necessary amendments. But the plan of Massachusetts is far preferable and will, I hope, be followed by those who are yet to decide. There are two amendments only which I am anxious for: 1. A bill of rights, which it is so much the interest of all to have that I conceive it must be yielded. . . . 2. The restoring the principle of necessary rotation, particularly to the Senate and Presidency, but most of all to the last. . . . Of the correction of this article, however, I entertain no present hope, because I find it has scarcely excited an objection in America. And if it does not take place ere long, it assuredly never will. The natural progress of things is for liberty to yield and government to gain ground. As yet our spirits are free. Our jealousy is only put to sleep by the unlimited confidence we all repose in the person to whom we all look as our president.

To Edward Carrington, Paris, May 27, 1788.

e This letter of Jefferson's was cited by Patrick Henry in opposing ratification of the Constitution by Virginia.

I wish to heaven that our new government may see the importance of putting themselves immediately into a respectable position. To make provision for the speedy payment of their foreign debts will be the first operation necessary. This will give them credit. A concomitant one should be magazines and manufactures of arms. . . . I am greatly anxious to hear that nine States accept our new constitution. We must be contented to accept of its good and to cure what is evil in it hereafter. It seems necessary for our happiness at home; I am sure it is so for our respectability abroad.

To John Brown, Paris, May 26, 1788.

General Washington writes me word he thinks Virginia will accept of the new Constitution. It appears to me, in fact, from all information, that its rejection would drive the States to despair and bring on events which cannot be foreseen, and that its adoption is become absolutely necessary. It will be easier to get the assent of nine States to correct what is wrong in the way pointed out by the Constitution itself than to get thirteen to concur in a new convention and another plan of confederation. I therefore sincerely pray that the remaining States may accept it, as Massachusetts has done, with standing instructions to their delegates to press for amendments till they are obtained. They cannot fail of being obtained when the delegates of eight States shall be under such perpetual instructions.

To Thomas Lee Shippen, Jr., Paris, June 19, 1788.

3. In General

Perhaps the best exposition of Jefferson's views on the Constitution was voiced in the following letter to Madison:

I like much the general idea of framing a government which should go on of itself peaceably, without needing continual recurrence to the State legislatures. I like the organization of the government into legislative, judiciary, and executive. I like the power given the legislature to levy taxes, and for that reason solely approve of the greater House being chosen by the people directly. For though I think a House chosen by them will be very illy qualified to legislate for the Union, for foreign nations, etc., yet this evil does not weigh against the good of preserving inviolate the fundamental principle that the people are not to be taxed but by representatives chosen immediately by themselves. I am captivated by the compromise of the opposite claims of the great and little States, of the latter to equal and the former to proportional influence. I am much pleased, too, with the substitution of the method of voting by persons instead of that of voting by States, and I like the negative given to the executive, with a third of either House, though I should have liked it better had the judiciary been associated for that purpose or invested with a similar and separate power. There are other good things of less moment. I will now add what I do not like. First, the omission of a bill of rights providing clearly and without the aid of sophisms for freedom of religion, freedom of the press, protection against standing armies, restriction against monopolies, the eternal and unremitting force of the habeas corpus laws, and trials by jury in all matters of fact triable by the laws of the land and not by the law of nations. . . . Let me add that a bill of rights is what the people are entitled to against every government on earth, general or particular, and what no just government should refuse or rest on inferences.

The second feature I dislike, and greatly dislike, is the abandonment in every instance of the necessity of rotation in office, and most particularly in the case of the President. . . . Smaller objections are the appeal in fact as well as law, and the binding all persons, legislative, executive, and judiciary, by oath to maintain that constitution. I do not pretend to decide what would be the best method of procuring the establishment of the manifold good things in this constitution and of getting rid of the bad.

To James Madison, Paris, December 20, 1787.

I sincerely rejoice at the acceptance of our new Constitution by nine States. It is a good canvas, on which some strokes only

want retouching. What these are I think are sufficiently manifested by the general voice from north to south, which calls for
a bill of rights. It seems pretty generally understood that this
should go to juries, habeas corpus, standing armies, printing,
religion, and monopolies. I conceive there may be difficulty in
finding general modifications of these, suited to the habits of all
the States. But if such cannot be found, then it is better to
establish trials by jury, the right of habeas corpus, freedom of
the press, and freedom of religion in all cases, and to abolish
standing armies in time of peace and monopolies in all cases
than not to do it in any. The few cases wherein these things
may do evil cannot be weighed against the multitude wherein
the want of them will do evil. In disputes between a foreigner
and a native a trial by jury may be improper. But if this exception
cannot be agreed to, the remedy will be to model the jury by
giving the *medietas linguae* in civil as well as criminal cases.
Why suspend the habeas corpus in insurrections and rebellions?
The parties who may be arrested may be charged instantly with
a well defined crime; of course the judge will remand them. If
the public safety requires that the government should have a man
imprisoned on less probable testimony in those than in other
emergencies, let him be taken and tried, retaken and retried,
while the necessity continues, only giving him redress against
the government for damages. Examine the history of England.
See how few of the cases of the suspension of the habeas corpus
law have been worthy of that suspension. They have been either
real treasons, wherein the parties might as well have been charged
at once, or sham plots, where it was shameful they should ever
have been suspected. Yet for the few cases wherein the suspension of the habeas corpus has done real good, that operation is
now become habitual and the minds of the nation almost prepared
to live under its constant suspension. A declaration that the
Federal Government will never restrain the presses from printing
anything they please will not take away the liability of the
printers for false facts printed. The declaration that religious
faith shall be unpunished does not give impunity to criminal
acts dictated by religious error. The saying there shall be no
monopolies lessens the incitements to ingenuity, which is spurred

on by the hope of a monopoly for a limited time, as of fourteen years, but the benefit even of limited monopolies is too doubtful to be opposed to that of their general suppression. If no check can be found to keep the number of standing troops within safe bounds, while they are tolerated as far as necessary, abandon them altogether, discipline well the militia, and guard the magazines with them. More than magazine guards will be useless if few, and dangerous if many. No European nation can ever send against us such a regular army as we need fear, and it is hard if our militia are not equal to those of Canada or Florida. My idea, then, is that though proper exceptions to these general rules are desirable and probably practicable, yet if the exceptions cannot be agreed on, the establishment of the rules in all cases will do ill in very few. I hope, therefore, a bill of rights will be formed to guard the people against the federal government, as they are already guarded against their State governments in most instances.

To James Madison, Paris, July 31, 1788.

My opinion originally was that the President of the United States should have been elected for seven years and forever ineligible afterwards. I have since become sensible that seven years is too long to be irremovable, and that there should be a peaceable way of withdrawing a man in midway who is doing wrong. The service for eight years with a power to remove at the end of the first four comes nearly to my principle as corrected by experience, and it is in adherence to that that I determine to withdraw at the end of my second term. The danger is that the indulgence and attachments of the people will keep a man in the chair after he becomes a dotard, that re-election through life shall become habitual, and election for life follow that. General Washington set the example of voluntary retirement after eight years. I shall follow it. And a few more precedents will oppose the obstacle of habit to anyone after awhile who shall endeavor to extend his term. Perhaps it may beget a disposition to establish it by an amendment of the Constitution.

To John Taylor, Washington, January 6, 1805.

I am for responsibilities at short periods, seeing neither reason nor safety in making public functionaries independent of the nation for life, or even for long terms of years. On this principle I prefer the Presidential term of four years to that of seven years, which I myself had at first suggested, annexing to it, however, ineligibility forever after, and I wish it were now annexed to the second quadrennial election of President.

To James Martin, Monticello, September 20, 1813.

Our new Constitution, of which you speak also, has succeeded beyond what I apprehended it would have done. I did not at first believe that eleven States out of thirteen would have consented to a plan consolidating them as much into one. A change in their dispositions, which had taken place since I left them, had rendered this consolidation necessary, that is to say, had called for a federal government which could walk upon its own legs without leaning for support on the State legislatures. A sense of necessity, and a submission to it, is to me a new and consolatory proof that, whenever the people are well-informed, they can be trusted with their own government; that, whenever things get so far wrong as to attract their notice, they may be relied on to set them to rights.

To Richard Price, Paris, January 8, 1789.

III. CONSTRUING THE CONSTITUTION

1. Constitutionality of Their Actions Determined by the Respective Branches

Jefferson was generally a strict constructionist, favoring amendment whenever necessary to bring the Constitution into accord with public opinion. However, he believed that in some cases (such as the Louisiana Purchase) officials should take action which they considered beneficial, whether authorized by law or not, and throw themselves on the mercy of the people for approbation or censure. He believed that each branch of the government must determine for itself questions of constitutionality when they arise in connection with its official functioning.

When an instrument admits two constructions, the one safe, the other dangerous, the one precise, the other indefinite, I prefer that which is safe and precise. I had rather ask an enlargement of power from the nation, where it is found necessary, than to assume it by a construction which would make our powers boundless. Our peculiar security is in the possession of a written Constitution. Let us not make it a blank paper by construction.[f] I say the same as to the opinion of those who consider the grant of the treaty-making power as boundless. If it is, then we have no Constitution. If it has bounds, they can be no others than the definitions of the powers which that instrument gives. It specifies and delineates the operations permitted to the Federal Government and gives all the powers necessary to carry these into execution. Whatever of these enumerated objects is proper for a law, Congress may make the law; whatever is proper to be executed by way of a treaty, the President and Senate may enter into the treaty; whatever is to be done by a judicial sentence, the judges may pass the sentence. Nothing is more likely than that their enumeration of powers is defective. This is the ordinary case of all human works. Let us go on then perfecting it by adding, by way of amendment to the Constitution, those powers which time and trial show are still wanting. But it has been taken too much for granted that by this rigorous construction the treaty power would be reduced to nothing. I had occasion once to examine its effect on the French treaty, made by the old Congress, and found that out of thirty-odd articles which that contained, there were one, two, or three only which could not now be stipulated under our present Constitution. I confess, then, I think it important, in the present case, to set an example against

[f] Of Jefferson's position as stated in this letter, Henry Adams says (*History of the United States*, II, 91–92): "He had declared that he would acquiesce with satisfaction in making blank paper of the constitution."

broad construction by appealing for new power to the people. If, however, our friends shall think differently, certainly I shall acquiesce with satisfaction, confiding that the good sense of our country will correct the evil of construction when it shall produce ill effects.

To Wilson C. Nicholas, Monticello, September 7, 1803.

The question you propose, whether circumstances do not sometimes occur which make it a duty in officers of high trust to assume authorities beyond the law, is easy of solution in principle but sometimes embarrassing in practice.g A strict observance of the written laws is doubtless *one* of the high duties of a good citizen, but it is not *the highest*. The laws of necessity, of self-preservation, of saving our country when in danger are of higher obligation. To lose our country by a scrupulous adherence to written law would be to lose the law itself, with life, liberty, property, and all those who are enjoying them with us, thus absurdly sacrificing the end to the means. When, in the battle of Germantown, General Washington's army was annoyed from Chew's house, he did not hesitate to plant his cannon against it, although the property of a citizen. When he besieged Yorktown, he leveled the suburbs, feeling that the laws of property must be postponed to the safety of the nation. . . .

From these examples and principles you may see what I think on the question proposed. They do not go to the case of persons charged with petty duties, where consequences are trifling and time allowed for a legal course, nor to authorize them to take such cases out of the written law. In these, the example of overleaping the law is of greater evil than a strict adherence to its imperfect provisions. It is incumbent on those only who accept of great charges to risk themselves on great occasions, when the safety of the nation or some of its very high interests are at stake.

To John B. Colvin, Monticello, September 20, 1810.

g The same thought is expressed in other letters: to W. C. Claiborne, Washington, February 3, 1807, *Writings,* XI, 151; to James Brown, Washington, October 27, 1808, *Writings,* XII, 183.

I have stated above that the original objects of the Federalists were: 1st, to warp our government more to the form and principles of monarchy; and, 2nd, to weaken the barriers of the State governments as co-ordinate powers. In the first they have been so completely foiled by the universal spirit of the nation that they have abandoned the enterprise, shrunk from the odium of their old appellation, taken to themselves a participation of ours, and under the pseudo-republican mask are now aiming at their second object and, strengthened by unsuspecting or apostate recruits from our ranks, are advancing fast towards an ascendancy. I have been blamed for saying that a prevalence of the doctrines of consolidation would one day call for reformation or *revolution*. I answer by asking if a single State of the Union would have agreed to the Constitution, had it given all powers to the general Government; if the whole opposition to it did not proceed from the jealousy and fear of every State of being subjected to the other States in matters merely its own; and if there is any reason to believe the States more disposed now than then to acquiesce in this general surrender of all their rights and powers to a consolidated government, one and undivided.

You request me, confidentially, to examine the question whether the Supreme Court has advanced beyond its constitutional limits and trespassed on those of the State authorities. I do not undertake it, my dear Sir, because I am unable. Age and the wane of mind consequent on it have disqualified me from investigations so severe and researches so laborious. And it is the less necessary in this case, as having been already done by others with a logic and learning to which I could add nothing. On the decision of the case of Cohens *vs.* The State of Virginia, in the Supreme Court of the United States, in March, 1821, Judge Roane, under the signature of Algernon Sidney, wrote for the *Enquirer* a series of papers on the law of that case. I considered these papers maturely as they came out and confess that they appeared to me to pulverize every word which had been delivered by Judge Marshall of the extrajudicial part of his opinion, and all was extrajudicial, except the decision that the act of Congress had not purported to give to the corporation of Washington the authority, claimed by their lottery law, of controlling the laws of the States within the States themselves. . . .

This practice of Judge Marshall of traveling out of his case to prescribe what the law would be in a moot case not before the court is very irregular and very censurable. I recollect another instance, and the more particularly, perhaps, because it in some measure bore on myself. Among the midnight appointments of Mr. Adams were commissions to some federal justices of the peace for Alexandria. These were signed and sealed by him but not delivered. I found them on the table of the department of State on my entrance into office, and I forbade their delivery. Marbury, named in one of them, applied to the Supreme Court for a mandamus to the Secretary of State (Mr. Madison) to deliver the commission intended for him. The Court determined at once that, being an original process, they had no cognizance of it, and therefore the question before them was ended. But the Chief Justice went on to lay down what the law would be, had they jurisdiction of the case, to wit: that they should command the delivery. . . . Yet this case of Marbury and Madison is continually cited by bench and bar as if it were settled law without any animadversion on its being merely an *obiter* dissertation of the Chief Justice.[h]

It may be impracticable to lay down any general formula of words which shall decide at once, and with precision in every case, this limit of jurisdiction. But there are two canons which will guide us safely in most of the cases: 1. The capital and leading object of the constitution was to leave with the States all authorities which respected their own citizens only and to transfer to the United States those which respected citizens of foreign or other States, to make us several as to ourselves but one as to all others. In the latter case, then, constructions should lean to the general jurisdiction, if the words will bear it, and in favor of the States in the former if possible to be so construed.

[h] The Supreme Court decisions commented on by Jefferson are *Cohens* v. *Virginia*, 6 Wheaton 264 (1821) and *Marbury* v. *Madison*, 1 Cranch 137 (1803). In both, Chief Justice Marshall wrote the opinion of the court.

. . . 2. On every question of construction, carry ourselves back to the time when the Constitution was adopted, recollect the spirit manifested in the debates and, instead of trying what meaning may be squeezed out of the text or invented against it, conform to the probable one in which it was passed. . . . Laws are made for men of ordinary understanding and should, therefore, be construed by the ordinary rules of common sense. Their meaning is not to be sought for in metaphysical subtleties which may make anything mean everything or nothing at pleasure. It should be left to the sophisms of advocates, whose trade it is to prove that a defendant is a plaintiff, though dragged into court, *torto collo* [summarily], like Bonaparte's volunteers into the field in chains, or that a power has been given because it ought to have been given, *et alia talia* [and other things of that sort]. The States supposed that by their tenth amendment they had secured themselves against constructive powers. They were not lessoned yet by Cohen's case, nor aware of the slipperiness of the eels of the law. I ask for no straining of words against the General Government, nor yet against the States. I believe the States can best govern our home concerns, and the General Government our foreign ones. I wish, therefore, to see maintained that wholesome distribution of powers established by the constitution for the limitation of both, and never to see all offices transferred to Washington, where, further withdrawn from the eyes of the people, they may more securely be bought and sold as at market.

But the Chief Justice says, "there must be an ultimate arbiter somewhere." True, there must, but does that prove it is either party? The ultimate arbiter is the people of the Union, assembled by their deputies in convention at the call of Congress or of two-thirds of the States. Let them decide to which they mean to give an authority claimed by two of their organs. And it has been the peculiar wisdom and felicity of our constitution to have provided this peaceable appeal where that of other nations is at once to force.

I rejoice in the example you set of *seriatim* [1] opinions. I have heard it often noticed and always with high approbation. Some of your brethren will be encouraged to follow it occasionally, and in time it may be felt by all as a duty, and the sound practice of the primitive court be again restored. Why should not every judge be asked his opinion and give it from the bench, if only by yea or nay? Besides ascertaining the fact of his opinion, which the public have a right to know in order to judge whether it is impeachable or not, it would show whether the opinions were unanimous or not and thus settle more exactly the weight of their authority.

To William Johnson, Monticello, June 12, 1823.

I did not see till last night the opinion of the Judge on the *subpoena duces tecum*[2] against the President. Considering the question there as *coram non judice*,[3] I did not read his argument with much attention. Yet I saw readily enough that, as is usual where an opinion is to be supported right or wrong, he dwells much on smaller objections and passes over those which are solid. Laying down the position generally that all persons owe obedience to subpoenas, he admits no exception unless it can be produced in his law books. But if the Constitution enjoins on a particular officer to be always engaged in a particular set of duties imposed on him, does not this supersede the general law, subjecting him to minor duties inconsistent with these? The Constitution enjoins his constant agency in the concerns of six millions of people. Is the law paramount to this, which calls on him on behalf of a single one?[1]

To George Hay, Washington, June 20, 1807.

The radical idea of the character of the constitution of our government which I have adopted as a key in cases of doubtful construction is that the whole field of government is divided into two departments, domestic and foreign (the States in their mutual relations being of the latter); that the former department is reserved exclusively to the respective States within their own limits and the latter assigned to a separate set of functionaries,

---

[1] Marshall's opinion here referred to was one rendered during the trial of Aaron Burr for treason. Burr sought to compel Jefferson to produce documents for the defense. David Robertson, *Reports of the Trials of Colonel Aaron Burr* (1808), I, 113-189; *U. S. v. Burr*, Fed. Cas. No. 14692d (D. Va. 1807).

constituting what may be called the foreign branch, which, instead of a federal basis, is established as a distinct government *quoad hoc*,[4] acting as the domestic branch does on the citizens directly and coercively; that these departments have distinct directories, co-ordinate and equally independent and supreme each within its own sphere of action. Whenever a doubt arises to which of these branches a power belongs, I try it by this test.

To Edward Livingston, Monticello, April 4, 1824.

You ask my opinion on the question whether the States can add any qualifications to those which the constitution has prescribed for their members of Congress? . . . Had the constitution been silent, nobody can doubt but that the right to prescribe all the qualifications and disqualifications of those they would send to represent them would have belonged to the State. So also the Constitution might have prescribed the whole and excluded all others. . . . But it does not declare, itself, that the member shall not be a lunatic, a pauper, a convict of treason, of murder, of felony, or other infamous crime, or a non-resident of his district; nor does it prohibit to the State the power of declaring these or any other disqualifications which its particular circumstances may call for, and these may be different in different States. . . .

I have always thought that where the line of demarcation between the powers of the General and the State governments was doubtfully or indistinctly drawn, it would be prudent and praiseworthy in both parties never to approach it but under the most urgent necessity. Is the necessity now urgent to declare that no non-resident of his district shall be eligible as a member of Congress? It seems to me that in practice the partialities of the people are a sufficient security against such an election, and that if, in any instance, they should ever choose a non-resident, it must be one of such eminent merit and qualifications as would make it a good rather than an evil, and that, in any event, the examples will be so rare as never to amount to a serious evil. If the case then be neither clear nor urgent, would it not be better to let it lie undisturbed?

To Joseph C. Cabell, Monticello, January 31, 1814.

On the question of the lawfulness of slavery, that is, of the right of one man to appropriate to himself the faculties of another without his consent, I certainly retain my early opinions. On that, however, of third persons to interfere between the parties and the effect of conventional modifications of that pretension, we are probably nearer together. I think with you, also, that the constitution of the United States is a compact of independent nations subject to the rules acknowledged in similar cases, as well that of amendment provided within itself as, in case of abuse, the justly dreaded but unavoidable *ultima ratio gentium.*[5]

To Edward Everett, Monticello, April 8, 1826.

The . . . question whether the judges are invested with exclusive authority to decide on the constitutionality of a law has been heretofore a subject of consideration with me in the exercise of official duties. Certainly there is not a word in the constitution which has given that power to them more than to the executive or legislative branches. Questions of property, of character, and of crime being ascribed to the judges through a definite course of legal proceeding, laws involving such questions belong of course to them, and as they decide on them ultimately and without appeal, they of course decide *for themselves*. The constitutional validity of the law or laws again prescribing executive action and to be administered by that branch ultimately and without appeal, the executive must decide *for themselves* also, whether under the constitution they are valid or not. So also as to laws governing the proceedings of the legislature, that body must judge *for itself* the constitutionality of the law and equally without appeal or control from its co-ordinate branches. And, in general, that branch which is to act ultimately and without appeal on any law is the rightful expositor of the validity of the law, uncontrolled by the opinions of the other co-ordinate authorities.

To William H. Torrance, Monticello, June 11, 1815.

I had read in the *Enquirer*, and with great approbation, the pieces signed Hampden, and have read them again with redoubled approbation in the copies you have been so kind as to send me. I subscribe to every tittle of them. They contain the true principles of the revolution of 1800, for that was as real a revolution in the principles of our government as that of 1776 was in its form, not effected indeed by the sword, as that, but by the rational and peaceable instrument of reform, the suffrage of the people. The nation declared its will by dismissing functionaries of one principle and electing those of another in the two branches, executive and legislative, submitted to their election. Over the judiciary department, the constitution had deprived them of their control. That, therefore, has continued the reprobated system and, although new matter has been occasionally incorporated into the old, yet the leaven of the old mass seems to assimilate to itself the new and, after twenty years' confirmation of the federated system by the voice of the nation declared through the medium of elections, we find the judiciary on every occasion still driving us into consolidation.

In denying the right they usurp of exclusively explaining the constitution, I go further than you do, if I understand rightly your quotation from the *Federalist* of an opinion that "the judiciary is the last resort in relation *to the other departments* of the government, but not in relation to the rights of the parties to the compact under which the judiciary is derived." If this opinion be sound, then indeed is our constitution a complete *felo de se.* For intending to establish three departments, co-ordinate and independent, that they might check and balance one another, it has given according to this opinion to one of them alone the right to prescribe rules for the government of the others, and to that one too which is unelected by and independent of the nation. For experience has already shown that the impeachment it has provided is not even a scarecrow; that such opinions as the one you combat, sent cautiously out, as you observe also, by detachment, not belonging to the case often but sought for out of it, as if to rally the public opinion beforehand to their views and to indicate the line they are to walk in, have been so quietly passed over as never to have excited animadversion, even in a speech of anyone of the body entrusted with impeachment. The constitution on this hypothesis is a mere thing of wax in the hands of the judiciary, which they may twist and shape into any form they please. It should be remembered, as an axiom of eternal truth in politics, that whatever power in any government is independent is absolute also; in theory only, at first, while the spirit of the people is up, but in practice as fast as that relaxes. Independence can be trusted nowhere but with the people in mass. They are inherently independent of all but moral law. My construction of the constitution is very different from that you quote. It is that each department is truly independent of the others and has an equal right to decide for itself what is the meaning of the constitution in the cases submitted to its action, and especially where it is to act ultimately and without appeal.

To Spencer Roane, Poplar Forest, September 6, 1819.

You seem . . . to consider the judges as the ultimate arbiters of all constitutional questions, a very dangerous doctrine indeed and one which would place us under the despotism of an oligarchy. Our judges are as honest as other men and not more so. They have with others the same passions for party, for power, and the privilege of their corps. Their maxim is *boni judicis est ampliare jurisdictionem,* [6] and their power the more dangerous as they are in office for life and not responsible, as the other functionaries are, to the elective control. The constitution has erected no such single tribunal, knowing that, to whatever hands confided, with the corruptions of time and party its members would become despots. It has more wisely made all the departments co-equal and co-sovereign within themselves. If the legislature fails to pass laws for a census, for paying the judges and other officers of government, for establishing a militia, for naturalization as prescribed by the constitution, or if they fail to meet in congress, the judges cannot issue their mandamus to them; if the President fails to supply the place of a judge, to appoint other civil or military officers, to issue requisite commissions, the judges cannot force him. . . .

. . . The judges certainly have more frequent occasion to act on constitutional questions, because the laws of mine and thine and of criminal action forming the great mass of the system of law constitute their particular department. When the legislative or executive functionaries act unconstitutionally, they are responsible to the people in their elective capacity. The exemption of the judges from that is quite dangerous enough. I know no safe depository of the ultimate powers of the society but the people themselves, and, if we think them not enlightened enough to exercise their control with a wholesome discretion, the remedy is not to take it from them but to inform their discretion by education. This is the true corrective of abuses of constitutional power.

To William C. Jarvis, Monticello, September 28, 1820.

I discharged every person under punishment or prosecution under the Sedition Law because I considered, and now consider, that law to be a nullity, as absolute and as palpable as if Congress had ordered us to fall down and worship a golden image, and that it was as much my duty to arrest its execution in every stage as it would have been to have rescued from the fiery furnace those who should have been cast into it for refusing to worship the image. It was accordingly done in every instance without asking what the offenders had done, or against whom they had offended, but whether the pains they were suffering were inflicted under the pretended sedition law.

To Abigail Adams, Washington, July 22, 1804.

You seem to think it devolved on the judges to decide on the validity of the Sedition Law. But nothing in the Constitution has given them a right to decide for the executive, more than to the executive to decide for them. Both magistrates are equally independent in the sphere of action assigned to them. The judges, believing the law constitutional, had a right to pass a sentence of fine and imprisonment, because the power was placed in their hands by the Constitution. But the executive, believing the law to be unconstitutional, were bound to remit the execution of it, because that power has been confided to them by the Constitution. That instrument meant that its co-ordinate branches should be checks on each other. But the opinion which gives to the judges the right to decide what laws are constitutional and what not, not only for themselves in their own sphere of action but for the Legislature and executive also in their spheres, would make the judiciary a despotic branch.

To Abigail Adams, Monticello, September 11, 1804.

2. States' Interpretation of Constitutionality

The Alien and Sedition laws, referred to in the preceding letters, were enacted by the Federalist party in a mad fury of fear and hatred directed principally against the influence of French, Irish, and other anti-British sympathizers. Enforcement of these laws, involving drastic measures against critics of the Adams administration and resulting in severe curtailment of freedom of speech and of the press, kindled public sentiment and contributed to the victory of Jefferson's party at the polls in 1800.

For the present, I should be for resolving the Alien and Sedition laws [7] to be against the Constitution and merely void and for addressing the other States to obtain similar declarations, and I would not do anything at this moment which should commit us further but reserve ourselves to shape our future measures or no measures by the events which may happen. It is a singular phenomenon that, while our State governments are the very *best in the world* without exception or comparison, our General Government has, in the rapid course of nine or ten years, become more arbitrary and has swallowed more of the public liberty than even that of England.

To John Taylor, Monticello, November 26, 1798.

In this State, however, the delusion has not prevailed. They are sufficiently on their guard to have justified the assurance that, should you choose it for your asylum, the laws of the land, administered by upright judges, would protect you from any exercise of power unauthorized by the Constitution of the United States. The habeas corpus secures every man here, alien or citizen, against everything which is not law, whatever shape it may assume.

To Archibald H. Rowan, Monticello, September 26, 1798.

The X. Y. Z.[8] fever has considerably abated through the country, as I am informed, and the Alien and Sedition Laws are working hard. I fancy that some of the State legislatures will take strong ground on this occasion. For my own part I consider those laws as merely an experiment on the American mind to see how far it will bear an avowed violation of the Constitution. If this goes down, we shall immediately see attempted another act of Congress, declaring that the President shall continue in office during life, reserving to another occasion the transfer of the succession to his heirs, and the establishment of the Senate for life.

To Stephens T. Mason, Monticello, October 11, 1798.

I enclose you a copy of the draft of the Kentucky resolutions. I think we should distinctly affirm all the important principles they contain, so as to hold to that ground in future and leave the matter in such a train as that we may not be committed absolutely to push the matter to extremities, and yet may be free to push as far as events will render prudent.

To James Madison, Monticello, November 17, 1798.

3. Jefferson's Draft of the Kentucky Resolutions

The Kentucky Resolutions referred to in the preceding letter were prepared by Jefferson and, with a few softening amendments, adopted by the legislature of that State. Similar resolutions drawn by Madison attacking the constitutionality of the Alien and Sedition laws were passed by the legislature of Virginia. Jefferson's draft of the Kentucky Resolutions follows:

1. *Resolved*, That the several States composing the United States of America are not united on the principle of unlimited submission to their general government, but that by a compact

under the style and title of a Constitution for the United States and of amendments thereto, they constituted a general government for special purposes, delegated to that government certain definite powers, reserving, each State to itself, the residuary mass of right to their own self-government; and that whensoever the general government assumes undelegated powers, its acts are unauthoritative, void, and of no force; that to this compact each State acceded as a State and is an integral party, its co-States forming, as to itself, the other party; that the government created by this compact was not made the exclusive or final judge of the extent of the powers delegated to itself, since that would have made its discretion, and not the Constitution, the measure of its powers; but that, as in all other cases of compact among powers having no common judge, each party has an equal right to judge for itself as well of infractions as of the mode and measure of redress.

2. *Resolved,* That the Constitution of the United States, having delegated to Congress a power to punish treason, counterfeiting the securities and current coin of the United States, piracies, and felonies committed on the high seas, and offenses against the law of nations, and no other crimes whatsoever, . . . the power to create, define, and punish such other crimes is reserved and of right appertains solely and exclusively to the respective States, each within its own territory.

3. *Resolved,* That it is true as a general principle and is also expressly declared by one of the amendments to the Constitution that "the powers not delegated to the United States by the Constitution, nor prohibited by it to the States, are reserved to the States respectively, or to the people"; and that no power over the freedom of religion, freedom of speech, or freedom of the press being delegated to the United States by the Constitution, . . . libels, falsehood, and defamation, equally with heresy and false religion, are withheld from the cognizance of federal tribunals. That, therefore, the act of Congress of the United States, passed on the 14th day of July, 1798, entitled "An Act in Addition to the Act Entitled An Act for the Punishment of Certain Crimes Against the United States," which does abridge

the freedom of the press, is not law but is altogether void and of no force.

4. *Resolved,* That alien friends are under the jurisdiction and protection of the laws of the State wherein they are: that no power over them has been delegated to the United States, nor prohibited to the individual States distinct from their power over citizens. And it being true as a general principle and one of the amendments to the Constitution having also declared that "the powers not delegated to the United States by the Constitution, nor prohibited by it to the States, are reserved to the States respectively, or to the people," the act of the Congress of the United States, passed on the — day of July, 1798, entitled "An Act Concerning Aliens," which assumes powers over alien friends not delegated by the Constitution, is not law but is altogether void and of no force.

5. *Resolved,* That, in addition to the general principle as well as the express declaration that powers not delegated are reserved, another and more special provision, inserted in the Constitution from abundant caution, has declared that "the migration or importation of such persons as any of the States now existing shall think proper to admit, shall not be prohibited by the Congress prior to the year 1808"; that this commonwealth does admit the migration of alien friends, described as the subject of the said act concerning aliens; that a provision against prohibiting their migration is a provision against all acts equivalent thereto, or it would be nugatory; that to remove them when migrated is equivalent to a prohibition of their migration and is, therefore, contrary to the said provision of the Constitution and void.

6. *Resolved,* That the imprisonment of a person under the protection of the laws of this commonwealth on his failure to obey the simple *order* of the President to depart out of the United States, as is undertaken by said act entitled "An Act Concerning Aliens," is contrary to the Constitution. . . .

7. *Resolved,* That the construction applied by the General Government (as is evidenced by sundry of their proceedings) to those parts of the Constitution of the United States which delegate to Congress a power "to lay and collect taxes, duties, im-

posts, and excises, to pay the debts, and provide for the common defense and general welfare of the United States," and "to make all laws which shall be necessary and proper for carrying into execution the powers vested by the Constitution in the government of the United States, or in any department or officer thereof," goes to the destruction of all limits prescribed to their power by the Constitution; that words meant by the instrument to be subsidiary only to the execution of limited powers ought not to be so construed as themselves to give unlimited powers, nor a part to be so taken as to destroy the whole residue of that instrument; that the proceedings of the General Government under color of these articles will be a fit and necessary subject of revisal and correction at a time of greater tranquility, while those specified in the preceding resolutions call for immediate redress.

8. *Resolved,* That a committee of conference and correspondence be appointed, who shall have in charge to communicate the preceding resolutions to the Legislatures of the several States; to assure them that this commonwealth continues in the same esteem of their friendship and union which it has manifested from that moment at which a common danger first suggested a common union; that it considers union for specified national purposes and particularly for those specified in their late federal compact to be friendly to the peace, happiness, and prosperity of all the States; that, faithful to that compact, according to the plain intent and meaning in which it was understood and acceded to by the several parties, it is sincerely anxious for its preservation; that it does also believe that to take from the States all the powers of self-government and transfer them to a general and consolidated government, without regard to the special delegations and reservations solemnly agreed to in that compact, is not for the peace, happiness, or prosperity of these States, and that therefore this commonwealth is determined, as it doubts not its co-States are, to submit to undelegated and consequently unlimited powers in no man or body of men on earth; that in cases of an abuse of the delegated powers, the members of the General Government being chosen by the people, a change by the people

would be the constitutional remedy, but, where powers are assumed which have not been delegated, a nullification of the act is the rightful remedy; that every State has a natural right in cases not within the compact, *casus non foederis*,[9] to nullify of their own authority all assumptions of power by others within their limits; that without this right they would be under the dominion, absolute and unlimited, of whosoever might exercise this right of judgment for them; that, nevertheless, this commonwealth, from motives of regard and respect for its co-States, has wished to communicate with them on the subject; that with them alone it is proper to communicate, they alone being parties to the compact and solely authorized to judge in the last resort of the powers exercised under it, Congress being not a party but merely the creature of the compact and subject as to its assumptions of power to the final judgment of those by whom and for whose use itself and its powers were all created and modified; that, if the acts before specified should stand, these conclusions would flow from them: that the general government may place any act they think proper on the list of crimes and punish it themselves whether enumerated or not enumerated by the Constitution as cognizable by them; that they may transfer its cognizance to the President, or any other person, who may himself be the accuser, counsel, judge, and jury, whose *suspicions* may be the evidence, his *order* the sentence, his *officer* the executioner, and his breast the sole record of the transaction; that a very numerous and valuable description of the inhabitants of these States being, by this precedent, reduced, as outlaws, to the absolute dominion of one man, and the barrier of the Constitution thus swept away from us all, no rampart now remains against the passions and the powers of a majority in Congress to protect from a like exportation or other more grievous punishment the minority of the same body, the legislatures, judges, governors, and counselors of the States, nor their other peaceable inhabitants who may venture to reclaim the constitutional rights and liberties of the States and people, or who for other causes, good or bad, may be obnoxious to the views or marked by the suspicions of the President, or be thought dangerous to his or their election, or other interests, public or personal; that the friendless alien has indeed been selected as the safest subject of a first experiment, but the citizen will soon follow, or rather has already followed, for already has a sedition act marked him as its prey; that these and successive acts of the same character, unless arrested at the threshold, necessarily drive these States into revolution and blood and will furnish new calumnies against republican government, and new pretexts for those who wish it to be believed that man cannot be governed but by a rod of iron; that it would be a dangerous delusion were a confidence in the men of our choice to silence our fears for the safety of our rights; that confidence is everywhere the parent of despotism—free government is founded in jealousy, and not in confidence; it is jealousy and not confidence which prescribes limited constitutions to bind down those whom we are obliged to trust with power; that our Constitution has accordingly fixed the limits to which, and no further, our confidence may go, and let the honest advocate of confidence read the Alien and Sedition acts and say if the Constitution has not been wise in fixing limits to the government it created, and whether we should be wise in destroying those limits. Let him say what the government is, if it be not a tyranny, which the men of our choice have conferred on our President, and the President of our choice has assented to, and accepted over the friendly strangers to whom the mild spirit of our country and its laws have pledged hospitality and protection; that the men of our choice have more respected the bare *suspicions* of the President than the solid right of innocence, the claims of justification, the sacred force of truth, and the forms and substance of law and justice. In questions of power, then, let no more be heard of confidence in man but bind him down from mischief by the chains of the Constitution. That this commonwealth does therefore call on its co-States for an expression of their sentiments on the acts concerning aliens and for the punishment of certain crimes herein before specified, plainly declaring whether these acts are or are not authorized by the federal compact. And it doubts not that their sense will be so announced as to prove their attachment unaltered to limited government, whether general or particular . . . and that the co-States, recurring to their natural right in cases not made federal, will concur in declaring these acts void and of no force, and will each take measures of its own for providing that neither these acts nor any others of the General Government not plainly and intentionally authorized by the Constitution shall be exercised within their respective territories.

9. *Resolved,* That the said committee be authorized to communicate by writing or personal conferences, at any times or places whatever, with any person or persons who may be appointed by any one or more co-States to correspond or confer with them, and that they lay their proceedings before the next session of Assembly.

4. Congressional Immunity

Even Congressmen of the Jeffersonian party were not free from molestation under the frenzy of the Alien and Sedition laws. A Federalist grand jury at Richmond in a presentment took notice of letters written to his onstituents by Congressman Samuel J. Cabell, who represented the district in which Jefferson resided. Seeking to make political capital of the incident, Jefferson prepared a protest for submission to the Virginia legislature.

The doubt which you suggest as to our jurisdiction over the case of the Grand Jury *vs.* Cabell had occurred to me and naturally occurs on first view of the question. But I knew that to send the petition to the House of Representatives in Congress would make bad worse, that a majority of that House would pass a vote of approbation. On examination of the question, too, it appeared to me that we could maintain the authority of our own government over it.

A right of free correspondence between citizen and citizen, on their joint interests, whether public or private, and under whatsoever laws these interests arise (to wit, of the State, of Congress, of France, Spain, or Turkey), is a natural right; it is not the gift of any municipal law, either of England, or Virginia, or of Congress, but in common with all our other natural rights, it is one of the objects for the protection of which society is formed and municipal laws established.

The courts of this commonwealth (and among them the General Court, as a court of impeachment) are originally competent to the cognizance of all infractions of the rights of one citizen by another citizen, and they still retain all their judiciary cognizances not expressly alienated by the federal Constitution.

The Federal Constitution alienates from them all cases arising, first, under the constitution; secondly, under the laws of Congress; thirdly, under treaties, etc. But this right of free correspondence, whether with a public representative in General Assembly, in Congress, in France, in Spain, or with a private one charged with pecuniary trust, or with a private friend the object of our esteem, or any other, has not been given to us under, first, the federal Constitution; secondly, any law of Congress; or thirdly, any treaty; but, as before observed, by nature. It is therefore not alienated, but remains under the protection of our courts.

Were the question even doubtful, that is no reason for abandoning it. The system of the General Government is to seize all doubtful ground. We must join in the scramble or get nothing. Where first occupancy is to give right, he who lies still loses all. Besides, it is not right for those who are only to act in a preliminary form to let their own doubts preclude the judgment of the court of ultimate decision. We ought to let it go to the House of Delegates for their consideration, and they, unless the contrary be palpable, ought to let it to go to the General Court, who are ultimately to decide on it.

It is of immense consequence that the States retain as complete authority as possible over their own citizens. The withdrawing themselves under the shelter of a foreign jurisdiction is so subversive of order and so pregnant of abuse that it may not be amiss to consider how far a law of *praemunire* [10] should be revived and modified against all citizens who attempt to carry their causes before any other than the State courts, in cases where those other courts have no right to their cognizance. A plea to the jurisdiction of the courts of their State or a reclamation of a foreign jurisdiction, if adjudged valid, would be safe, but, if adjudged invalid, would be followed by the punishment of *praemunire* for the attempt.

To James Monroe, Monticello, September 7, 1797.

To the Speaker and House of Delegates of the Commonwealth of Virginia, being a Protest against interference of Judiciary between Representative and Constituent—1797

The petition of the subscribers, inhabitants of the counties of Amherst, Albemarle, Fluvanna, and Goochland, shows:

That at the general partition of this commonwealth into districts, each of which was to choose a representative to Congress, the counties of Amherst, Albemarle, Fluvanna, and Goochland were laid off into one district; that at the elections held for the said district, in the month of April, in the years 1795 and 1797, the electors thereof made choice of Samuel Jordan Cabell, of the county of Amherst, to be their representative in the legislature of the General Government; that the said Samuel Jordan Cabell accepted the office, repaired at the due periods to the legislature of the General Government, exercised his functions there as became a worthy member and, as a good and dutiful representative, was in the habit of corresponding with many of his constituents and communicating to us, by way of letter, information of the public proceedings, of asking and receiving our opinions and advice, and of contributing, as far as might be with right, to preserve the transactions of the general government in unison with the principles and sentiments of his constituents; that, while the said Samuel J. Cabell was in the exercise of his functions as a representative from this district and was in the course of that correspondence which his duty and the will of his constituents imposed on him, the right of thus communicating with them, deemed sacred under all the forms in which our government has hitherto existed, never ques-

tioned or infringed even by Royal judges or governors, was
openly and directly violated at a Circuit court of the General
Government held at the city of Richmond for the district of
Virginia in the month of May of this present year, 1797; that
at the said court, A, B, etc., some of whom were foreigners, having been called upon to serve in the office of grand jurors, . . .
made a presentment of the act of the said Samuel J. Cabell, in
writing letters to his constituents, in the following words, to wit:
"We, of the grand jury of the United States for the district of
Virginia, present as a real evil the circular letters of several
members of the late Congress, and particularly letters with the
signature of Samuel J. Cabell, endeavoring at a time of real
public danger to disseminate unfounded calumnies against the
happy government of the United States and thereby to separate
the people therefrom, and to increase or produce a foreign influence, ruinous to the peace, happiness, and independence of these
United States."

That the grand jury is a part of the Judiciary, not permanent
indeed, but in office *pro hac vice* and responsible as other judges
are for their actings and doings while in office; that for the
Judiciary to interpose in the legislative department between the
constituent and his representative, to control them in the exercise
of their functions or duties towards each other, to overawe the
free correspondence which exists and ought to exist between
them, to dictate what communications may pass between them,
and to punish all others, to put the representative into jeopardy
of criminal prosecution, of vexation, expense, and punishment
before the Judiciary if his communications, public or private,
do not exactly square with their ideas of fact or right or
with their designs of wrong, is to put the legislative department under the feet of the Judiciary, is to leave us, indeed, the
shadow but to take away the substance of representation which
requires essentially that the representative be as free as his constituents would be, that the same interchange of sentiment be
lawful between him and them as would be lawful among themselves were they in the personal transaction of their own business,
is to do away the influence of the people over the proceedings of

their representatives by excluding from their knowledge, by the terror of punishment, all but such information or misinformation as may suit their own views, and is the more vitally dangerous when it is considered that grand jurors are selected by officers nominated and holding their places at the will of the Executive; that they are exposed to influence from the judges who are nominated immediately by the Executive and who, although holding permanently their commissions as judges, yet from the career of additional office and emolument *actually* opened to them of late, whether *constitutionally* or not, are under all those motives which interest or ambition inspire, of courting the favor of that branch from which appointments flow; that grand juries are frequently composed in part of bystanders, often foreigners, of foreign attachments and interests, and little knowledge of the laws they are most improperly called to decide on; and, finally, is to give to the Judiciary and through them to the Executive a complete preponderance over the legislature, rendering ineffectual that wise and cautious distribution of powers made by the Constitution between the three branches, and subordinating to the other two that branch which most immediately depends on the people themselves and is responsible to them at short periods. . . .

We, your petitioners, therefore pray that you will be pleased to take your constitutional cognizance of the premises and institute such proceedings for impeaching and punishing the said A, B, etc., as may secure to the citizens of this commonwealth their constitutional right that their representatives shall in the exercise of their functions be free and independent of the other departments of government, may guard that full intercourse between them and their constituents which the nature of their relations and the laws of the land establish, may save to them the natural right of communicating their sentiments to one another by speaking and writing, and may serve as a terror to others attempting hereafter to subvert those rights and the fundamental principles of our Constitution, . . .

5. Protest Against the Federal Government's Encroachments

To the end of his life Jefferson adhered to the principles which animated the American patriots during the Revolution, and regarded submission to a government of unlimited powers as the greatest of all political evils. When it seemed to him that the federal government was claiming powers in excess of those granted by the Constitution, he prepared a protest, somewhat reminiscent of the Resolutions of the Continental Congress in 1774 against the unconstitutional excesses of the British government.

The solemn Declaration and Protest of the Commonwealth of Virginia on the principles of the Constitution of the United States of America and on the violations of them (1825)

We, the General Assembly of Virginia, on behalf and in the name of the people thereof, do declare as follows:

The States in North America which confederated to establish their independence of the government of Great Britain, of which Virginia was one, became, on that acquisition, free and independent States and, as such, authorized to constitute governments, each for itself, in such form as it thought best.

They entered into a compact (which is called the Constitution of the United States of America) by which they agreed to unite in a single government as to their relations with each other and with foreign nations, and as to certain other articles particularly specified. They retained at the same time, each to itself, the other rights of independent government, comprehending mainly their domestic interests.

For the administration of their federal branch, they agreed to appoint, in conjunction, a distinct set of functionaries, legislative, executive, and judiciary, in the manner settled in that compact; while to each, severally and of course, remained its original right of appointing, each for itself, a separate set of functionaries, . . .

These two sets of officers, each independent of the other, constitute thus a *whole* of government for each State separately; . . .

To this construction of government and distribution of its powers the commonwealth of Virginia does religiously and affectionately adhere, opposing, with equal fidelity and firmness, the usurpation of either set of functionaries on the rightful powers of the other.

But the federal branch has assumed in some cases and claimed in others a right of enlarging its own powers by constructions, inferences, and indefinite deductions from those directly given, which this assembly does declare to be usurpations of the powers retained to the independent branches, mere interpolations into the compact, and direct infractions of it. . . .

While the General Assembly thus declares the rights retained by the States, rights which they have never yielded and which this State will never voluntarily yield, they do not mean to raise the banner of disaffection or of separation from their sister States, co-parties with themselves to this compact. They know and value too highly the blessings of their Union, as to foreign nations and questions arising among themselves, to consider every infraction as to be met by actual resistance. They respect too affectionately the opinions of those possessing the same rights under the same instrument to make every difference of construction a ground of immediate rupture. They would, indeed, consider such a rupture as among the greatest calamities which could befall them, but not the greatest. There is yet one greater, submission to a government of unlimited powers. It is only when the hope of avoiding this shall become absolutely desperate that further forbearance could not be indulged. Should a majority of the co-parties, therefore, contrary to the expectation and hope of this assembly, prefer, at this time, acquiescence in these assumptions of power by the federal member of the government, we will be patient and suffer much, under the confidence that time, ere it be too late, will prove to them also the bitter consequences in which that usurpation will involve us all. In the meanwhile we will breast with them, rather than separate from them, every misfortune save that only of living under a government of unlimited powers. We owe every other sacrifice to ourselves, to our federal brethren, and to the world at large to pursue with temper and perseverance the great experiment which shall prove that man is capable of living in society, governing itself by laws self-imposed, and securing to its members the enjoyment of life, liberty, property, and peace, and further to show that even when the government of its choice shall manifest a tendency to degeneracy, we are not at once to despair but that the will and the watchfulness of its sounder parts will reform its aberrations, recall it to original and legitimate principles, and restrain it within the rightful limits of self-government. And these are the objects of this Declaration and Protest. . . .

Proposed Declaration and Protest of Virginia.

I see, as you do, and with the deepest affliction, the rapid strides with which the federal branch of our government is advancing towards the usurpation of all the rights reserved to the States, and the consolidation in itself of all powers, foreign and domestic, and that, too, by constructions which, if legitimate, leave no limits to their power. Take together the decisions of the Federal Court, the doctrines of the President, and the misconstructions of the constitutional compact acted on by the legislature of the federal branch, and it is but too evident that the three ruling branches of that department are in combination to strip their colleagues, the State authorities, of the powers reserved by them, and to exercise themselves all functions foreign and domestic. Under the power to regulate commerce they assume indefinitely that also over agriculture and manufactures and call it regulation to take the earnings of one of these branches of industry, and that, too, the most depressed, and put them into the pockets of the other, the most flourishing of all. Under the authority to establish post roads, they claim that of cutting down mountains for the construction of roads, of digging canals, and, aided by a little sophistry on the words "general welfare," a right to do not only the acts to effect that which are specifically enumerated and permitted, but whatsoever they shall think or pretend will be for the general welfare. And what is our resource for the preservation of the constitution? Reason and argument? You might as well reason and argue with the marble columns encircling them. The representatives chosen by ourselves? They are joined in the combination, some from incorrect views of government, some from corrupt ones, sufficient voting together to outnumber the sound parts; and with majorities only of one, two, or three, bold enough to go forward in defiance. Are we then *to stand to our arms . . . ?* No! That must be the last resource, not to be thought of until much longer and greater sufferings. If every infraction of a compact of so many parties is to be resisted at once as a dissolution of it, none can ever be formed which would last one year. We must have patience and longer endurance then with our brethren while under delusion; give them time for reflection and experience of consequences; keep ourselves in a situation to profit by the chapter of accidents; and separate from our companions only when the sole alternatives left are the dissolution of our Union with them or submission to a government without limitation of powers. Between these two evils, when we must make a choice, there can be no hesitation. But, in the meanwhile, the States should be watchful to note every material usurpation on their rights, to denounce them as they occur in the most peremptory terms, to protest against them as wrongs to which our present submission shall be considered, not as acknowledgments or precedents of right but as a temporary yielding to the lesser evil, until their accumulation shall overweigh that of separation. I would go still further and give to the federal member, by a regular amendment of the constitution, a right to make roads and canals of intercommunication between the States, providing sufficiently against corrupt practices in Congress (log-rolling, etc.) by declaring that the federal proportion of each State of the moneys so employed shall be in works within the State, or elsewhere with its consent, and with a due *salvo* of jurisdiction. This is the course which I think safest and best as yet.

To William B. Giles, Monticello, December 26, 1825.

IV. CONSTITUTIONAL ADMINISTRATION AND USAGE

Jefferson's *Manual of Parliamentary Practice* begins with a section on the importance of adhering to rules. The forms and rules of proceeding are described as the only weapons by which the minority can defend themselves against improper measures on the part of those in power. At all times Jefferson was sensitive to niceties of procedure.

The ordinary business of every day is done by consultation between the President and the head of the department alone to which it belongs. For measures of importance or difficulty, a consultation is held with the heads of departments, either assembled or by taking their opinions separately in conversation or in writing. The latter is most strictly in the spirit of the constitution. Because the President, on weighing the advice of all, is left free to make up an opinion for himself. In this way they are not brought together, and it is not necessarily known to any what opinion the others have given. This was General Washington's practice for the first two or three years of his administration, till the affairs of France and England threatened to embroil us and rendered consideration and discussion desirable. In these discussions, Hamilton and myself were daily pitted in the cabinet like two cocks. We were then but four in number, and, according to the majority, which of course was three to one, the President decided. The pain was for Hamilton and myself, but the public experienced no inconvenience. I practiced this last method because the harmony was so cordial among us all that we never failed, by a contribution of mutual views on the subject, to form an opinion acceptable to the whole. I think there never was one instance to the contrary, in any case of consequence. Yet this does, in fact, transform the executive into a directory, and I hold the other method to be more constitutional. It is better calculated, too, to prevent collision and irritation, and to cure it, or at least suppress its effects when it has already taken place.

To Walter Jones, Monticello, March 5, 1810.

In my report on How's case where I state that it should go to the President, it will become a question with the House whether they shall refer it to the President themselves, or give it back to the petitioner and let him so address it, as he ought to have done at first. I think the latter proper: (1) because it is a case belonging purely to the Executive; (2) the legislature should never show itself in a matter with a foreign nation, but where the case is very serious and they mean to commit the nation on its issue; (3) because if they indulge individuals in handing through the legislature their applications to the Executive, all applicants will be glad to avail themselves of the weight of so powerful a solicitor. Similar attempts have been repeatedly made by individuals to get the President to hand in their petitions to the legislature, which he has constantly refused. It seems proper that every person should address himself directly to the department to which the constitution has allotted his case, and that the proper answer to such from any other department is that "it is not to us that the constitution has assigned the transaction of this business." I suggest these things to you, that if they may appear to you to be right this kind of business may in the first instance be turned into its proper channel.

To James Madison, Monticello, November 11, 1791.

The functions of the Executive are not competent to the decision of questions of property between individuals. These are ascribed to the judiciary alone and, when either persons or property are taken into their custody, there is no power in this country that can take them out. You will, therefore, be sensible, Sir, that though the President is not the organ for doing what is just in the present case, it will be effectually done by those to whom the Constitution has ascribed the duty.

To Edmond C. Genêt, Philadelphia, June 17, 1793.

I have been still reflecting on the draft of the letter from the Secretary of the Treasury to the custom house officers, instructing them to be on the watch as to all infractions or tendencies to infraction of the laws of neutrality by our citizens, and to communicate the same to him. . . . By this proposal the collectors of the customs are to be made an established corps of spies or informers against their fellow citizens, whose actions they are to watch in secret, inform against in secret to the Secretary of the Treasury, who is to communicate it to the President. . . . The object of this new institution is to be to prevent infractions of the laws of neutrality and preserve our peace with foreign nations. Acts involving war or proceedings which respect foreign nations seem to belong either to the department of war, or to that which is charged with the affairs of foreign nations, but I cannot possibly conceive how the superintendence of the laws of neutrality, or the preservation of our peace with foreign nations, can be ascribed to the department of the treasury, which I suppose to comprehend merely matters of revenue. It would be to add a new and a large field to a department already amply provided with business, patronage, and influence. It was urged as a reason that the collectors of the customs are in convenient positions for this espionage. They are in convenient positions too for building ships of war, but will that business be transplanted from its department merely because it can be conveniently done in another? It seemed the desire that, if this means was disapproved, some other equivalent might be adopted. Though we consider the acts of a foreigner making a captive within our limits as an act of public hostility and therefore to be turned over to the military rather than the civil power; yet the acts of our own citizens infringing the laws of neutrality, or contemplating that, are offenses against the ordinary laws and cognizable by them. Grand juries are the constitutional inquisitors and informers of the country; they are scattered everywhere, see everything, see it while they suppose themselves mere private persons and not with the prejudiced eye of a permanent and systematic spy. Their information is on *oath*, is public; it is in the vicinage of the party charged and can be at once refuted. These officers taken only occasionally from among the people are familiar to them, the office respected, and the experience of centuries has shown that it is safely entrusted with our character, property, and liberty. A grand juror cannot carry on systematic persecution against a neighbor whom he hates, because he is not permanent in the office. The judges generally, by a charge, instruct the grand jurors in the infractions of law which are to be noticed by them, and our judges are in the habit of printing their charges in the newspapers. . . . I am not quite certain what was considered as agreed upon yesterday; it cannot be too late, however, to suggest the substitution of the judges and grand jurors in place of the collectors of the customs.

To Edmund Randolph, Philadelphia, May 8, 1793.

The commission of consul to M. Dannery ought to have been addressed to the President of the United States. He being the only channel of communication between this country and foreign nations, it is from him alone that foreign nations or their agents are to learn what is or has been the will of the nation, . . . I had observed to you that we were persuaded, in the case of the consul Dannery, the error in the address had proceeded from no intention in the Executive Council of France to question the functions of the President, and therefore no difficulty was made in issuing the commissions. We are still under the same persuasion. But in your letter of the 14th instant, you *personally* question the authority of the President and, in consequence of that, have not addressed to him the commission of Messrs. Pennevert and Chervi. Making a point of this formality on your part, it becomes necessary to make a point of it on ours also, and I am therefore charged to return you those commissions and to inform you that, bound to enforce respect to the order of things established by our Constitution, the President will issue no exequatur to any consul or vice-consul not directed to him in the usual form, after the party from whom it comes has been apprised that such should be the address.

To Edmond C. Genêt, Germantown, November 22, 1793.

I was against writing letters to judiciary officers. I thought them independent of the Executive, not subject to its coercion, and, therefore, not obliged to attend to its admonitions.

Anas, September 4, 1793.

As to the mode of correspondence between the general and particular executives, I do not think myself a good judge. Not because my position gives me any prejudice on the occasion; for, if it be possible to be certainly conscious of anything, I am conscious of feeling no difference between writing to the highest and lowest being on earth, but because I have ever thought that forms should yield to whatever should facilitate business. Comparing the two governments together, it is observable that, in all those cases where the independent or reserved rights of the States are in question, the two executives, if they are to act together, must be exactly co-ordinate; they are, in these cases, each the supreme head of an independent government. In other cases, to wit, those transferred by the Constitution to the General Government, the general executive is certainly pre-ordinate, *e. g.,* in a question respecting the militia and others easily to be recollected. Were there, therefore, to be a stiff adherence to etiquette, I should say that in the former cases the correspondence should be between the two heads, and that in the latter the Governor must be subject to receive orders from the war department as any other subordinate officer would. And were it observed that either party set up unjustifiable pretensions, perhaps the other might be right in opposing them by a tenaciousness of his own rigorous rights. But I think the practice in General Washington's administration was most friendly to business and was absolutely equal; sometimes he wrote to the Governors, and sometimes the heads of departments wrote. . . . If this be practiced promiscuously in both classes of cases, each party setting examples of neglecting etiquette, both will stand on equal ground, and convenience alone will dictate through whom any particular communication is to be made. On the whole, I think a free correspondence best and shall never hesitate to write myself to the Governors in every federal case where the occasion presents itself to me particularly.

To James Monroe, Washington, July 11, 1801.

Coming all of us into executive office, new and unfamiliar with the course of business previously practiced, it was not to be expected we should, in the first outset, adopt in every part a line of proceeding so perfect as to admit no amendment. The mode and degrees of communication, particularly between the President and heads of departments, have not been practiced exactly on the same scale in all of them. Yet it would certainly be more safe and satisfactory for ourselves as well as the public that not only the best but also a uniform course of proceeding as to manner and degree should be observed. Having been a member of the first administration under General Washington, I can state with exactness what our course then was. Letters of business came addressed sometimes to the President but most frequently to the heads of departments. If addressed to himself, he referred them to the proper department to be acted on; if to one of the secretaries, the letter, if it required no answer, was communicated to the President simply for his information. If an answer was requisite, the secretary of the department communicated the letter and his proposed answer to the President. Generally they were simply sent back after perusal, which signified his approbation. Sometimes he returned them with an informal note suggesting an alteration or a query. If a doubt of any importance arose, he reserved it for conference. By this means he was always in accurate possession of all facts and proceedings in every part of the Union and to whatsoever department they related; he formed a central point for the different branches; preserved a unity of object and action among them; exercised that participation in the suggestion of affairs which his office made incumbent on him; and met himself the due responsibility for whatever was done. During Mr. Adams' administration, his long and habitual absences from the seat of government rendered this kind of communication impracticable, removed him from any share in the transaction of affairs, and parceled out the government, in fact, among four independent heads, drawing sometimes in opposite directions. That the former is preferable to the latter course cannot be doubted. It gave, indeed, to the heads of departments the trouble of making up, once a day, a packet of all their communications for the perusal of the President; it commonly also retarded one day their despatches by mail. But in pressing cases this injury was prevented by presenting that case singly for immediate attention, and it produced us in return the benefit of his sanction for every act we did. Whether any change of circumstances may render a change in this procedure necessary, a little experience will show us. But I cannot withhold recommending to heads of departments that we should adopt this course for the present, leaving any necessary modifications of it to time and trial.

Circular to the Heads of the Departments, Washington,
November 6, 1801.

[Your] preference of a plural over a singular executive will probably not be assented to here. When our present government was first established, we had many doubts on this question and many leanings towards a supreme executive counsel. It happened that at that time the experiment of such a one was commenced in France, while the single executive was under trial here. We watched the motions and effects of these two rival plans with an interest and anxiety proportioned to the importance of a choice between them. The experiment in France failed after a short course, and not from any circumstance peculiar to the times or nation but from those internal jealousies and dissensions in the Directory which will ever arise among men equal in power without a principal to decide and control their differences. We had tried a similar experiment in 1784 by establishing a committee of the States composed of a member from every State, then thirteen, to exercise the executive functions during the recess of Congress. They fell immediately into schisms and dissensions, which became at length so inveterate as to render all co-operation among them impracticable; they dissolved themselves, abandoning the helm of government, and it continued without a head until Congress met the ensuing winter. This was then imputed to the temper of two or three individuals, but the wise ascribed it to the nature of man. . . . During the administration of our first President, his cabinet of four members was equally divided by as marked an opposition of principle as monarchism and republicanism could bring into conflict. Had that cabinet been a directory, like positive and negative quantities in algebra the opposing wills would have balanced each other and produced a state of absolute inaction. But the President heard with calmness the opinions and reasons of each, decided the course to be pursued, and kept the government steadily in it, unaffected by the agitation. The public knew well the dissensions of the cabinet but never had an uneasy thought on their account, because they knew also they had provided a regulating power which would keep the machine in steady movement. I speak with an intimate knowledge of these scenes, *quorum pars fui;* [11] as I may of others of a character entirely opposite. The third administration, which was of eight years, presented an example of harmony in a cabinet of six persons to which perhaps history has furnished no parallel. There never arose, during the whole time, an instance of an unpleasant thought or word between the members. We sometimes met under differences of opinion but scarcely ever failed, by conversing and reasoning, so to modify each other's ideas as to produce a unanimous result. Yet, able and amicable as these members were, I am not certain this would have been the case had each possessed equal and independent powers. . . .

I am still, however, sensible of the solidity of your principle, that, to insure the safety of the public liberty, its depository should be subject to be changed with the greatest ease possible and without suspending or disturbing for a moment the movements of the machine of government. You apprehend that a single executive, with eminence of talent and destitution of principle equal to the object, might, by usurpation, render his powers hereditary. Yet I think history furnishes as many examples of a single usurper arising out of a government by a plurality as of temporary trusts of power in a single hand rendered permanent by usurpation. I do not believe, therefore, that this danger is lessened in the hands of a plural executive. . . . But the true barriers of our liberty in this country are our State governments, and the wisest conservative power ever contrived by man is that of which our Revolution and present government found us possessed. Seventeen distinct States, amalgamated into one as to their foreign concerns but single and independent as to their internal administration, regularly organized with a legislature and governor resting on the choice of the people and enlightened by a free press, can never be so fascinated by the arts of one man as to submit voluntarily to his usurpation. Nor can they be constrained to it by any force he can possess. . . .

Dangers of another kind might more reasonably be apprehended from this perfect and distinct organization, civil and military, of the States; to wit, that certain States from local and occasional discontents might attempt to secede from the Union. This is certainly possible and would be befriended by this regular organization. But it is not probable that local discontents can spread to such an extent as to be able to face the sound parts of so extensive a Union, and if ever they should reach the majority, they would then become the regular government, acquire the ascendency in Congress, and be able to redress their own grievances by laws peaceably and constitutionally passed. And even the States in which local discontents might engender a commencement of fermentation would be paralyzed and self-checked by that very division into parties into which we have fallen, into which all States must fall wherein men are at liberty to think, speak, and act freely, according to the diversities of their individual conformations, and which are, perhaps, essential to preserve the purity of the government, by the censorship which these parties habitually exercise over each other.

To Antoine L. C. Destutt de Tracy, Monticello, January 26, 1811.

For if experience has ever taught a truth, it is that a plurality in the supreme executive will forever split into discordant factions, distract the nation, annihilate its energies, and force the nation to rally under a single head, generally a usurper. We have, I think, fallen on the happiest of all modes of constituting the executive, that of easing and aiding our President by permitting him to choose Secretaries of State, of finance, of war, and of the navy, with whom he may advise, either separately or all together, and remedy their divisions by adopting or controlling their opinions at his discretion; this saves the nation from the evils of a divided will and secures to it a steady march in the systematic course which the president may have adopted for that of his administration.

To Adamantios Coray, Monticello, October 31, 1823.

I presume you will now remain at London to see the trial of Hastings.[12] Without suffering yourself to be imposed on by the pomp in which it will be enveloped, I would recommend to you to consider and decide for yourself these questions: If his offense is to be decided by the law of the land, why is he not tried in that court in which his fellow citizens are tried, that is, the King's bench? If he is cited before another court that he may be judged not according to the law of the land but by the discretion of his judges, is he not disfranchised of his most precious right, the benefit of the laws of his country, in common with his fellow citizens? I think you will find, in investigating this subject, that every solid argument is against the extraordinary court, and that every one in its favor is specious only. It is a transfer from a judicature of learning and integrity to one the greatness of which is both illiterate and unprincipled. Yet such is the force of prejudice with some, and of the want of reflection in others, that many of our constitutions have copied this absurdity without suspecting it to be one.

To William Rutledge, Paris, February 2, 1788.

CHAPTER SIX

THE GREAT FAMILY OF MANKIND

I. FREE GOVERNMENT AND PEACE

Jefferson believed that peace was favorable to the preservation of free government, and also that free government was favorable to the preservation of peace.

Peace, then, has been our principle, peace is our interest, and peace has saved to the world this only plant of free and rational government now existing in it. If it can still be preserved, we shall soon see the final extinction of our national debt and liberation of our revenues for the defense and improvement of our country. . . . However, therefore, we may have been reproached for pursuing our Quaker system, time will affix the stamp of wisdom on it and the happiness and prosperity of our citizens will attest its merit. And this, I believe, is the only legitimate object of government and the first duty of governors, and not the slaughter of men and devastation of the countries placed under their care in pursuit of a fantastic honor unallied to virtue or happiness; or in gratification of the angry passions or the pride of administrators excited by personal incidents in which their citizens have no concern.

To Thaddeus Kosciusko, Monticello, April 13, 1811.

What course the government will pursue, I know not. But if we are left in peace, I have no doubt the wonderful turn in the public opinion now manifestly taking place and rapidly increasing will, in the course of this summer, become so universal and so weighty that friendship abroad and freedom at home will be firmly established by the influence and constitutional powers of the people at large. If we are forced into war, we must give up political differences of opinion and unite as one man to defend our country. But whether at the close of such a war we should be as free as we are now, God knows. In fine, if war takes place, republicanism has everything to fear; if peace, be assured that your forebodings and my alarms will prove vain, and that the spirit of our citizens, now rising as rapidly as it was then running crazy, and rising with a strength and majesty which show the loveliness of freedom, will make this government in practice what it is in principle, a model for the protection of man in a state of freedom and order.

To Thaddeus Kosciusko, Philadelphia, February 21, 1799.

II. PEACEABLE COERCION [1]

1. Justice by Negotiation

He also believed that commercial regulations could be used so as to induce other nations, for their own advantage, to deal justly with the United States, thus avoiding the need of avenging injuries by resort to war. A notable example of this policy was the Embargo adopted during Jefferson's presidency. Opinions are divided as to the efficacy of that experiment, some believing that, like war itself, it was "as much a punishment to the punisher as to the sufferer."

As to myself, I love peace, and I am anxious that we should give the world still another useful lesson by showing to them other modes of punishing injuries than by war, which is as much a punishment to the punisher as to the sufferer. I love, therefore . . . [the] proposition of cutting off all communications with the nation which has conducted itself so atrociously. This, you will say, may bring on war. If it does, we will meet it like men, but it may not bring on war and then the experiment will have been a happy one.

To Tench Coxe, Monticello, May 1, 1794.

War is not the best engine for us to resort to. Nature has given us one in our commerce which, if properly managed, will be a better instrument for obliging the interested nations of Europe to treat us with justice.

To Thomas Pinckney, Philadelphia, May 29, 1797.

The English are still our enemies. The spirit existing there and rising in America has a very lowering aspect. To what events it may give birth, I cannot foresee. We are young and can survive them, but their rotten machine must crush under the trial. The animosities of sovereigns are temporary and may be allayed, but those which seize the whole body of a people, and of a people, too, who dictate their own measures, produce calamities of long duration. I shall not wonder to see the scenes of ancient Rome and Carthage renewed in our day, and if not pursued to the same issue, it may be because the republic of modern powers will not permit the extinction of any one of its members. Peace and friendship with all mankind is our wisest policy, and I wish we may be permitted to pursue it. But the temper and folly of our enemies may not leave this in our choice.

To Charles W. F. Dumas, Paris, May 6, 1786.

Calculation has convinced me that circumstances may arise, and probably will arise, wherein all the resources of taxation will be necessary for the safety of the State. For though I am decidedly of opinion we should take no part in European quarrels but cultivate peace and commerce with all, yet who can avoid seeing the source of war in the tyranny of those nations who deprive us of the natural right of trading with our neighbors? The produce of the United States will soon exceed the European demand; what is to be done with the surplus, when there shall be one? It will be employed, without question, to open by force a market for itself with those placed on the same continent with us, and who wish nothing better. Other causes, too, are obvious, which may involve us in war, and war requires every resource of taxation and credit. The power of making war often prevents it and in our case would give efficacy to our desire of peace. If the new government wears the front which I hope it will, I see no impossibility in the availing ourselves of the wars of others to open the other parts of America to our commerce as the price of our neutrality.

To George Washington, Paris, December 4, 1788.

Never was so much false arithmetic employed on any subject as that which has been employed to persuade nations that it is their interest to go to war. Were the money which it has cost to gain at the close of a long war a little town, or a little territory, the right to cut wood here or to catch fish there, expended in improving what they already possess, in making roads, opening rivers, building ports, improving the arts, and finding employment for their idle poor, it would render them much stronger, much wealthier and happier. This I hope will be our wisdom. And, perhaps, to remove as much as possible the occasions of making war, it might be better for us to abandon the ocean altogether, that being the element whereon we shall be principally exposed to jostle with other nations; to leave to others to bring what we shall want and to carry what we can spare. This would make us invulnerable to Europe by offering none of our property to their prize and would turn all our citizens to the cultivation of the earth, and, I repeat it again, cultivators of the earth are the most virtuous and independent citizens. It might be time enough to seek employment for them at sea when the land no longer offers it. But the actual habits of our countrymen attach them to commerce. They will exercise it for themselves. Wars then must sometimes be our lot, and all the wise can do will be to avoid that half of them which would be produced by our own follies and our own acts of injustice, and to make for the other half the best preparations we can.

Notes on Virginia, Query XXII.

Our people are decided in the opinion that it is necessary for us to take a share in the occupation of the ocean, and their established habits induce them to require that the sea be kept open to them, and that that line of policy be pursued which will render the use of that element to them as great as possible. I think it a duty in those entrusted with the administration of their affairs to conform themselves to the decided choice of their constituents, and that, therefore, we should, in every instance, preserve an equality of right to them in the transportation of commodities, in the right of fishing, and in the other uses of the sea.

But what will be the consequence? Frequent wars without a doubt. . . . The justest dispositions possible in ourselves will not secure us against it. It would be necessary that all other nations were just also. Justice, indeed, on our part will save us from those wars which would have been produced by a contrary disposition. But how can we prevent those produced by the wrongs of other nations? By putting ourselves in a condition to punish them. Weakness provokes insult and injury, while a condition to punish often prevents them. This reasoning leads to the necessity of some naval force, that being the only weapon by which we can reach an enemy. I think it to our interest to punish the first insult, because an insult unpunished is the parent of many others.

To John Jay, Paris, August 23, 1785.

My hope of preserving peace for our country is not founded in the Quaker principles of nonresistance under every wrong, but in the belief that a just and friendly conduct on our part will procure justice and friendship from others.

To the Earl of Buchan, Washington, July 10, 1803.

2. Justice Maintained by International Naval Force

While minister to France, Jefferson urged the establishment of an international naval force to protect commerce from the Mediterranean pirates, to whom the principal commercial powers of Europe were paying tribute. The project fell through. The United States was not willing to undertake the burden of furnishing its share of the naval force (one frigate); and England (according to Lafayette) preferred the continuance of unsafe conditions as a deterrent to the commercial ventures of rival nations.

There is little prospect of accommodation between the Algerines and the Portuguese and Neapolitans. A very valuable capture, too, lately made by them on the Empress of Russia, bids fair to draw her on them. The probability is, therefore, that these three nations will be at war with them, and the probability is that, could we furnish a couple of frigates, a convention might be formed with those powers, establishing a perpetual cruise on the coast of Algiers which would bring them to reason. Such a convention, being left open to all powers willing to come into it, should have for its object a general peace to be guaranteed to each by the whole. Were only two or three to begin a confederacy of this kind, I think every power in Europe would soon fall into it, except France, England, and perhaps Spain and Holland. Of these, there is only England who would give any real aid to the Algerines. Morocco, you perceive, will be at peace with us. Were the honor and advantage of establishing such a confederacy out of the question, yet the necessity that the United States should have some marine force, and the happiness of this as the ostensible cause for beginning it, would decide on its propriety. It will be said there is no money in the treasury. There never will be money in the treasury till the confederacy shows its teeth. The States must see the rod; perhaps it must be felt by some one of them. I am persuaded all of them would rejoice to see every one obliged to furnish its contributions. It is not the difficulty of furnishing them which beggars the treasury, but the fear that others will not furnish as much. Every rational citizen must wish to see an effective instrument of coercion and should fear to see it on any other element than the water. A naval force can never endanger our liberties, nor occasion bloodshed; a land force would do both. It is not in the choice of the States whether they will pay money to cover their trade against the Algerines. If they obtain a peace by negotiation, they must pay a great sum of money for it; if they do nothing, they must pay a great sum of money in the form of insurance; and, in either way, as great a one as in the way of force and probably less effectual.

To James Monroe, Paris, August 11, 1786.

III. ONE CODE OF MORALITY FOR MEN AND NATIONS

Jefferson vigorously rejected the view that only individuals are bound by the moral code, and that nations are free to act in accordance with self-interest without any restraints.

To say, . . . that gratitude is never to enter into the motives of national conduct is to revive a principle which has been buried for centuries with its kindred principles of the lawfulness of assassination, poison, perjury, etc. All of these were legitimate principles in the dark ages, which intervened between ancient and modern civilization, but exploded and held in just horror in the eighteenth century. I know but one code of morality for men, whether acting singly or collectively.[2] He who says I will be a rogue when I act in company with a hundred others, but an honest man when I act alone, will be believed in the former assertion but not in the latter. I would say with the poet, *hic niger est, hunc tu, Romane, caveto.*[3] If the morality of one man produces a just line of conduct in him acting individually, why should not the morality of one hundred men produce a just line of conduct in them acting together? But I indulge myself in these reflections, because my own feelings run me into them; with you they were always acknowledged. Let us hope that our new government will take some other occasions to show that they mean to proscribe no virtue from the canons of their conduct with other nations.

To James Madison, Paris, August 28, 1789.

I have but one system of ethics for men and for nations—to be grateful, to be faithful to all engagements under all circumstances, to be open and generous, promoting in the long run even the interests of both, and I am sure it promotes their happiness.

To the Duchesse d'Anville, New York, April 2, 1790.

As to the English, notwithstanding their base example, we wish not to expose them to the inhumanities of a savage enemy. Let this reproach remain on them, but for ourselves we would not have our national character tarnished with such a practice. If indeed they strike the Indians, these will have a natural right to punish the aggressors and we none to hinder them. It will then be no act of ours. But to incite them to a participation of the war is what we would avoid by all possible means.

To George Rogers Clark, Williamsburg, January 29, 1780.

IV. THE LAW OF NATIONS

International law arose when the doctrines of natural law were applied to the relations of states as well as of individuals. The law of nature and of nations formed a single subject in the thinking of legal scholars. Jefferson, like other eighteenth century statesmen, turned to the writings of Grotius, Vattel, and Pufendorf to determine the rights and duties of nations.

The law of nations, by which this question is to be determined, is composed of three branches: 1. The moral law of our nature; 2. The usages of nations; 3. Their special conventions. The first of these only concerns this question, that is to say, the moral law to which man has been subjected by his creator and of which his feelings or conscience, as it is sometimes called, are the evidence with which his creator has furnished him. The moral duties which exist between individual and individual in a state of nature accompany them into a state of society, and the aggregate of the duties of all the individuals composing the society constitutes the duties of that society towards any other; so that between society and society the same moral duties exist as did between the individuals composing them while in an unassociated state, their Maker not having released them from those duties on their forming themselves into a nation. Compacts, then, between nation and nation are obligatory on them by the same moral law which obliges individuals to observe their compacts. There are circumstances, however, which sometimes excuse the non-performance of contracts between man and man; so are there also between nation and nation. When performance, for instance, becomes *impossible,* nonperformance is not immoral; so if performance becomes *self-destructive* to the party, the law of self-preservation overrules the laws of obligation to others. For the reality of these principles I appeal to the true fountains of evidence, the head and heart of every rational and honest man. It is there nature has written her moral laws, and where every man may read them for himself.

Cabinet Opinion, April 28, 1793.

You think, Sir, that this opinion is also contrary to the law of nature and usage of nations. We are of opinion it is dictated by that law and usage, and this had been very maturely inquired into before it was adopted as a principle of conduct. . . . By our treaties with several of the belligerent powers, which are a part of the laws of our land, we have established a state of peace with them. But, without appealing to treaties, we are at peace with them all by the law of nature. For by nature's law, man is at peace with man till some aggression is committed, which, by the same law, authorizes one to destroy another as his enemy.

To Edmond C. Genêt, Philadelphia, June 17, 1793.

But our right [to navigate the Mississippi] is built on ground still broader and more unquestionable, to wit: on the law of nature and nations.

If we appeal to this, as we feel it written on the heart of man, what sentiment is written in deeper characters than that the ocean is free to all men and their rivers to all their inhabitants? Is there a man, savage or civilized, unbiased by habit, who does not feel and attest this truth? Accordingly, in all tracts of country united and under the same political society, we find this natural right universally acknowledged and protected by laying the navigable rivers open to all their inhabitants. When their rivers enter the limits of another society, if the right of the upper inhabitants to descend the stream is in any case obstructed, it is an act of force by a stronger society against a weaker, condemned by the judgment of mankind. . . .

Report on Negotiations with Spain, March 18, 1792.

My opinion on the right of Expatriation has been, so long ago as the year 1776, consigned to record in the act of the Virginia code, drawn by myself, recognizing the right expressly and prescribing the mode of exercising it. The evidence of this natural right, like that of our right to life, liberty, the use of our faculties, the pursuit of happiness, is not left to the feeble and sophistical investigations of reason but is impressed on the sense of every man. We do not claim these under the charters of kings or legislators, but under the King of kings. If he has made it a law in the nature of man to pursue his own happiness, he has left him free in the choice of place as well as mode, and we may safely call on the whole body of English jurists to produce the map on which Nature has traced, for each individual, the geographical line which she forbids him to cross in pursuit of happiness.

To John Manners, Monticello, June 12, 1817.

APPENDIX NOTES

CHAPTER ONE

[1] In addition to the writers mentioned here by Jefferson as having possibly influenced the Declaration of Independence, he recommended to inquiring students various other political treatises: the *Federalist* (1788); Montesquieu's *Spirit of Laws* (1748); James Burgh, *Political Disquisitions* (Philadelphia, 1775); Joseph Priestley, *An Essay on the First Principles of Government* (2d ed., London, 1771); Nathaniel Chipman, *Sketches of the Principles of Government* (Rutland, Vt., 1793); and Antoine L. C. Destutt de Tracy, *A Commentary and Review of Montesquieu's Spirit of Laws* (Philadelphia, 1811), the translation of which into English Jefferson himself revised and which he described as "the best elementary book on government which has ever been published." To Francis Eppes, Monticello, June 27, 1821 (Huntington Library, Jefferson Manuscripts). See also to Thomas M. Randolph, Jr., New York, May 30, 1790, *Works*, VI, 63; to John Norvell, Washington, June 11, 1807, *ibid.*, X, 416; to George W. Lewis, Monticello, October 25, 1825, A. A. Lipscomb and A. E. Bergh, eds., *The Writings of Thomas Jefferson* (Washington, 1903), XVI, 128. Jefferson told Norvell that "as we have employed some of the best materials of the British constitution in the construction of our own government, a knowledge of British history becomes useful to the American politician." But the "elegant" history of David Hume (1711–1776) "is so plausible and pleasing in its style and manner" as to plant Tory doctrines unwittingly in the minds of "unwary readers."

A "republicanized" edition of Hume was recommended by Jefferson. This was John Baxter, *A New and Impartial History of England* (London, 1796–1801), regarding which see Sowerby, I, 174. The spread of Tory principles was also promoted by the "honeyed Mansfieldism" of the *Commentaries on the Laws of England* (1765–1769), by Sir William Blackstone (1723–1783). To James Madison, Monticello, February 17, 1826, *Works*, XII, 456; to John Tyler, Monticello, June 17, 1812, *Writings*, XIII, 165–67. Instead of Blackstone's "elegant digest," Jefferson preferred that law students begin with the sound Whig principles of Sir Edward Coke (1552–1634), in spite of the difficult and crabbed style which had made Jefferson in his youth exclaim, "I do wish the Devil had old Coke, for I am sure I never was so tired of an old dull scoundrel in my life." To John Page, Fairfield, December 25, 1762. *Works*, I, 436.

Jefferson wished to forbid citation in American courts of any English decisions since Lord Mansfield went on the bench. To John B. Cutting, Paris, October 2, 1788. *Writings*, XIII, 155. Lord Mansfield (1705–1793) is now best known for his liberalization of commercial law (the "law merchant") by infusion of equitable principles from the Civil Law. In Jefferson's day, however, he was most prominent for his opposition in Parliament to the claims of the Colonists, and for his decisions adverse to freedom of speech in cases involving seditious libel.

The works of Locke, Algernon Sidney, the Declaration of Independence, the *Federalist*, the Virginia Resolutions of 1799 on the Alien and Sedition Laws, and Washington's Farewell Address were adopted as the approved materials for instruction in political science by a resolution of the Board of Visitors of the University of Virginia on March 4, 1825. *Writings*, XIX, 461.

[2] Scot and lot: a local English tax imposed in accordance with ability to pay.

[3] Gavelkind was a mode of descent of property which prevailed in certain localities in England. All sons shared equally. It differed from the usual English practice of giving everything to the eldest son. Blackstone, *Commentaries on the Laws of England*, II, *84.

[4] Allodial tenure of land was absolute ownership, unlike feudal tenure. Under feudalism the owner held his land from his liege lord to whom he owed certain duties (especially military service) and from whom he received protection. In England all land was held ultimately from the king, those who held directly from him, without there being any intermediate or mesne lord, being known as tenants *in capite*. Blackstone, II, *47, 59f. Jefferson was anxious to abolish in America the vestiges of feudalism and to restore the "ancient Saxon laws" displaced at the Norman conquest. He recurs to this topic in the *Summary View*, p. 29f., and he also discussed it in correspondence with Edmund Pendleton, who favored retention of the traditional land law. Julian P. Boyd, ed., *The Papers of Thomas Jefferson* (Princeton, 1950–), I, 491, 507.

⁵ The designation of "Federalists" here means those who favored adoption of the federal Constitution of 1787. Later the term came to be used to describe the political faction headed by Alexander Hamilton. Following the election of its antagonist, Jefferson, to the presidency in 1800, that party lost influence and disappeared. Its policy gave preference to manufacture, banking, and commerce over agriculture; England over France; the North over the South; centralization over localism; and strong government over popular liberty. The Jeffersonian party were known as "Republicans" or "Democrats," and should not be confused with the present Republican party, which first offered a candidate for President in 1856 and in 1860 was successful at the polls, electing Abraham Lincoln.

⁶ While American minister in London, John Adams published there in 1787 the first volume of *A Defence of the Constitutions of Government of the United States of America*. This work was hurriedly composed of extracts from historians and philosophers describing the form of government and vicissitudes of public affairs in numerous "democratic," "aristocratic," and "monarchical" republics during ancient and modern times. The lesson Adams extracted from this record of experience was the necessity of a balanced government, such as the English, with one branch representing the people, in combination with a strong executive, and a separate aristocratic senate for the rich, well-born, and able. To concentrate all power in a single democratic assembly, Adams concluded, would be fatal. See also pp. 51, 132, 134.

CHAPTER TWO

¹ *The Spirit of Laws* by Charles de Secondat, Baron de Montesquieu (1689–1755), was an influential work in the eighteenth century. He was an admirer of the English constitution. That the laws of a country are connected with its climate and that each form of government has its own characteristics and tends to flourish under particular conditions were main features of his doctrine. For other comments by Jefferson on Montesquieu, see pp. 54, 191. Extensive extracts from Montesquieu were copied by Jefferson in his *Commonplace Book*. Cf. G. Chinard, ed., *The Commonplace Book of Thomas Jefferson* (Baltimore and Paris, 1926).

[2] The Missouri question which alarmed Jefferson was the debate whether any restriction against slavery should be imposed in connection with the admission of that State into the Union. The "Missouri Compromise" of 1820 authorized the admission of Maine as a free State and of Missouri as a slave State, but provided that in all remaining portions of the Louisiana Purchase north of 36° 30′ N. latitude slavery should be forever prohibited. Jefferson feared that "if Congress has the power to regulate the inhabitants of the States, within the States, it will be but another exercise of that power to declare that all shall be free." Randall, *Life of Thomas Jefferson* (1858), III, 459. In deference to Stephen A. Douglas's doctrine of "squatter sovereignty," the Missouri Compromise was repealed in 1854 by the Kansas-Nebraska Act which enabled the population of those territories to determine whether or not slavery should be permitted there. Opposition to that legislation and desire to prevent the further spread of slavery led to formation of the present Republican party, which by 1856 was organized on a national scale and put forward its first candidate for the Presidency, John C. Frémont, who was defeated by James Buchanan. But four years later Abraham Lincoln was elected.

[3] The Cincinnati, deriving their name from the Roman Cincinnatus, were a society of ex-officers who had served in the United States Army during the Revolution. Jefferson feared that the organization might result in the establishment of a hereditary aristocracy. Washington was a member of the Society of the Cincinnati.

[4] I prefer adventurous liberty to quiet servitude.

[5] Conservatives were considerably upset by Shays's Rebellion in Massachusetts. High taxes and hard times caused a group of insurgents, led by Daniel Shays, a veteran of the Revolutionary War, to prevent foreclosures and sheriffs' sales by keeping the courts from sitting. (Iowa farmers during the 1932 depression similarly interfered with the functioning of the judiciary.)

[6] Joseph F. Correa y Serra, Portuguese diplomat and botanist, was a favorite companion of Jefferson's. See Edward Dumbauld, *Thomas Jefferson, American Tourist* (1946), p. 194.

[7] Jefferson seems to refer to the reaction of European nations to the Latin American wars of independence, especially to the statements by the members of the Holy Alliance at the Congress of

Vienna that they intended to help reconquer these areas for Spain. These events prompted the message to Congress in 1823 by President Monroe, known as the Monroe Doctrine, that any attempt to extend the rule of European nations to any part of the Western Hemisphere would be considered a threat to the safety of the United States.

[8] That in every political society there is a natural division into parties, one of which is composed of those who trust and "cherish" the people, and the other of those who fear the people and prefer a powerful government, is a theme to which Jefferson repeatedly recurs. See to John Adams, Monticello, June 27, 1813, *Writings*, XIII, 279; to James Sullivan, Monticello, February 9, 1797, *Works*, VIII, 281; to John Taylor, Philadelphia, June 1, 1798, *ibid.*, 431; to Joel Barlow, Washington, May 3, 1802, *ibid.*, IX, 371; to John Melish, Monticello, January 13, 1813, *ibid.*, XI, 276; to Lafayette, Monticello, November 4, 1823, *ibid.*, XII, 323; to Henry Lee, Monticello, August 10, 1824, *ibid.*, 375; to William Short, Monticello, January 8, 1825, *ibid.*, 397.

CHAPTER THREE

[1] Jefferson frequently voiced his fear that not all peoples were ripe for self-government. France, he felt, should be content with reforming its government in accordance with the example of England, before advancing to the degree of liberty attained in America. Louisiana could not immediately be received into the Union on the same footing as the original States, but must gradually progress towards an increasing degree of self-government. South American states could hardly be expected to throw off at once the habits which had become ingrained through ages of submission to despotic rule. See pp. 85; 196, n. 3; and the following: to Lafayette, Monticello, November 30, 1813, *Works*, XI, 357; to Lafayette, Monticello, February 14, 1815, *ibid.*, 455; to Alexander Humboldt, Monticello, December 6, 1813, *ibid.*, 351; to John Adams, Monticello, May 17, 1818, *Works*, XII, 95–96; to John Adams, Monticello, January 22, 1821, *ibid.*, 199; to Joseph Priestley, Washington, November 29, 1802, *Works*, IX, 404; to Samuel Brown, Monticello, July 14, 1813, *Writings*, XIII, 311.

[2] See note 5, p. 194.

CHAPTER FOUR

[1] As the term indicates.

[2] *Habeas corpus*: that you shall have the body. This is a well-known writ guaranteeing the liberty of Englishmen and Americans by preventing arbitrary imprisonment without legal ground at the pleasure of the government. The officer having custody of the prisoner is directed to produce his body in court, together with the grounds for his detention, and if these grounds are not sufficient in law the prisoner is released.

[3] "With more boldness than wisdom" Jefferson also drafted a constitution for the Louisiana territory, based upon frank recognition of the fact that "our new fellow citizens are as yet as incapable of self-government as children." To John Breckinridge, Washington, November 24, 1803, *Works*, X, 51; to De Witt Clinton, Washington, December 2, 1803, *ibid.*, X, 55.

CHAPTER FIVE

[1] *Seriatim* opinions: Jefferson wished the Supreme Court to follow the old English practice where each member of the court in turn gave his own opinion. Under the modern practice one member of the court writes the opinion stating the views of the majority of the court, and unless one or more of the minority judges wishes to file a dissenting opinion there is no occasion for each member of the court to record his individual views.

[2] *Subpoena duces tecum*: A *subpoena* is a judicial writ directing the person to whom it is addressed to appear in court "under penalty" to be suffered in case of failure to appear. A *subpoena duces tecum* is used if it is desired that the witness bring with him and produce documents in his possession.

[3] *Coram non judice*: not in the presence of a duly qualified judge.

[4] *Quoad hoc*: insofar as this is concerned.

[5] *Ultima ratio gentium*: the last resort of nations, i.e., war.

[6] It is characteristic of a good judge to expand his jurisdiction.

[7] On the Alien and Sedition Laws, see Adrienne Koch, *Jefferson and Madison* (New York, 1950), pp. 174–211; Frank M. Anderson, "Contemporary Opinion of the Virginia and Kentucky Resolutions," *American Historical Review*, V (1899), 45–63;

ibid., V (1900), 225–252; Anderson, "The Enforcement of the Alien and Sedition Laws," *Annual Report of the American Historical Association for 1912,* pp. 115–126.

[8] X, Y, and Z were inserted in place of the names of the French emissaries Hottenguer, Bellamy, and Hauteval when the dispatches from the United States mission to France (composed of John Marshall, Elbridge Gerry, and Charles Cotesworth Pinckney) were published in 1798. War with France seemed imminent when it became known that the American envoys had not been officially received by the French government and that a loan or bribe from the United States had been solicited by the French before any serious negotiation would be commenced. Pinckney's irate reply "No, not a sixpence" as it passed from mouth to mouth became the more rhetorical "Millions for defense, but not a cent for tribute." Hamilton's Federalist partisans saw their eagerly anticipated military honors slipping from their grasp when President Adams, on his own initiative, announced that he would send another mission to France if assurance were given that it would be received with proper respect for its diplomatic status.

During the excitement the Quaker physician Dr. James Logan went to Paris in an effort of his own to maintain peace between the two countries. He bore a personal letter of introduction from Jefferson, who was then Vice-President, and the Federalists blamed Jefferson for Logan's mission, which they regarded as an officious intermeddling with public business by a private citizen.

[9] *Casus non foederis:* a case not covered by the compact.

[10] *Praemunire* was a writ to prevent interference with jurisdiction of the Court of King's Bench in England by any other tribunal. It issued under statutes enacted to curb the ecclesiastical courts of the Church of Rome. Blackstone, *Commentaries on the Laws of England,* IV, *103. The writ of *praemunire* was involved in the controversies between Lord Coke and the King of England with respect to the powers of the crown and the liberties of the subject.

[11] *Quorum pars fui:* of which I was part. See Virgil *Aeneid* ii. 6.

[12] The trial of Warren Hastings for peculation as governor general of India gave Edmund Burke the opportunity to display his eloquence as Cicero had done in the case of Verres. Macaulay also found the career of Hastings a suitable subject on which to exercise his literary gifts.

CHAPTER SIX

[1] For other references to peaceable coercion, see to Peregrine Fitzhugh, Philadelphia, February 23, 1798, *Works*, VIII, 376; to Robert R. Livingston, Monticello, September 9, 1801, *ibid.*, IX, 300; to Albert Gallatin, Monticello, September 1, 1804, *ibid.*, X, 100; to William H. Cabell, Washington, June 29, 1807, *ibid.*, 433; to George Logan, Monticello, October 3, 1813, *ibid.*, XI, 340; to Cabanis, Washington, July 12, 1803, *Writings*, X, 405; to Meriwether Lewis, Monticello, August 21, 1808, *Writings*, XII, 143.

[2] For further letters where this idea is stated, see: to Albert Gallatin, Monticello, March 28, 1803, *Works*, IX, 455–56; to Valentine de Foronda, Monticello, October 4, 1809, *ibid.*, XI, 120; to George Logan, Poplar Forest, November 12, 1816, *ibid.*, XII, 43.

[3] "This is the villain, beware of him, O Roman." Horace *Sat.* i, 4, 85.

BIOGRAPHICAL INDEX

ADAMS, ABIGAIL (1744–1818). Wife of John Adams and noted letter writer.

ADAMS, JOHN (1735–1826). Delegate to First Continental Congress; commissioner to France; with Jay and Franklin, negotiated Treaty of Paris ending Revolution; second President of the United States.

BARLOW, JOEL (1754–1812). Liberal American statesman; poet; friend of Thomas Paine; consul for Algiers (1795); minister to France (1811).

BLACKSTONE, SIR WILLIAM (1723–1780). Famous English jurist. His *Commentaries on the Laws of England* (1765–1769) exerted a strong influence on British and American jurisprudence.

BLAIR, JOHN (1732–1800). Jurist; delegate to Constitutional Convention; supported Madison and Jefferson in struggle to frame and adopt a constitution.

BRECKINRIDGE, JOHN (1760–1806). Lawyer; statesman; United States senator; Attorney-General of the United States.

BROWN, JAMES (1766–1835). United States senator; diplomat; secretary of territory of New Orleans; minister to France.

BROWN, JOHN (1757–1837). United States senator; out-standing supporter of the interests of the Western country.

BURKE, EDMUND (1729–1797). British statesman and political writer. He eloquently espoused the cause of the American colonies for more self-government. Author a.o. of *On the Sublime and Beautiful* and *Reflections on the French Revolution* (1790). Best remembered for his speeches: "American Taxation" (1744) and "Conciliation with America" (1775).

BURR, AARON (1756–1836). Revolutionary soldier; lawyer; United States senator; Vice-President of the United States during Jefferson's first administration; killed Alexander Hamilton in a duel (1804); tried for treason (1807) and acquitted.

CABELL, JOSEPH C. (1778–1856). Principal assistant to Jefferson in founding University of Virginia; rector of the university.

CABELL, SAMUEL J., (1756–1818). Revolutionary soldier; lawyer; congressman; an original member of the Society of the Cincinnati (Cf. p. 194, note 3.

CABELL, WILLIAM H. (1772–1853). Governor of Virginia; one of board of commissioners to select site of University of

Virginia and plan its organization.

CARMICHAEL, WILLIAM (d. 1795). Diplomat; secretary to Benjamin Franklin, Deane, and Lee, when they were commissioners to France.

CHIPMAN, NATHANIEL (1752–1843). Jurist; United States senator; a Federalist.

CLAIBORNE, WILLIAM C. C. (1775–1817). Governor of territory of Louisiana and State of Louisiana after its admission to the Union.

CLARK, GEORGE ROGERS (1752–1818). Conqueror of Northwest during the Revolution. This territory was ceded to the United States by Britain in the Treaty of Paris, 1783.

CLINTON, DE WITT (1769–1828). Lawyer; philanthropist; mayor of New York; governor of New York; sponsor of Erie and Champlain-Hudson canals.

COKE, SIR EDWARD (1552–1634). Lord chief justice of England; author of the famous *Reports* and *Institutes*.

COOPER, THOMAS (1759–1839). Scientist; agitator; pamphleteer noted for his attacks on Sedition Act (Cf. p. 196, note 7.)

COXE, TENCH (1755–1824). Political economist; wrote pamphlet, "An Examination of the Constitution for the United States," supporting adoption of the Constitution.

DICKINSON, JOHN (1732–1808). Statesman; member of Consti-

tutional Convention; pamphleteer.

DUMAS, CHARLES WILLIAM FREDERICK. An American diplomatic agent in the Netherlands.

DUPONT DE NEMOURS, PIERRE SAMUEL (1739–1817). French statesman and author; father of Eléuthère Irénée.

EPPES, JOHN W. (1773–1823). Nephew and son-in-law of Jefferson; congressman; senator.

FRANKLIN, BENJAMIN (1706–1790). American printer, author, statesman, diplomat, scientist, and Revolutionary leader. He stands today as the symbol of the far-sighted businessman, sincere and able patriot, and above all as a practical man of affairs. America has produced few statesmen and almost no diplomats to rival him.

GALLATIN, ALBERT (1761–1849). Secretary of the Treasury during the administrations of Jefferson and Madison; diplomat.

GENÊT, EDMOND C. E. (1763–1834). First minister of the French Republic to the United States. Became involved in American domestic politics and Washington asked for his recall.

GERRY, ELBRIDGE (1744–1814). Statesman; member of the X.Y.Z. mission (Cf. p. 197, note 8.); Vice-President under Madison.

GILES, WILLIAM B. (1762–1830). Statesman; studied law

under George Wythe; congressman; governor of Virginia.

GRANGER, GIDEON (1767–1822). Lawyer; United States Postmaster-General in Jefferson's administration.

HAMILTON, ALEXANDER (1757–1804). Revolutionary soldier, statesman, and first Secretary of the Treasury under Washington. Hamilton was the founder and guiding genius of the Federalist party. He met an untimely death in a duel with Aaron Burr in 1804. With James Madison and John Jay, he wrote *The Federalist*.

HAY, GEORGE (1765–1830). Jurist; as United States attorney for Virginia prosecuted Aaron Burr for treason.

HENRY, PATRICK (1736–1799). Revolutionary statesman; orator; governor of Virginia.

HOPKINSON, FRANCIS (1737–1791). Statesman; musician; author; pamphleteer during Revolution; designer of the American flag.

HUMPHREYS, DAVID (1752–1818). Soldier; statesman; poet; commissioner of Algerian affairs; minister to Spain; negotiated treaty (with Barlow) with Algerian states for freeing American prisoners.

HUNTER, WILLIAM (1774–1849). United States senator; minister to Brazil.

JARVIS, WILLIAM C. (1770–1859). Agriculturist; merchant; chargé d'affaires and consul in Lisbon.

JAY, JOHN (1745–1829). States-man and diplomat. From 1784 to 1790 he was Secretary of Foreign Affairs under the Articles of Confederation, and then became the first Chief Justice of the Supreme Court. Co-author with Alexander Hamilton and James Madison of *The Federalist*.

KOSCIUSKO, THADDEUS (1746–1817). Revolutionary soldier and Polish patriot; one of the founders of the Society of the Cincinnati.

LAFAYETTE, MARIE JOSEPH PAUL YVES ROCH GILBERT DU MOTIER, MARQUIS DE (1757–1834). Volunteered his services in the cause of the Revolution; friend of Washington; played a significant part in the earlier phases of the French Revolution.

LEE, RICHARD HENRY (1732–1794). Revolutionary statesman and signer of the Declaration of Independence. He offered the resolution for independence in the Continental Congress on June 7, 1776. His proposal was seconded by John Adams, adopted on July 2, and proclaimed as the Declaration of Independence on July 4, 1776.

LEWIS, MERIWETHER (1774–1809). Explorer and governor; private secretary to Jefferson during his first administration; co-leader with William Clark of expedition to explore land route to Pacific (1803–1806).

LIVINGSTON, EDWARD (1764–1836). Statesman; congressman; mayor of New York City; senator from Louisiana; minister to France.

LIVINGSTON, ROBERT R. (1746–1813). Jurist; statesman; one of committee of five who drew up Declaration of Independence; first United States Secretary of Foreign Affairs; minister to France.

LOCKE, JOHN (1632–1704). English philosopher. His major political work, the *Two Treatises of Government* (1689), strongly influenced English and American political thought.

LOGAN, GEORGE (1753–1821). Physician; senator; went to France as a private citizen (1798) in an attempt to improve relations with that country. So-called "Logan Act" was passed on this account (Cf. p. 197, note 8.).

MADISON, JAMES (1750–1836). Statesman; writer; member of Congress; fourth President of the United States. He was one of the most influential members of the Constitutional Convention. He later served in Congress as a leader of the party of Jefferson, was Secretary of State under Jefferson, and succeeded Jefferson in the Presidency. Co-author with Alexander Hamilton and John Jay of *The Federalist*.

MARSHALL, JOHN (1755–1835). Revolutionary soldier; leader of the Federalist party in Virginia; judicial statesman. He was appointed Chief Justice of the Supreme Court of the United States by President John Adams, and served from 1801 to 1835. In this capacity, he established his reputation as one of America's greatest constitutional statesmen. The decisions of the Supreme Court under his leadership had a major influence in formulating a legal interpretation of the Constitution designed to strengthen the union of the states.

MASON, STEPHENS T. (1760–1803). Revolutionary soldier; senator; opponent of Sedition Act.

MONROE, JAMES (1758–1831). Fifth President of the United States; law student of Jefferson; U. S. senator; minister to France; governor of Virginia; Secretary of State under Madison; formulated policy of the United States which came to be known as the Monroe Doctrine (Cf. p. 194, note 7.).

MONTESQUIEU, CHARLES DE SECONDAT (1689–1755). French philosophical historian. Best known for his exposition, in his *The Spirit of Laws,* of the doctrine of the separation of powers.

MORRIS, GOUVERNEUR (1752–1816). Revolutionary patriot; member of Continental Congress; member of Constitutional Convention; commissioner to England; minister to France.

NELSON, THOMAS (1738–1789). Signer of the Declaration of Independence; Revolutionary soldier; governor of Virginia.

OTIS, JAMES (1725–1783). Massachusetts lawyer, politician, and publicist. He is probably best known for his opposition to the "Writs of Assistance," which allowed customs collectors wide discretion to search for and seize contraband goods.

PAGE, JOHN (1743–1808). Revolutionary patriot; congressman; governor of Virginia.

PAINE, THOMAS (1737–1809). A native of England; Revolutionary pamphleteer, agitator, and author. His political tract, "Common Sense," which advocated in ringing terms separation of the colonies from England, was widely read and influential. His other well-known political work is *Rights of Man*. (Part I, 1791; Part II, 1792).

PENDLETON, EDMUND (1721–1803). Leader of the Virginia bar; presided over Court of Chancery; served on Virginia Court of Appeals; presided at Virginia convention which ratified the U. S. Constitution.

PICKERING, TIMOTHY (1745–1826). Revolutionary soldier; member of Washington's cabinet; a Federalist.

PINCKNEY, CHARLES (1757–1824). Author of "Pinckney draft" of the Constitution; governor of South Carolina; senator; minister to Spain.

PINCKNEY, CHARLES C. (1746–1825). Revolutionary soldier; member of Constitutional Convention; assisted in drafting the Constitution; minister to France; member of the X.Y.Z.

mission to France (Cf. p. 197, note 8.).

PINCKNEY, THOMAS (1750–1824). Revolutionary soldier; governor of South Carolina; special commissioner to Spain; congressman; negotiated "Pinckney Treaty" with Spain (1795).

PLEASANTS, JOHN H. (1797–1846). Journalist and politician.

PRIESTLEY, JOSEPH (1733–1804). Educator; scientist; Jefferson consulted him when first planning the University of Virginia.

RANDOLPH, EDMUND (1753–1815). Lawyer; first United States Attorney-General; succeeded Jefferson as Secretary of State.

RANDOLPH, JOHN (1773–1833). Best known as John Randolph of Roanoke; statesman; orator; long-time member of Congress. Early in his career, he was a Jeffersonian, but later abandoned Jefferson.

RANDOLPH, THOMAS M., JR. (1768–1828). Son-in-law of Jefferson; congressman; governor of Virginia.

ROANE, SPENCER (1762–1822). Political writer; jurist; son-in-law of Patrick Henry.

RUSH, BENJAMIN (1745–1813). One of best-known American physicians; signer of the Declaration of Independence; great teacher, professor of chemistry at the College of Philadelphia, today the University of Pennsylvania.

RUTLEDGE, EDWARD (1749–1800). Signer of the Declaration of Independence; governor of South Carolina; a Federalist.

SHAYS, DANIEL (?1747–1825). Revolutionary soldier who led insurrection in Massachusetts known as Shays's Rebellion. He was condemned to death but was pardoned (Cf. p. 194, note 5.).

SHORT, WILLIAM (1759–1849). Diplomat; private secretary to Jefferson in France, later secretary of legation; minister to the Netherlands.

SIDNEY, ALGERNON (1622–1683). English politician and political philosopher who died as a martyr of English liberty. Jefferson's copy of his *Discourses Concerning Government* is preserved in the Library of Congress.

STUART, ARCHIBALD (1757–1832). Revolutionary soldier; jurist, studied law with Jefferson; legislator.

SULLIVAN, JAMES (1744–1808). Jurist; member of Continental Congress; governor of Massachusetts.

TAYLOR, JOHN (1753–1824). Best known as John Taylor of Caroline (Virginia); political writer and agriculturist; United States senator three different times.

TYLER, JOHN (1747–1813). Revolutionary patriot; governor of Virginia; state and federal judge.

VANDERKEMP, FRANCIS A. 1752–1829). Author, scholar, friend of John Adams.

WEBSTER, NOAH (1758–1843). Lexicographer and author; Revolutionary soldier; publisher of *An American Dictionary of the English Language* (1st ed. 1828).

WILSON, JAMES (1742–1798). Jurist; congressman; member of committee who drafted Constitution; held first chair of law at College of Philadelphia; Associate Justice of Supreme Court of the United States.

WYTHE, GEORGE (1726–1806). Jefferson's law teacher; jurist and statesman; signer of the Declaration of Independence; held the first law professorship in America, established by Jefferson when he was governor of Virginia.

THE AMERICAN HERITAGE SERIES

THE MIDDLE PERIOD

THE LATE NINETEENTH CENTURY

THE TWENTIETH CENTURY